ALL·NEW X·MEN

ONE DOWN

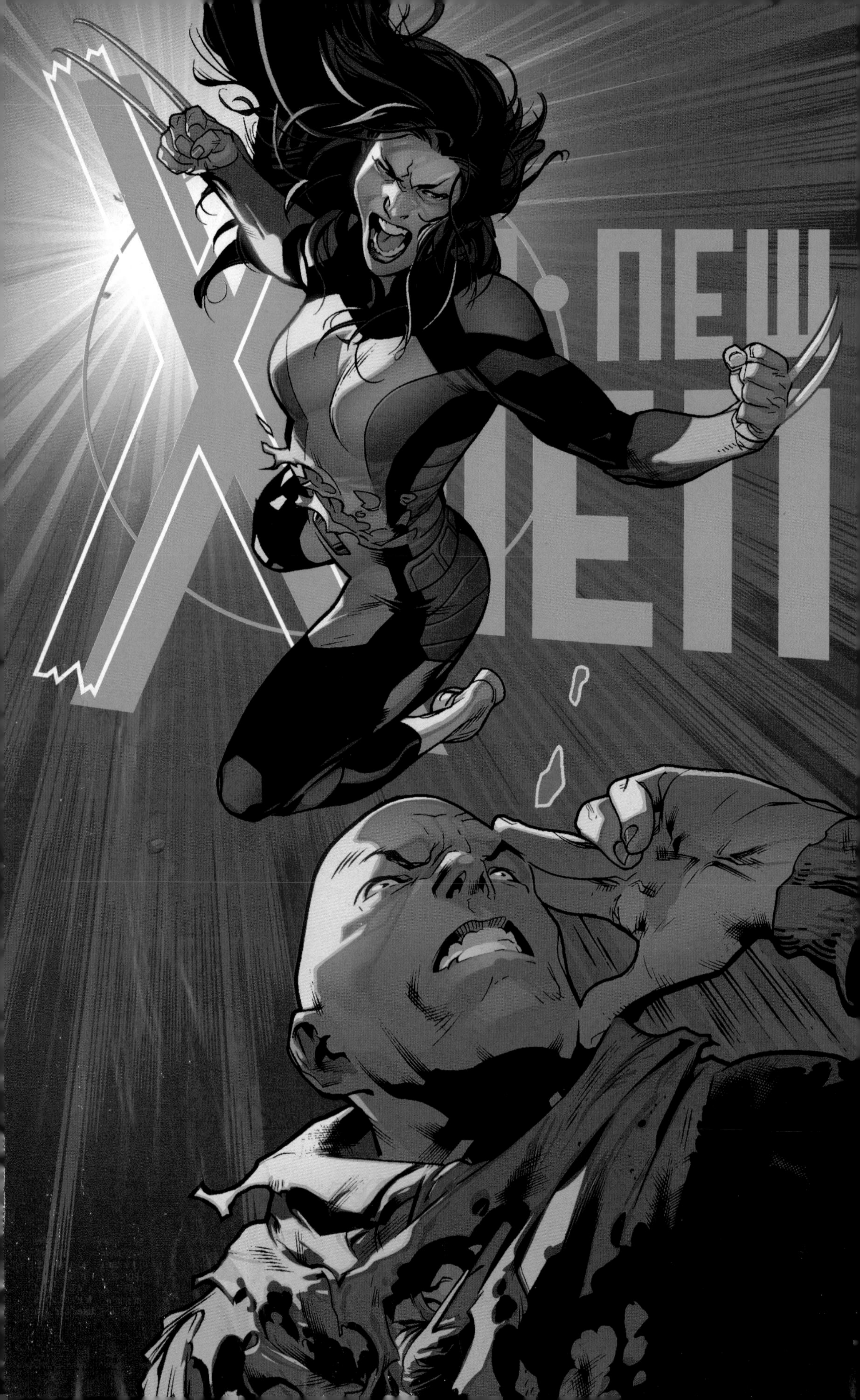
NEW

BEAST
HANK McCOY

MARVEL GIRL
JEAN GREY

CYCLOPS
SCOTT SUMMERS

ANGEL
WARREN WORTHINGTON III

ICEMAN
BOBBY DRAKE

ONE DOWN

BRIAN MICHAEL
BENDIS
WRITER

STUART
IMMONEN
PENCILER. #26-29

WADE VON
GRAWBADGER
INKER, #26-29

ADDITIONAL ART, #25:
BRUCE TIMM & LAURA MARTIN; DAVID MACK; SKOTTIE YOUNG & JASON KEITH; ROBBI RODRIGUEZ & JUSTIN
PONSOR; LEE BERMEJO & MARTE GRACIA; KENT WILLIAMS; ARTHUR ADAMS & JUSTIN PONSOR; J.G. JONES; RONNIE
DEL CARMEN; J. SCOTT CAMPBELL & NEI RUFFINO; MARIS WICKS; JASON SHIGA; DAN HIPP; MAX WITTERT; JAKE
PARKER & MATTHEW WILSON; JILL THOMPSON; AND PAUL SMITH, BOB WIACEK & JORDIE BELLAIRE

SARA
PICHELLI
ARTIST, #30

JUSTIN
PONSOR
COLORIST, #25

MARTE
GRACIA
COLORIST, #26-30
WITH JASON KEITH (#29)

CORY
PETIT
LETTERER

XANDER
JAROWEY
ASSISTANT EDITOR

JORDAN D.
WHITE
ASSOCIATE EDITOR

NICK   MIKE
LOWE & MARTS
EDITORS

COVER ART: **STUART IMMONEN, WADE VON GRAWBADGER & MARTE GRACIA**

X-MEN CREATED BY STAN LEE & JACK KIRBY

COLLECTION EDITOR: **JENNIFER GRÜNWALD** ASSOCIATE MANAGING EDITOR: **ALEX STARBUCK**
EDITOR, SPECIAL PROJECTS: **MARK D. BEAZLEY** SENIOR EDITOR, SPECIAL PROJECTS: **JEFF YOUNGQUIST**
SVP PRINT, SALES & MARKETING: **DAVID GABRIEL** BOOK DESIGNER: **RODOLFO MURAGUCHI**

EDITOR IN CHIEF: **AXEL ALONSO** CHIEF CREATIVE OFFICER: **JOE QUESADA**
PUBLISHER: **DAN BUCKLEY** EXECUTIVE PRODUCER: **ALAN FINE**

ALL-NEW X-MEN VOL. 5: ONE DOWN. Contains material originally published in magazine form as ALL-NEW X-MEN #25-30. First printing 2015. ISBN# 978-0-7851-8968-8. Published by MARVEL WORLDWIDE,
INC., a subsidiary of MARVEL ENTERTAINMENT, LLC. OFFICE OF PUBLICATION: 135 West 50th Street, New York, NY 10020. Copyright © 2015 MARVEL No similarity between any of the names, characters,
persons, and/or institutions in this magazine with those of any living or dead person or institution is intended, and any such similarity which may exist is purely coincidental. **Printed in the U.S.A.** ALAN FINE,
President, Marvel Entertainment; DAN BUCKLEY, President, TV, Publishing and Brand Management; JOE QUESADA, Chief Creative Officer; TOM BREVOORT, SVP of Publishing; DAVID BOGART, SVP of Operations
& Procurement, Publishing; C.B. CEBULSKI, SVP of Creator & Content Development; DAVID GABRIEL, SVP Print, Sales & Marketing; JIM O'KEEFE, VP of Operations & Logistics; DAN CARR, Executive Director of
Publishing Technology; SUSAN CRESPI, Editorial Operations Manager; ALEX MORALES, Publishing Operations Manager; STAN LEE, Chairman Emeritus. For information regarding advertising in Marvel Comics
or on Marvel.com, please contact Jonathan Rheingold, VP of Custom Solutions & Ad Sales, at jrheingold@marvel.com. For Marvel subscription inquiries, please call 800-217-9158. **Manufactured between**
3/13/2015 and 4/20/2015 by R.R. DONNELLEY, INC., SALEM, VA, USA.
10 9 8 7 6 5 4 3 2 1

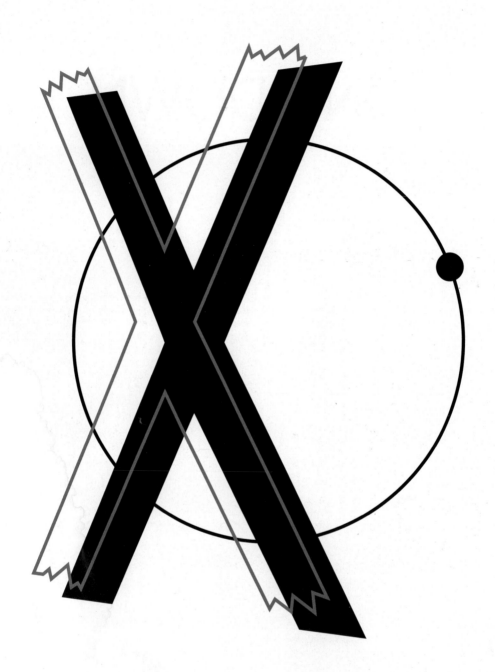

Born with genetic mutations that gave them abilities beyond those of normal humans, mutants are the next stage in evolution. As such, they are feared and hated by humanity. A group of mutants known as the X-Men fight for peaceful coexistence between mutants and humankind. But not all mutants see peaceful coexistence as a reality.

ALL·NEW X·MEN

Despite the future Brotherhood of Evil's best efforts, the All-New X-Men cannot return to their original time. Kitty Pryde, the only member of the Jean Grey school who stood up for the All-New X-Men's right to make their own decision about returning to the past, felt betrayed by her teammates and left, deciding to join Cyclops and the Uncanny X-Men at the New Xavier School. Feeling an allegiance to their professor, the All-New X-Men joined her...

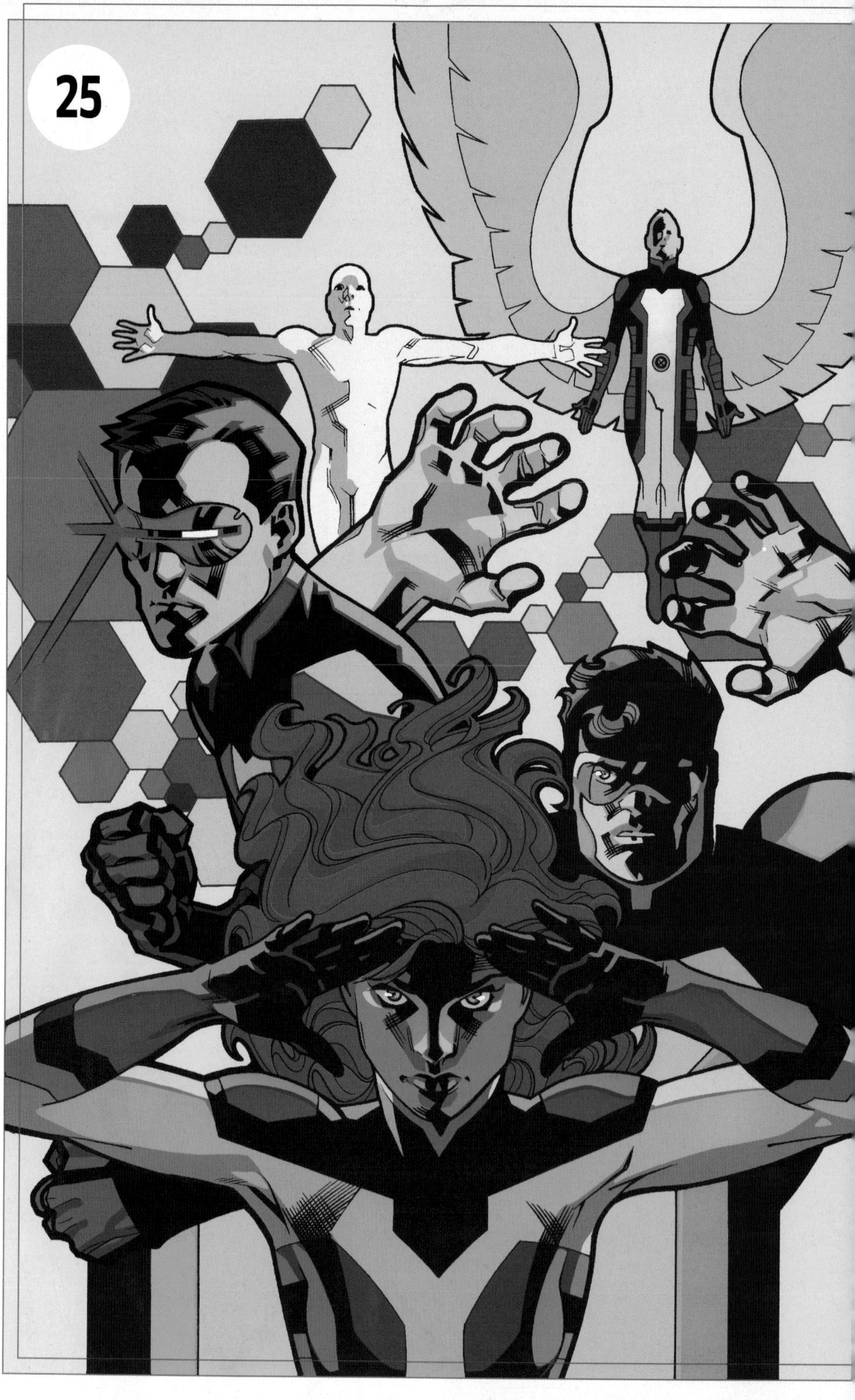
25

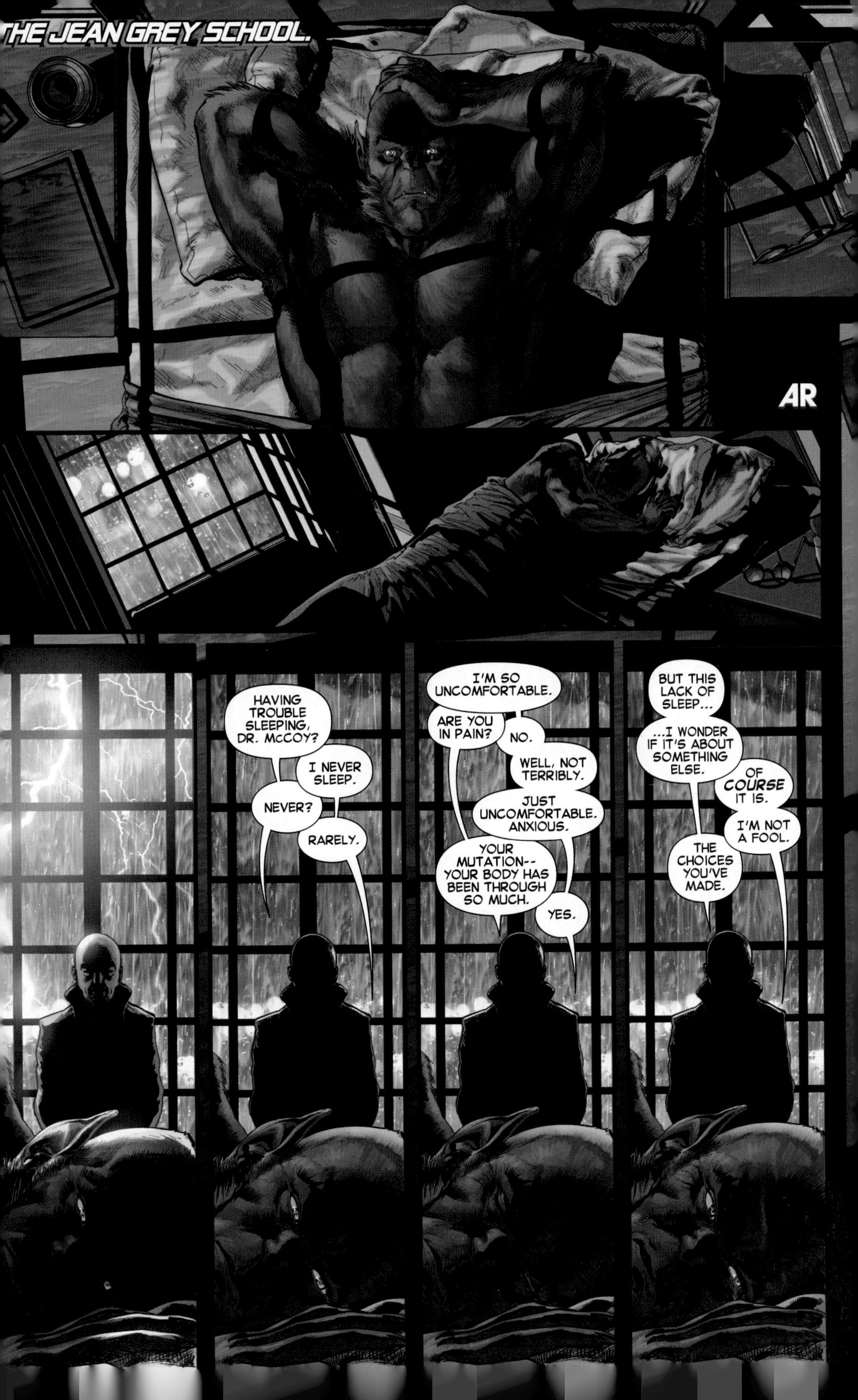
THE JEAN GREY SCHOOL.
AR
HAVING TROUBLE SLEEPING, DR. McCOY?
I NEVER SLEEP.
NEVER?
RARELY.
I'M SO UNCOMFORTABLE.
ARE YOU IN PAIN?
NO.
WELL, NOT TERRIBLY.
JUST UNCOMFORTABLE. ANXIOUS.
YOUR MUTATION-- YOUR BODY HAS BEEN THROUGH SO MUCH.
YES.
BUT THIS LACK OF SLEEP...
...I WONDER IF IT'S ABOUT SOMETHING ELSE.
OF COURSE IT IS.
I'M NOT A FOOL.
THE CHOICES YOU'VE MADE.

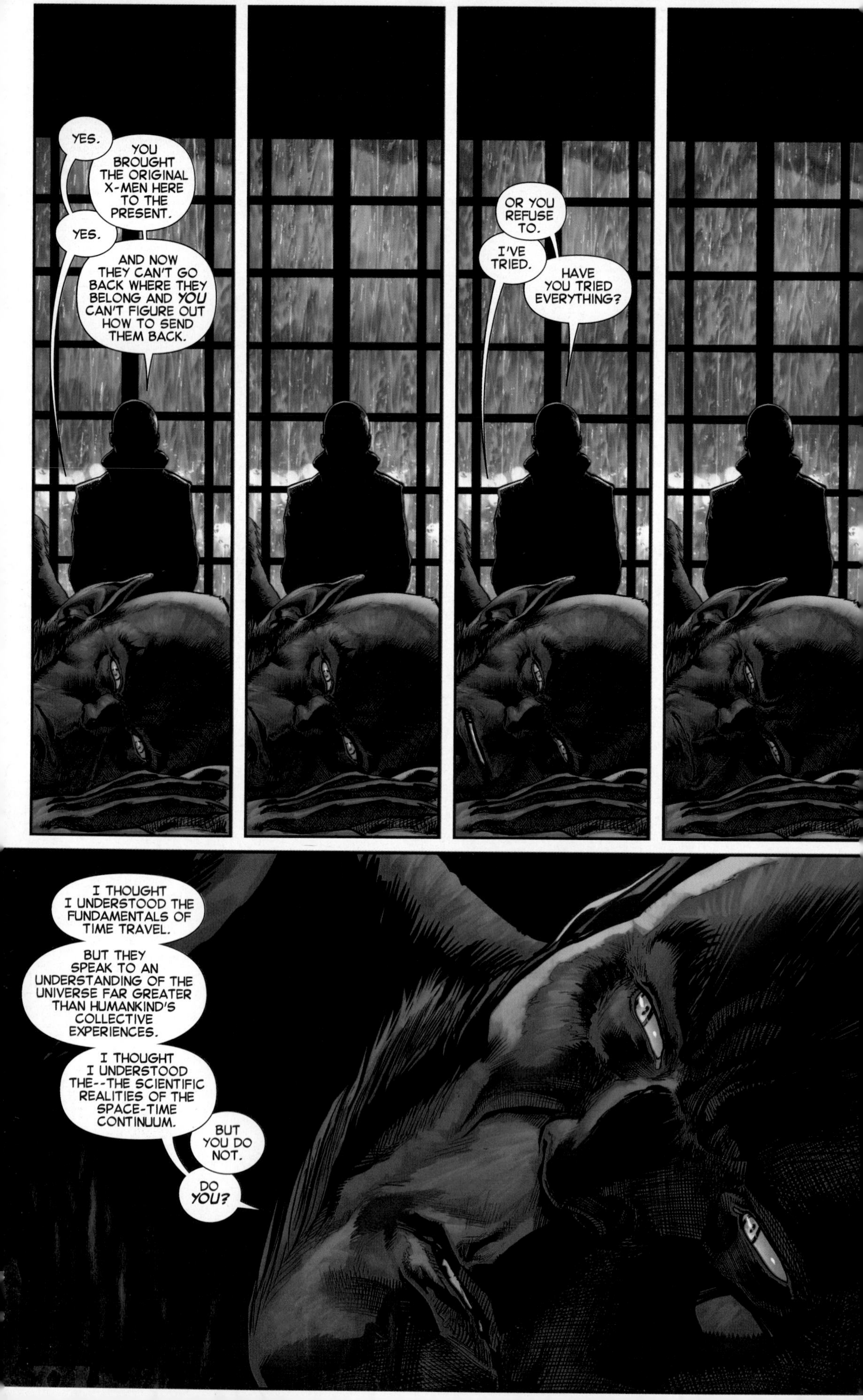
YES.
YOU BROUGHT THE ORIGINAL X-MEN HERE TO THE PRESENT.
YES.
AND NOW THEY CAN'T GO BACK WHERE THEY BELONG AND YOU CAN'T FIGURE OUT HOW TO SEND THEM BACK.
OR YOU REFUSE TO.
I'VE TRIED.
HAVE YOU TRIED EVERYTHING?
I THOUGHT I UNDERSTOOD THE FUNDAMENTALS OF TIME TRAVEL.
BUT THEY SPEAK TO AN UNDERSTANDING OF THE UNIVERSE FAR GREATER THAN HUMANKIND'S COLLECTIVE EXPERIENCES.
I THOUGHT I UNDERSTOOD THE--THE SCIENTIFIC REALITIES OF THE SPACE-TIME CONTINUUM.
BUT YOU DO NOT.
DO YOU?

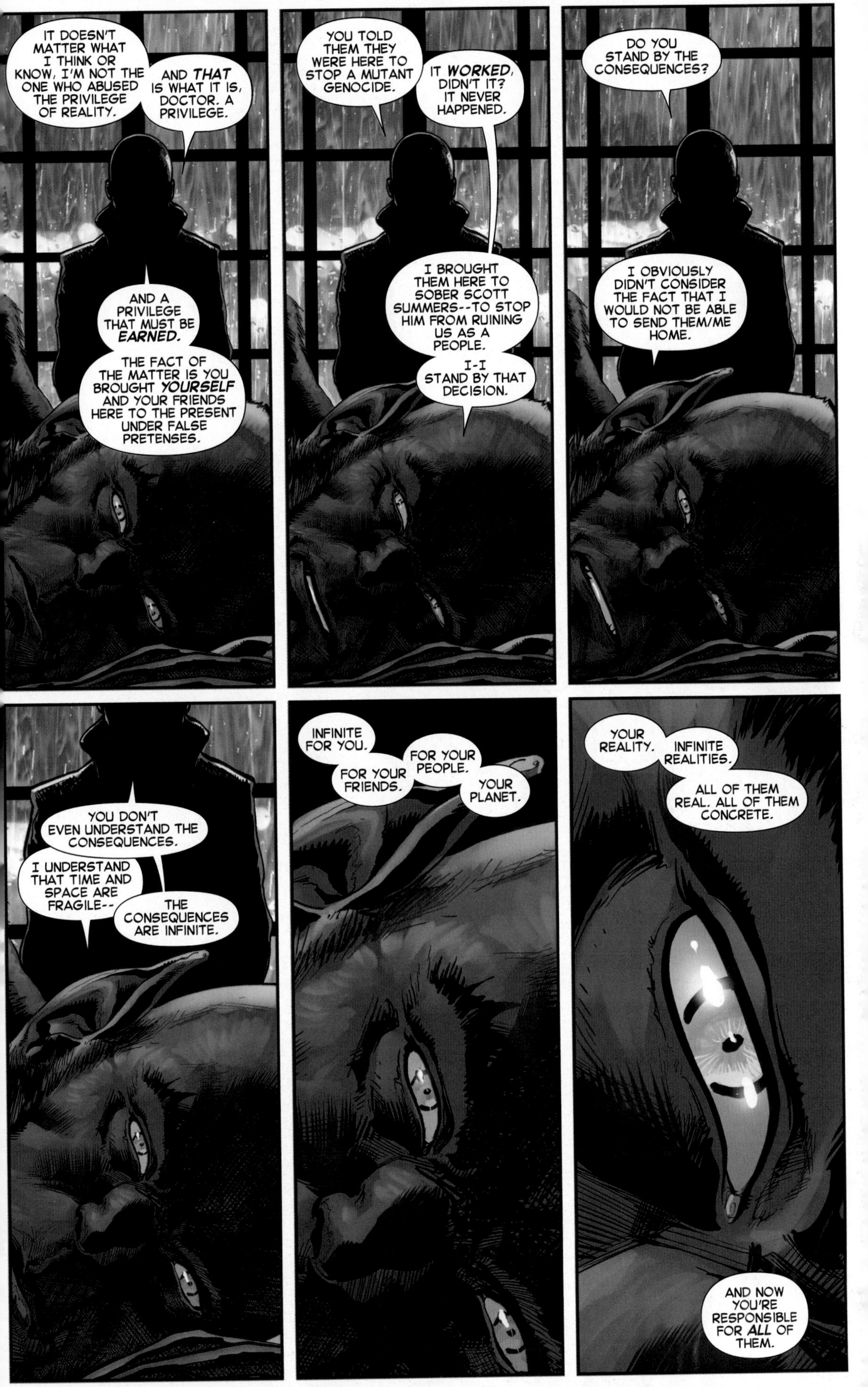

IT DOESN'T MATTER WHAT I THINK OR KNOW, I'M NOT THE ONE WHO ABUSED THE PRIVILEGE OF REALITY.
AND THAT IS WHAT IT IS, DOCTOR. A PRIVILEGE.
AND A PRIVILEGE THAT MUST BE EARNED.
THE FACT OF THE MATTER IS YOU BROUGHT YOURSELF AND YOUR FRIENDS HERE TO THE PRESENT UNDER FALSE PRETENSES.
YOU TOLD THEM THEY WERE HERE TO STOP A MUTANT GENOCIDE.
IT WORKED, DIDN'T IT? IT NEVER HAPPENED.
I BROUGHT THEM HERE TO SOBER SCOTT SUMMERS--TO STOP HIM FROM RUINING US AS A PEOPLE.
I-I STAND BY THAT DECISION.
DO YOU STAND BY THE CONSEQUENCES?
I OBVIOUSLY DIDN'T CONSIDER THE FACT THAT I WOULD NOT BE ABLE TO SEND THEM/ME HOME.
YOU DON'T EVEN UNDERSTAND THE CONSEQUENCES.
I UNDERSTAND THAT TIME AND SPACE ARE FRAGILE--
THE CONSEQUENCES ARE INFINITE.
INFINITE FOR YOU.
FOR YOUR FRIENDS.
FOR YOUR PEOPLE.
YOUR PLANET.
YOUR REALITY.
INFINITE REALITIES.
ALL OF THEM REAL. ALL OF THEM CONCRETE.
AND NOW YOU'RE RESPONSIBLE FOR ALL OF THEM.

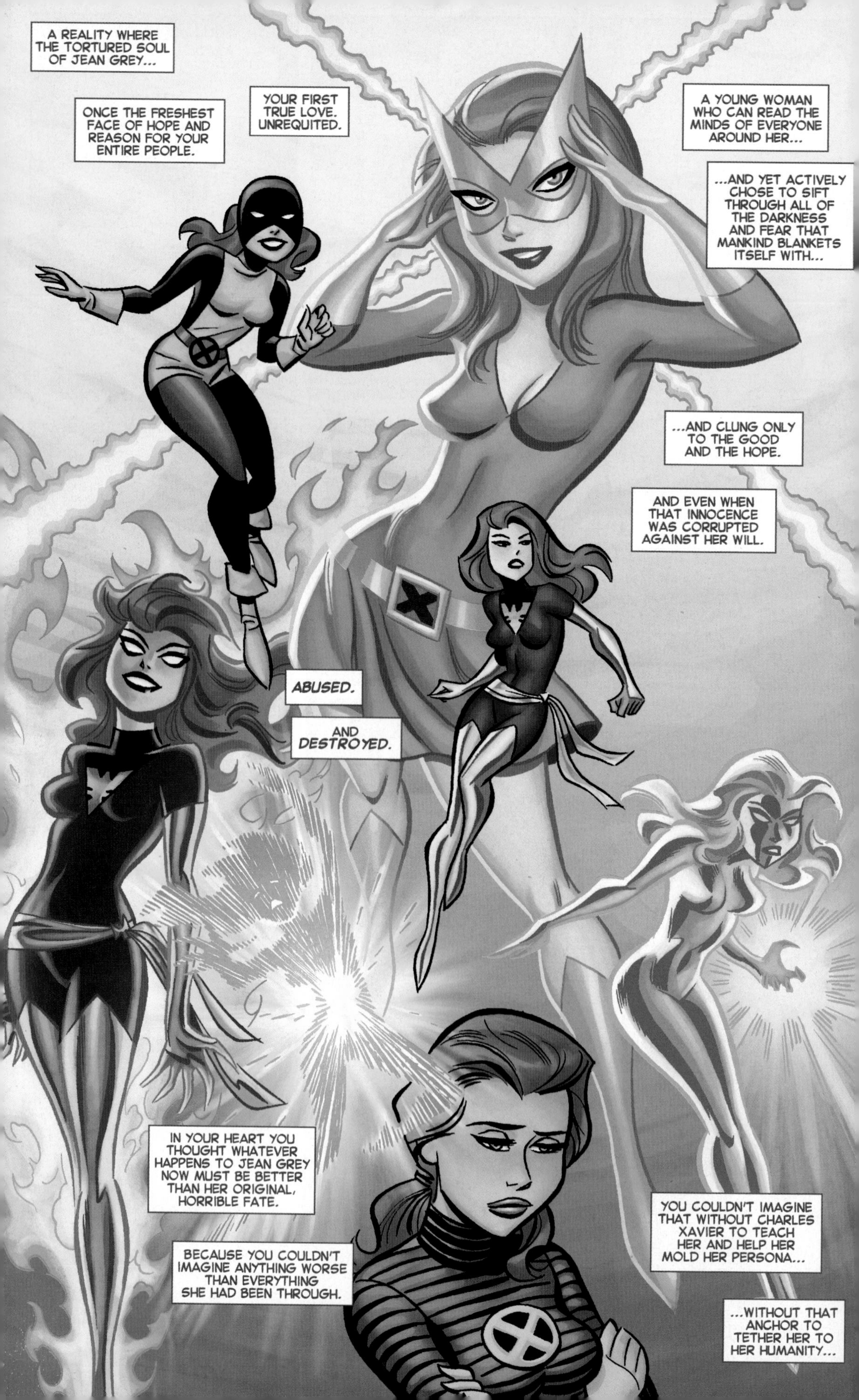
A REALITY WHERE THE TORTURED SOUL OF JEAN GREY...
ONCE THE FRESHEST FACE OF HOPE AND REASON FOR YOUR ENTIRE PEOPLE.
YOUR FIRST TRUE LOVE. UNREQUITED.
A YOUNG WOMAN WHO CAN READ THE MINDS OF EVERYONE AROUND HER...
...AND YET ACTIVELY CHOSE TO SIFT THROUGH ALL OF THE DARKNESS AND FEAR THAT MANKIND BLANKETS ITSELF WITH...
...AND CLUNG ONLY TO THE GOOD AND THE HOPE.
AND EVEN WHEN THAT INNOCENCE WAS CORRUPTED AGAINST HER WILL.
ABUSED.
AND DESTROYED.
IN YOUR HEART YOU THOUGHT WHATEVER HAPPENS TO JEAN GREY NOW MUST BE BETTER THAN HER ORIGINAL, HORRIBLE FATE.
BECAUSE YOU COULDN'T IMAGINE ANYTHING WORSE THAN EVERYTHING SHE HAD BEEN THROUGH.
YOU COULDN'T IMAGINE THAT WITHOUT CHARLES XAVIER TO TEACH HER AND HELP HER MOLD HER PERSONA...
...WITHOUT THAT ANCHOR TO TETHER HER TO HER HUMANITY...

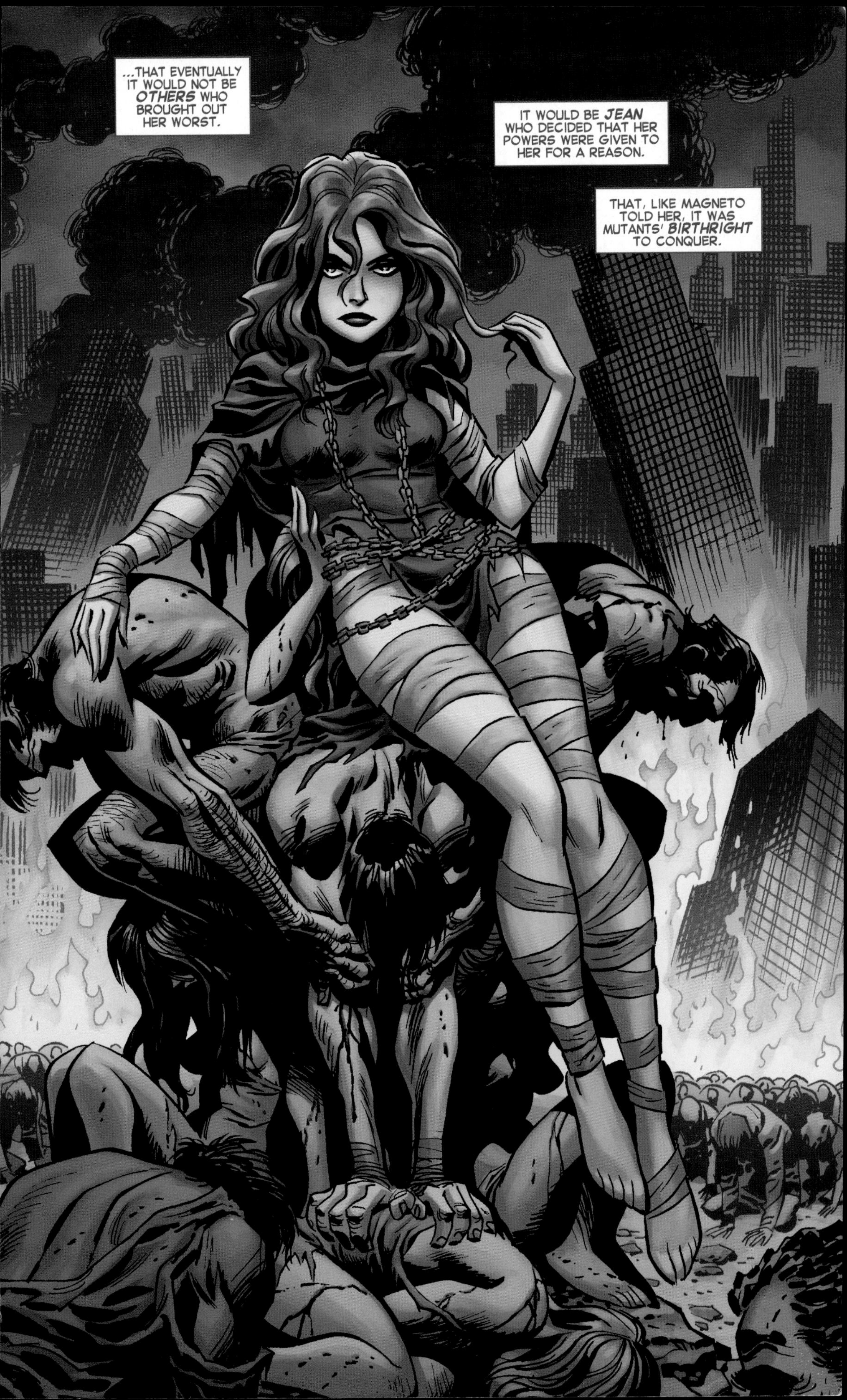
...THAT EVENTUALLY IT WOULD NOT BE OTHERS WHO BROUGHT OUT HER WORST.
IT WOULD BE JEAN WHO DECIDED THAT HER POWERS WERE GIVEN TO HER FOR A REASON.
THAT, LIKE MAGNETO TOLD HER, IT WAS MUTANTS' BIRTHRIGHT TO CONQUER.

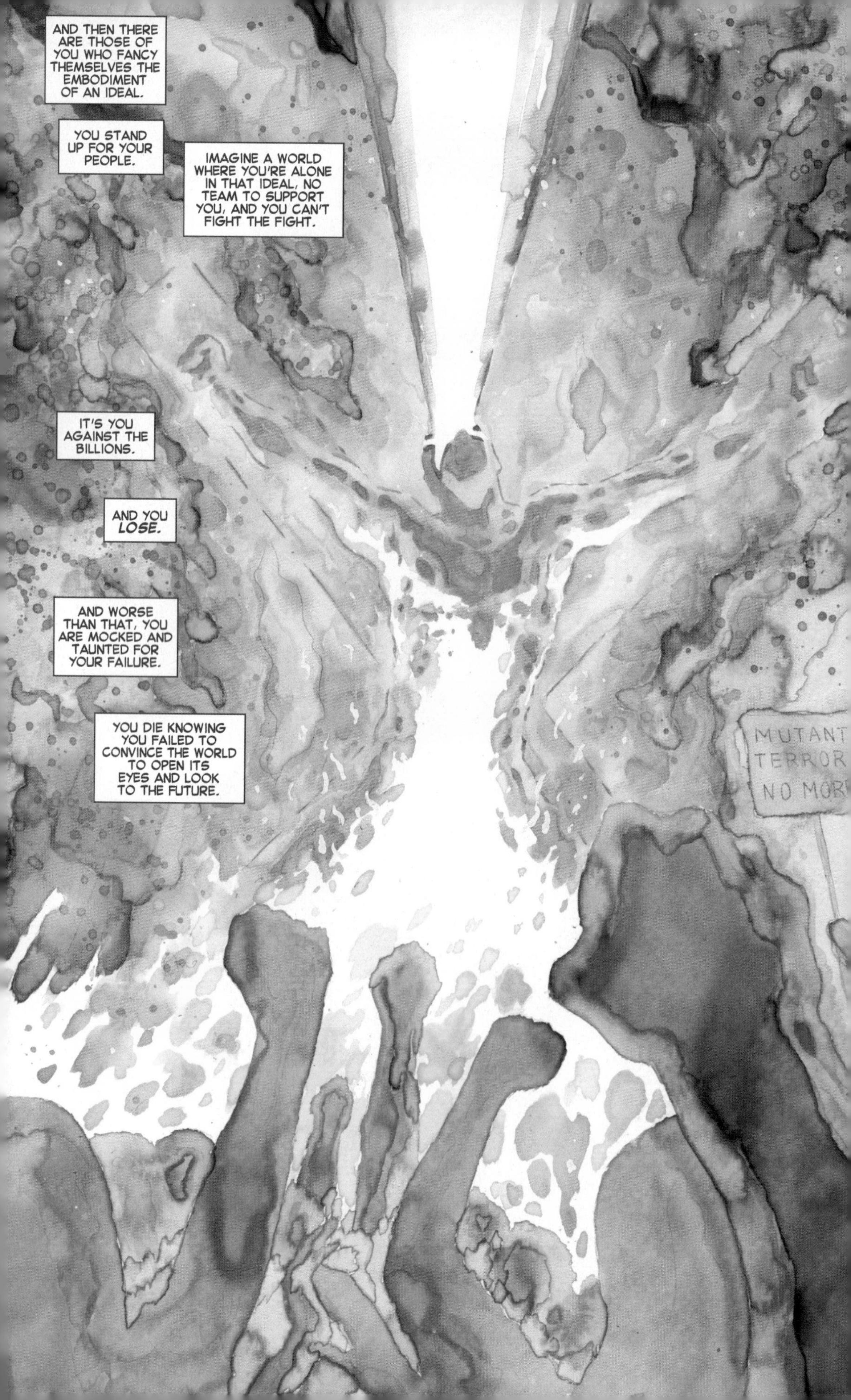
AND THEN THERE ARE THOSE OF YOU WHO FANCY THEMSELVES THE EMBODIMENT OF AN IDEAL.
YOU STAND UP FOR YOUR PEOPLE.
IMAGINE A WORLD WHERE YOU'RE ALONE IN THAT IDEAL, NO TEAM TO SUPPORT YOU, AND YOU CAN'T FIGHT THE FIGHT.
IT'S YOU AGAINST THE BILLIONS.
AND YOU *LOSE.*
AND WORSE THAN THAT, YOU ARE MOCKED AND TAUNTED FOR YOUR FAILURE.
YOU DIE KNOWING YOU FAILED TO CONVINCE THE WORLD TO OPEN ITS EYES AND LOOK TO THE FUTURE.
MUTANT TERROR NO MOR

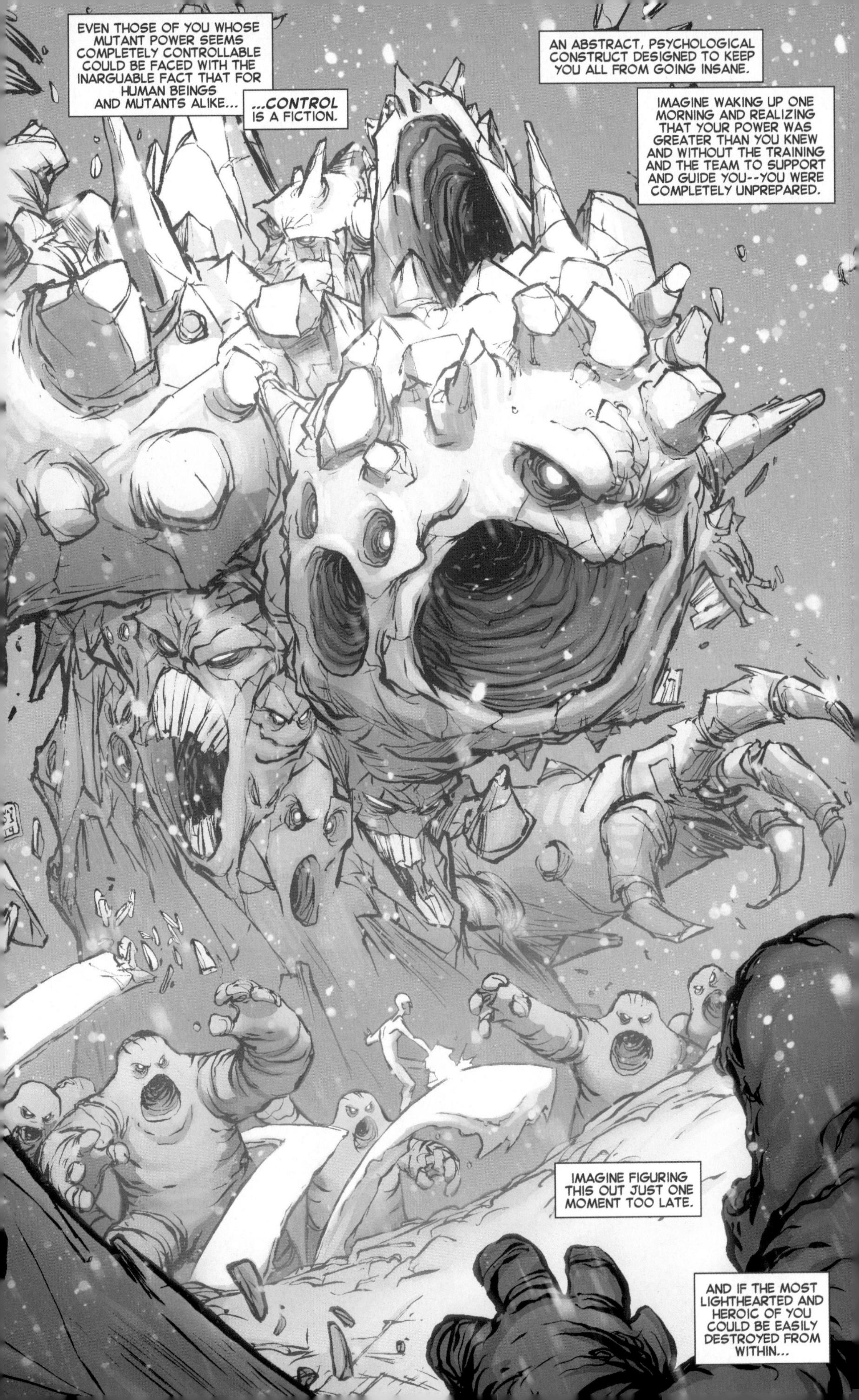
EVEN THOSE OF YOU WHOSE MUTANT POWER SEEMS COMPLETELY CONTROLLABLE COULD BE FACED WITH THE INARGUABLE FACT THAT FOR HUMAN BEINGS AND MUTANTS ALIKE...
...CONTROL IS A FICTION.
AN ABSTRACT, PSYCHOLOGICAL CONSTRUCT DESIGNED TO KEEP YOU ALL FROM GOING INSANE.
IMAGINE WAKING UP ONE MORNING AND REALIZING THAT YOUR POWER WAS GREATER THAN YOU KNEW AND WITHOUT THE TRAINING AND THE TEAM TO SUPPORT AND GUIDE YOU--YOU WERE COMPLETELY UNPREPARED.
IMAGINE FIGURING THIS OUT JUST ONE MOMENT TOO LATE.
AND IF THE MOST LIGHTHEARTED AND HEROIC OF YOU COULD BE EASILY DESTROYED FROM WITHIN...

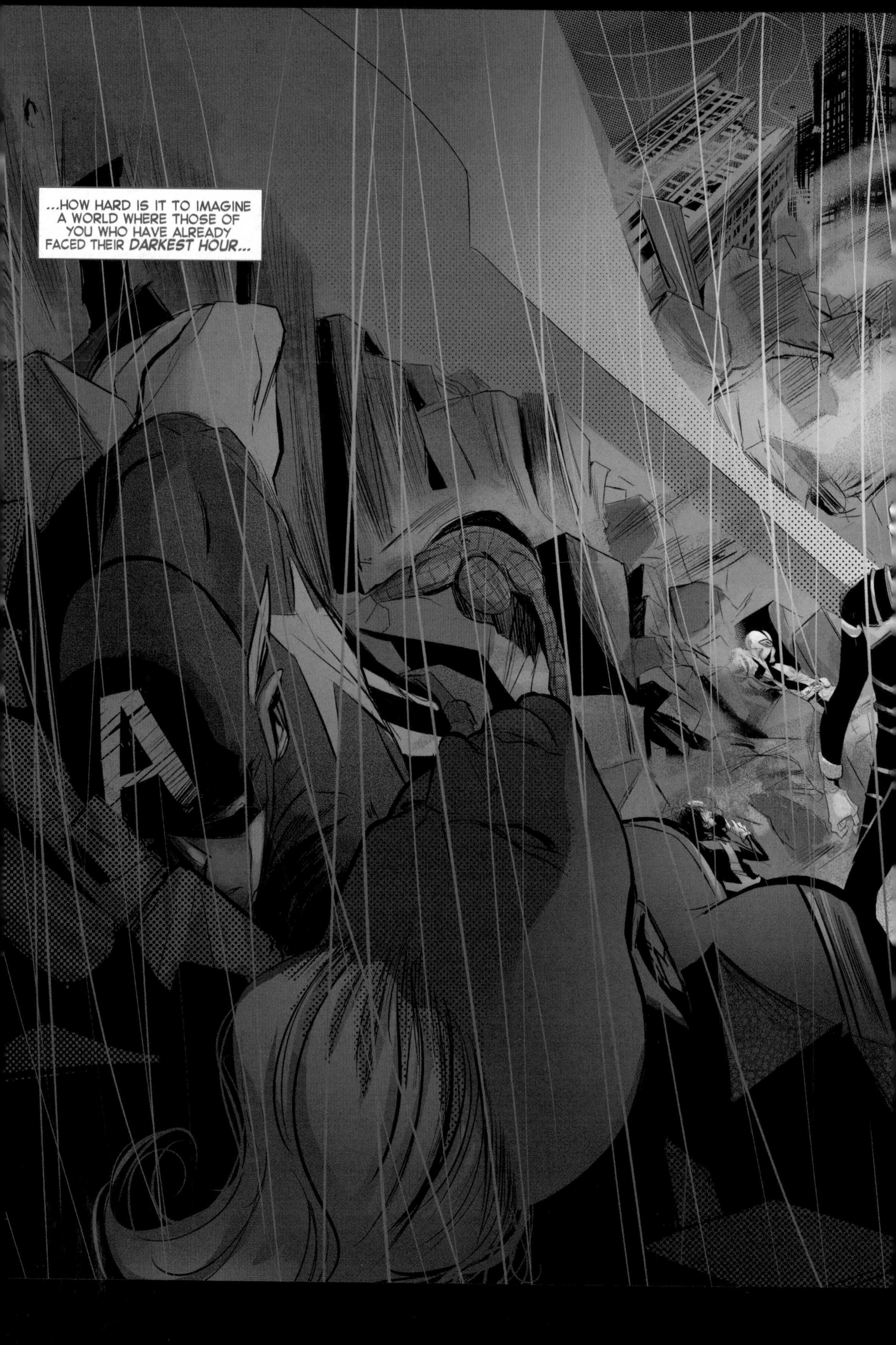
...HOW HARD IS IT TO IMAGINE A WORLD WHERE THOSE OF YOU WHO HAVE ALREADY FACED THEIR DARKEST HOUR...

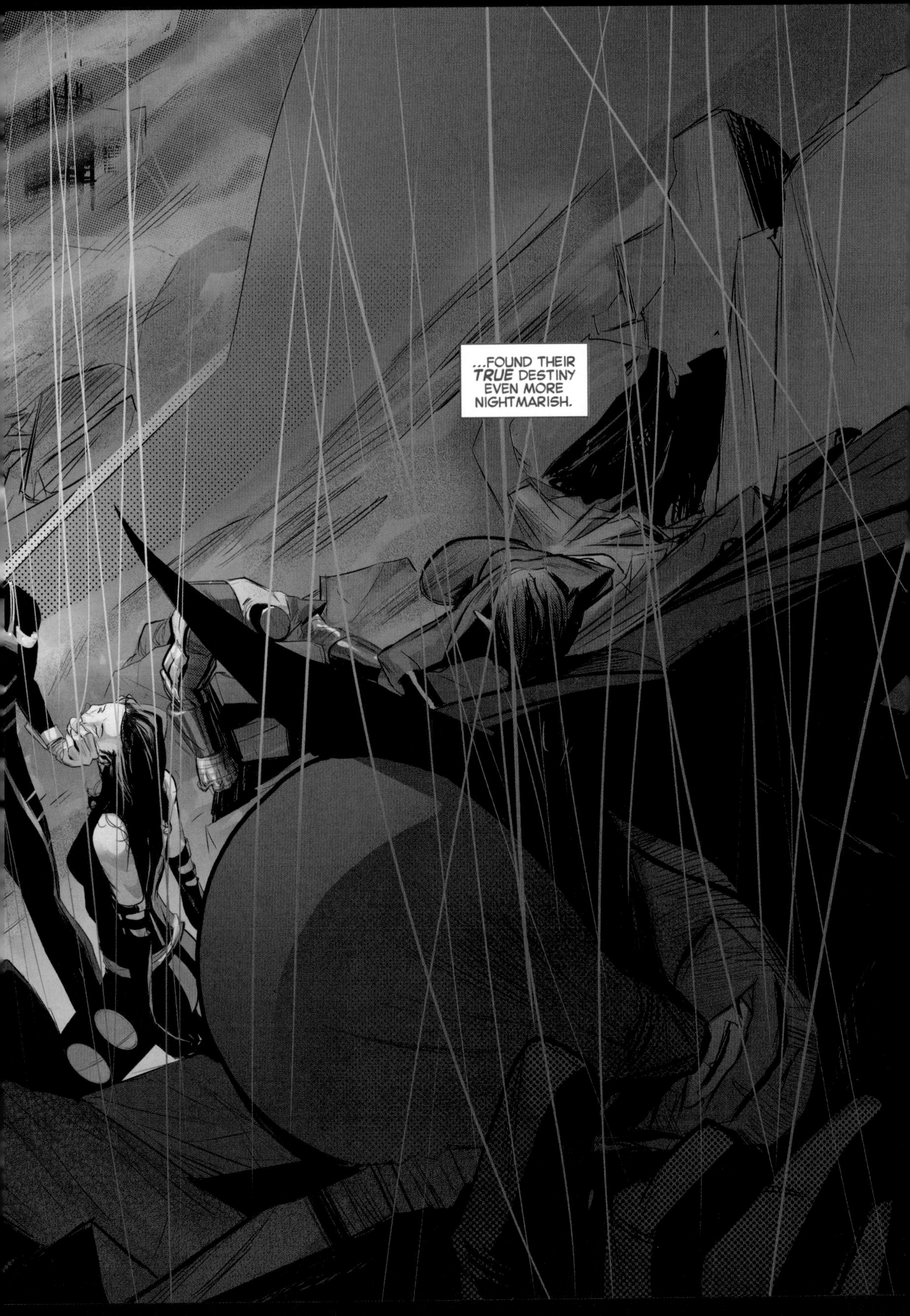
...FOUND THEIR TRUE DESTINY EVEN MORE NIGHTMARISH.

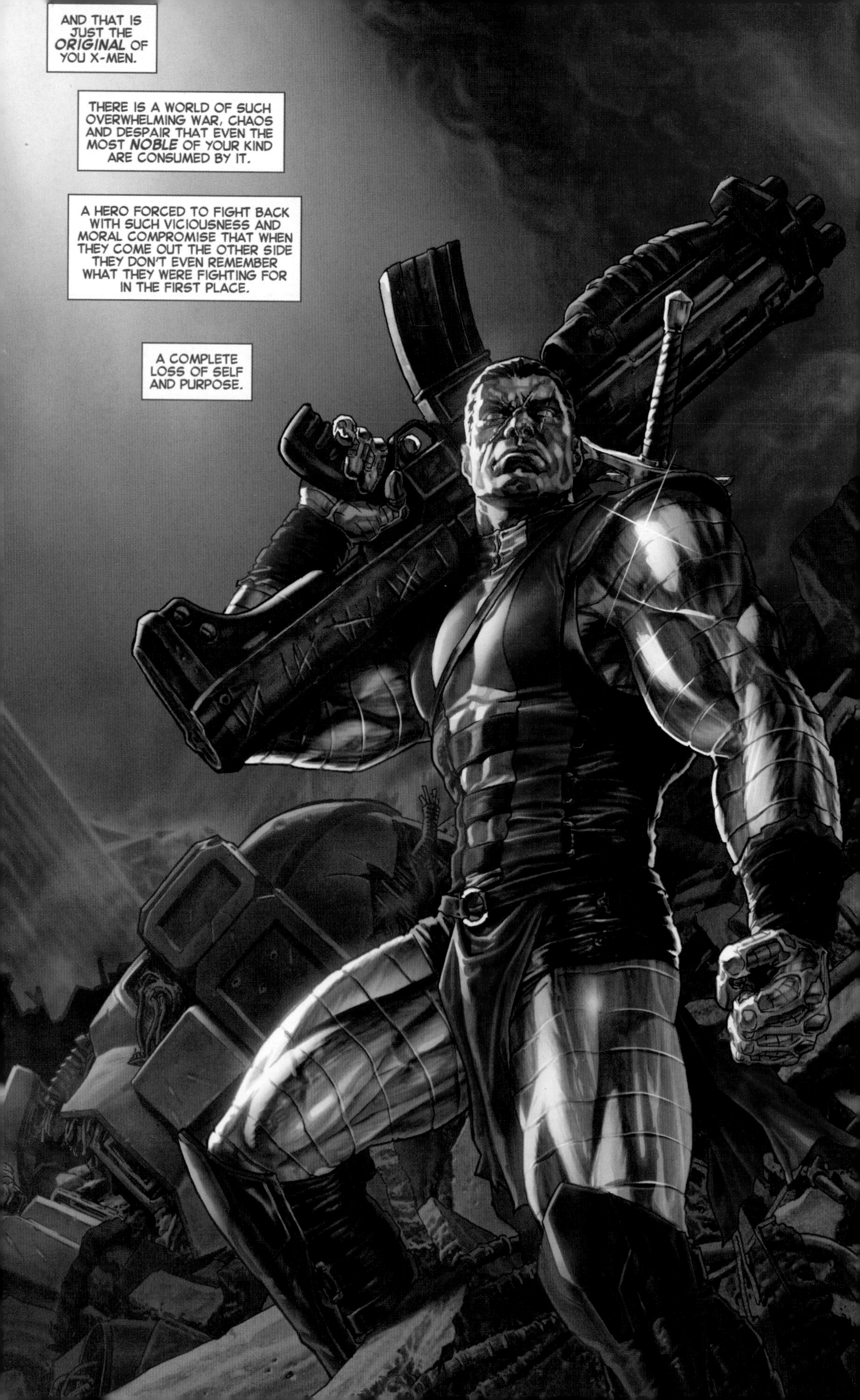
AND THAT IS JUST THE *ORIGINAL* OF YOU X-MEN.
THERE IS A WORLD OF SUCH OVERWHELMING WAR, CHAOS AND DESPAIR THAT EVEN THE MOST *NOBLE* OF YOUR KIND ARE CONSUMED BY IT.
A HERO FORCED TO FIGHT BACK WITH SUCH VICIOUSNESS AND MORAL COMPROMISE THAT WHEN THEY COME OUT THE OTHER SIDE THEY DON'T EVEN REMEMBER WHAT THEY WERE FIGHTING FOR IN THE FIRST PLACE.
A COMPLETE LOSS OF SELF AND PURPOSE.

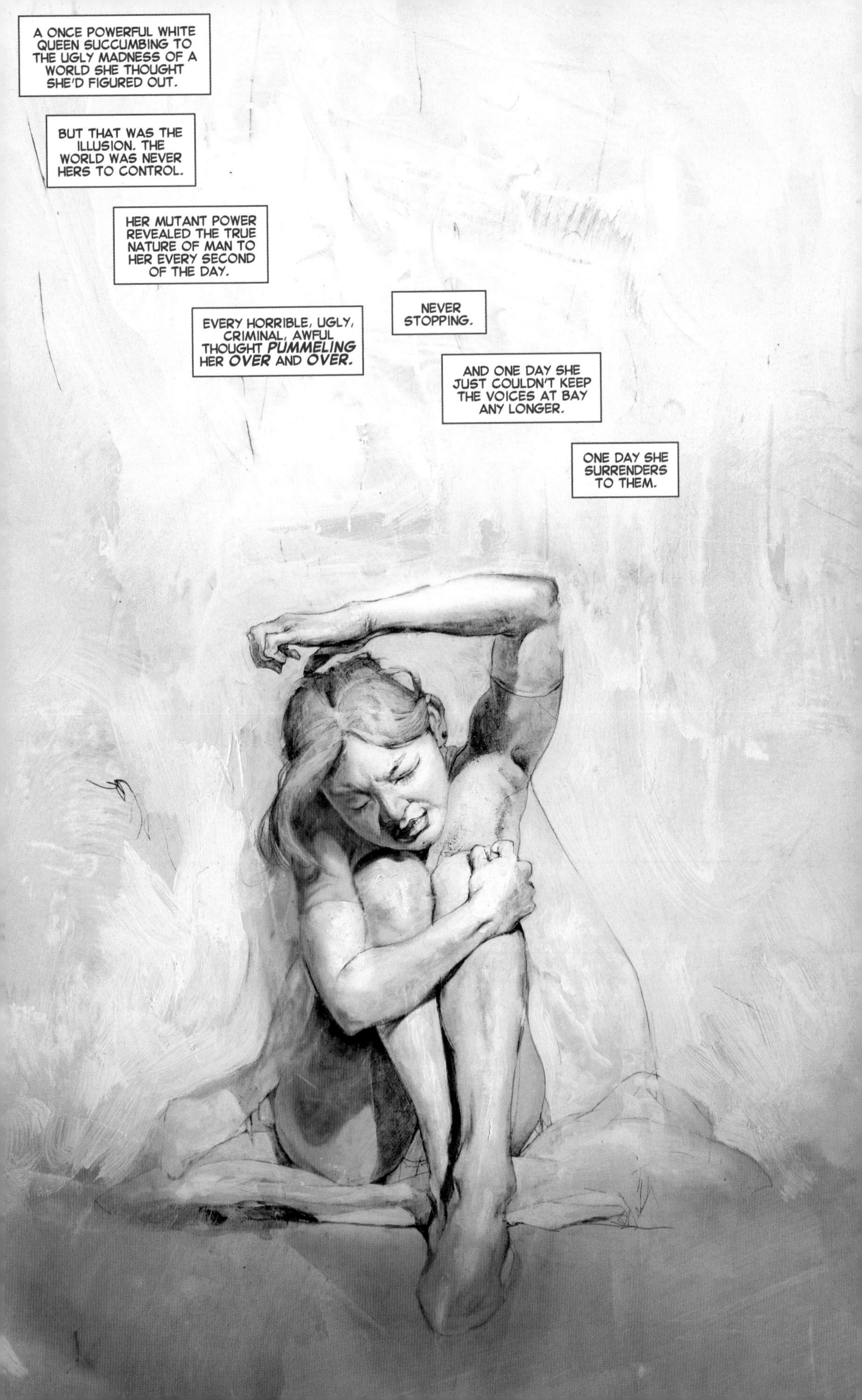
A ONCE POWERFUL WHITE QUEEN SUCCUMBING TO THE UGLY MADNESS OF A WORLD SHE THOUGHT SHE'D FIGURED OUT.
BUT THAT WAS THE ILLUSION. THE WORLD WAS NEVER HERS TO CONTROL.
HER MUTANT POWER REVEALED THE TRUE NATURE OF MAN TO HER EVERY SECOND OF THE DAY.
EVERY HORRIBLE, UGLY, CRIMINAL, AWFUL THOUGHT *PUMMELING* HER *OVER* AND *OVER*.
NEVER STOPPING.
AND ONE DAY SHE JUST COULDN'T KEEP THE VOICES AT BAY ANY LONGER.
ONE DAY SHE SURRENDERS TO THEM.

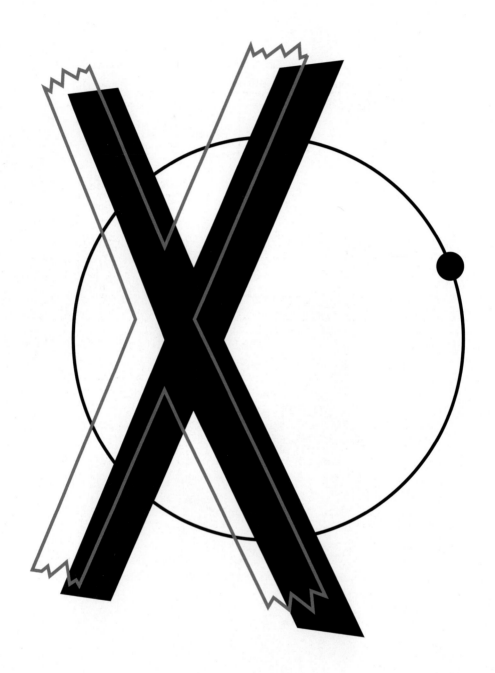

A REALITY WHERE THOSE OF YOU EVEN CLOSER TO THE EDGE OF YOUR OWN HUMANITY GIVE WAY TO YOUR TRUE NATURE.

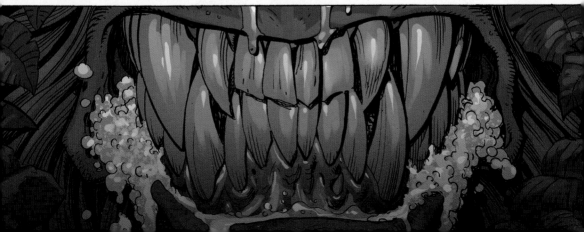

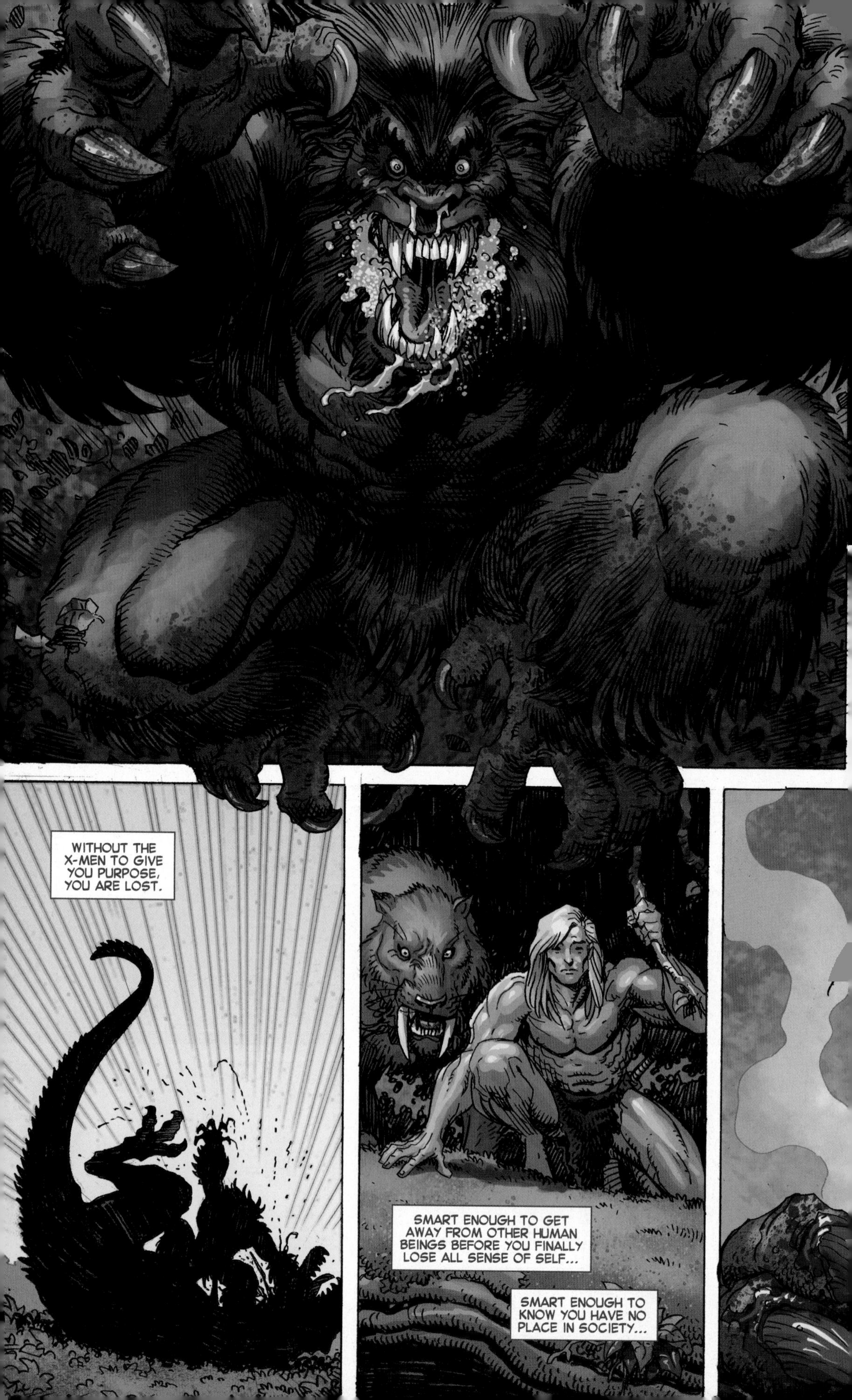
WITHOUT THE X-MEN TO GIVE YOU PURPOSE, YOU ARE LOST.
SMART ENOUGH TO GET AWAY FROM OTHER HUMAN BEINGS BEFORE YOU FINALLY LOSE ALL SENSE OF SELF...
SMART ENOUGH TO KNOW YOU HAVE NO PLACE IN SOCIETY...

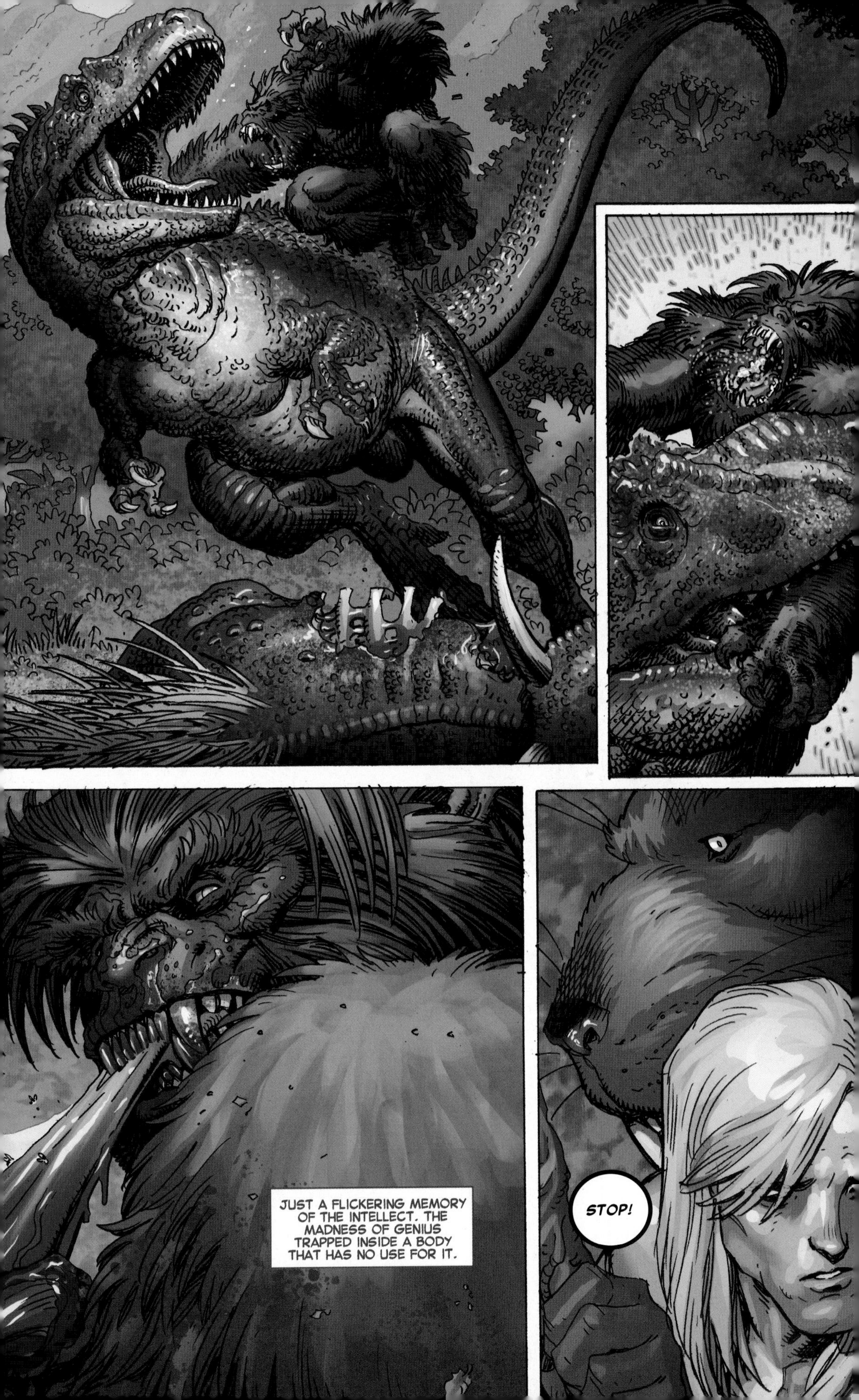
JUST A FLICKERING MEMORY OF THE INTELLECT. THE MADNESS OF GENIUS TRAPPED INSIDE A BODY THAT HAS NO USE FOR IT.
STOP!

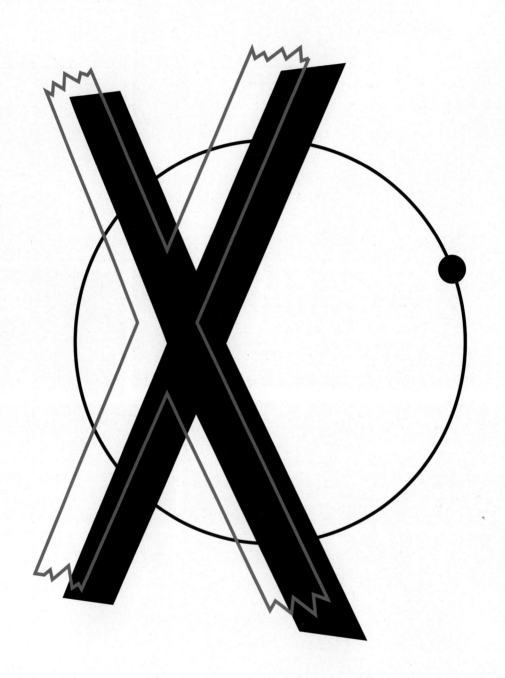

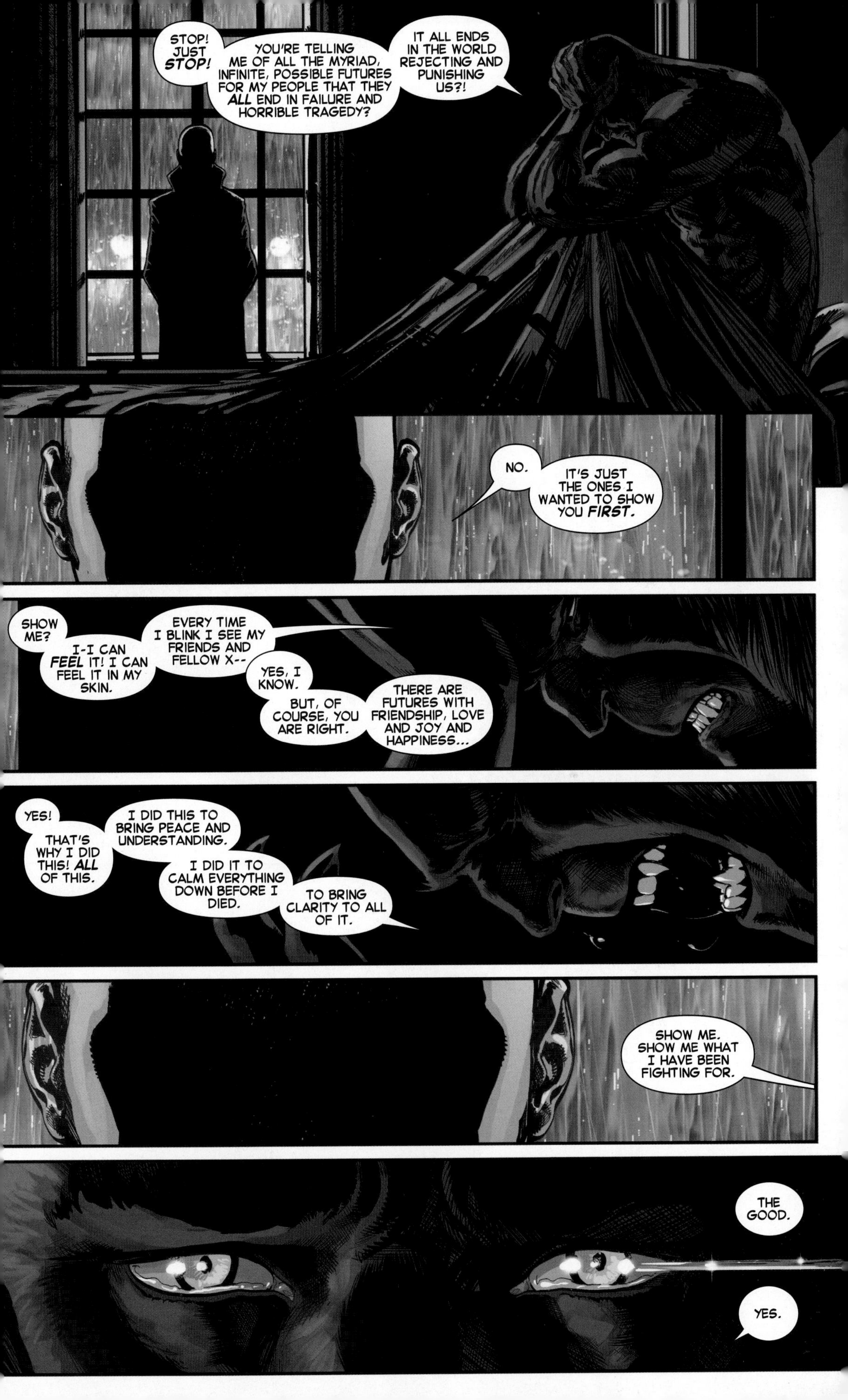
STOP! JUST STOP!
YOU'RE TELLING ME OF ALL THE MYRIAD, INFINITE, POSSIBLE FUTURES FOR MY PEOPLE THAT THEY ALL END IN FAILURE AND HORRIBLE TRAGEDY?
IT ALL ENDS IN THE WORLD REJECTING AND PUNISHING US?!
NO.
IT'S JUST THE ONES I WANTED TO SHOW YOU FIRST.
SHOW ME?
I-I CAN FEEL IT! I CAN FEEL IT IN MY SKIN.
EVERY TIME I BLINK I SEE MY FRIENDS AND FELLOW X--
YES, I KNOW.
BUT, OF COURSE, YOU ARE RIGHT.
THERE ARE FUTURES WITH FRIENDSHIP, LOVE AND JOY AND HAPPINESS...
YES!
THAT'S WHY I DID THIS! ALL OF THIS.
I DID THIS TO BRING PEACE AND UNDERSTANDING.
I DID IT TO CALM EVERYTHING DOWN BEFORE I DIED.
TO BRING CLARITY TO ALL OF IT.
SHOW ME. SHOW ME WHAT I HAVE BEEN FIGHTING FOR.
THE GOOD.
YES.

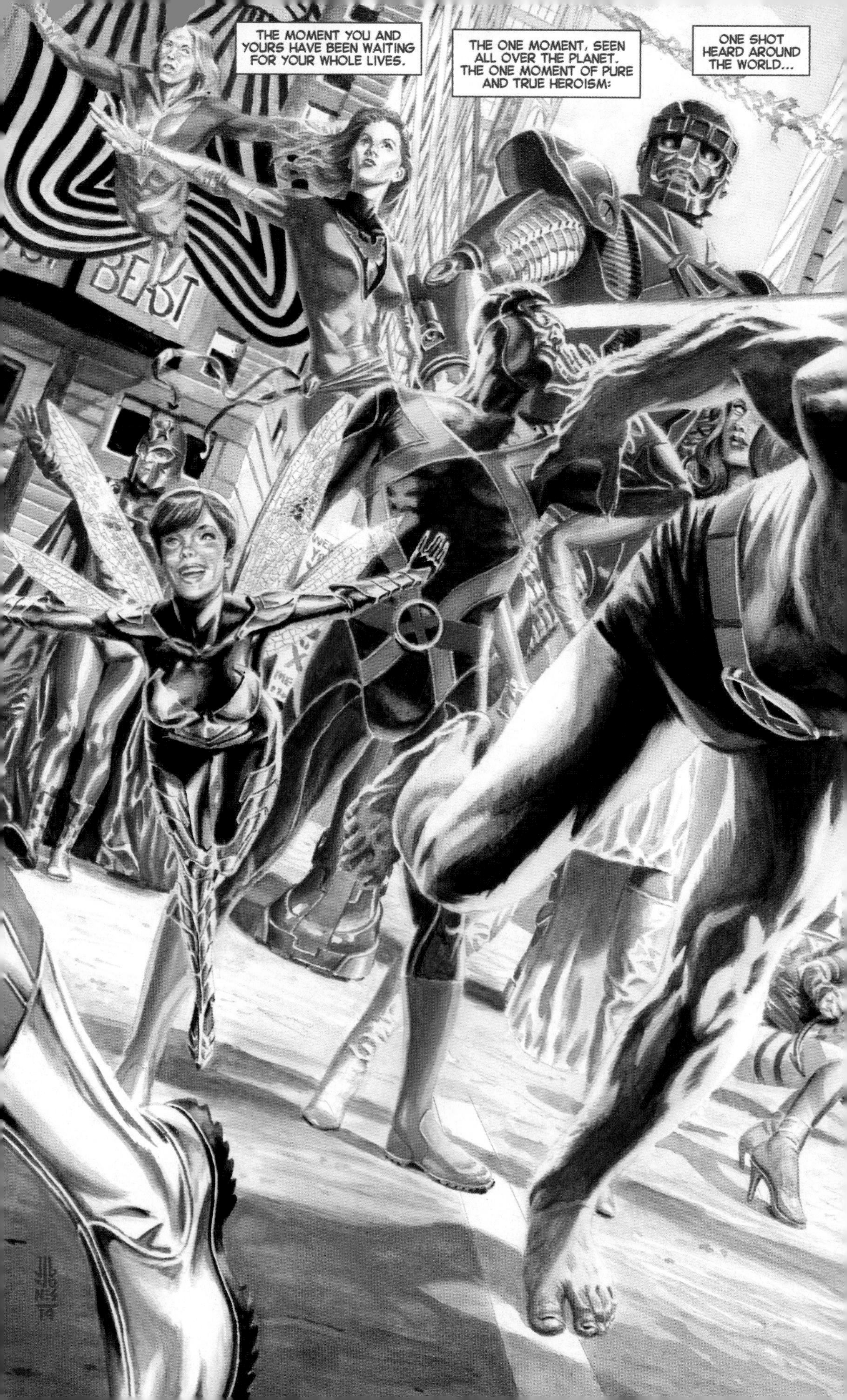
THE MOMENT YOU AND YOURS HAVE BEEN WAITING FOR YOUR WHOLE LIVES.
THE ONE MOMENT, SEEN ALL OVER THE PLANET. THE ONE MOMENT OF PURE AND TRUE HEROISM:
ONE SHOT HEARD AROUND THE WORLD...
BEAST

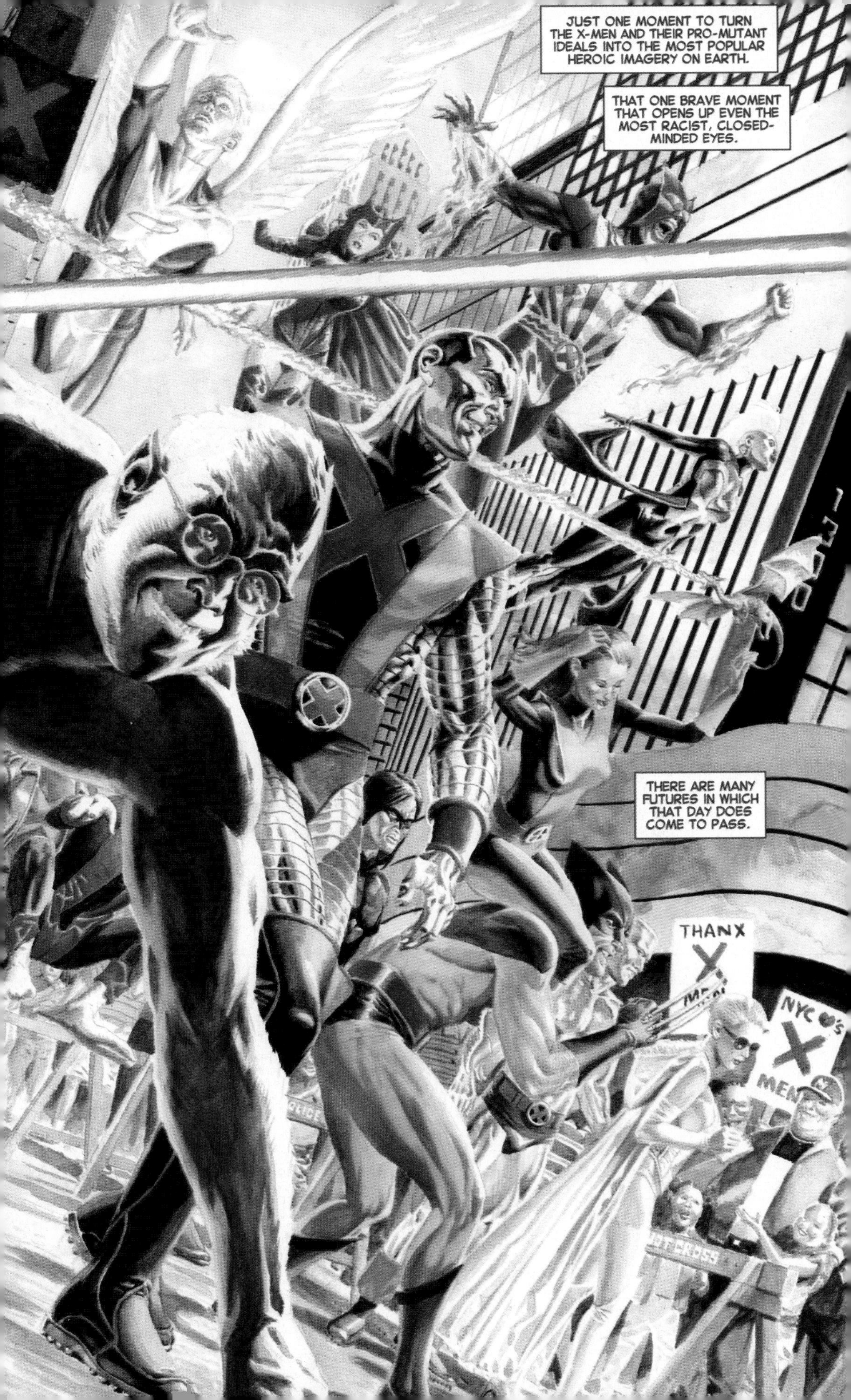
JUST ONE MOMENT TO TURN THE X-MEN AND THEIR PRO-MUTANT IDEALS INTO THE MOST POPULAR HEROIC IMAGERY ON EARTH.
THAT ONE BRAVE MOMENT THAT OPENS UP EVEN THE MOST RACIST, CLOSED-MINDED EYES.
THERE ARE MANY FUTURES IN WHICH THAT DAY DOES COME TO PASS.
THANX X
NYC ♥'S X MEN

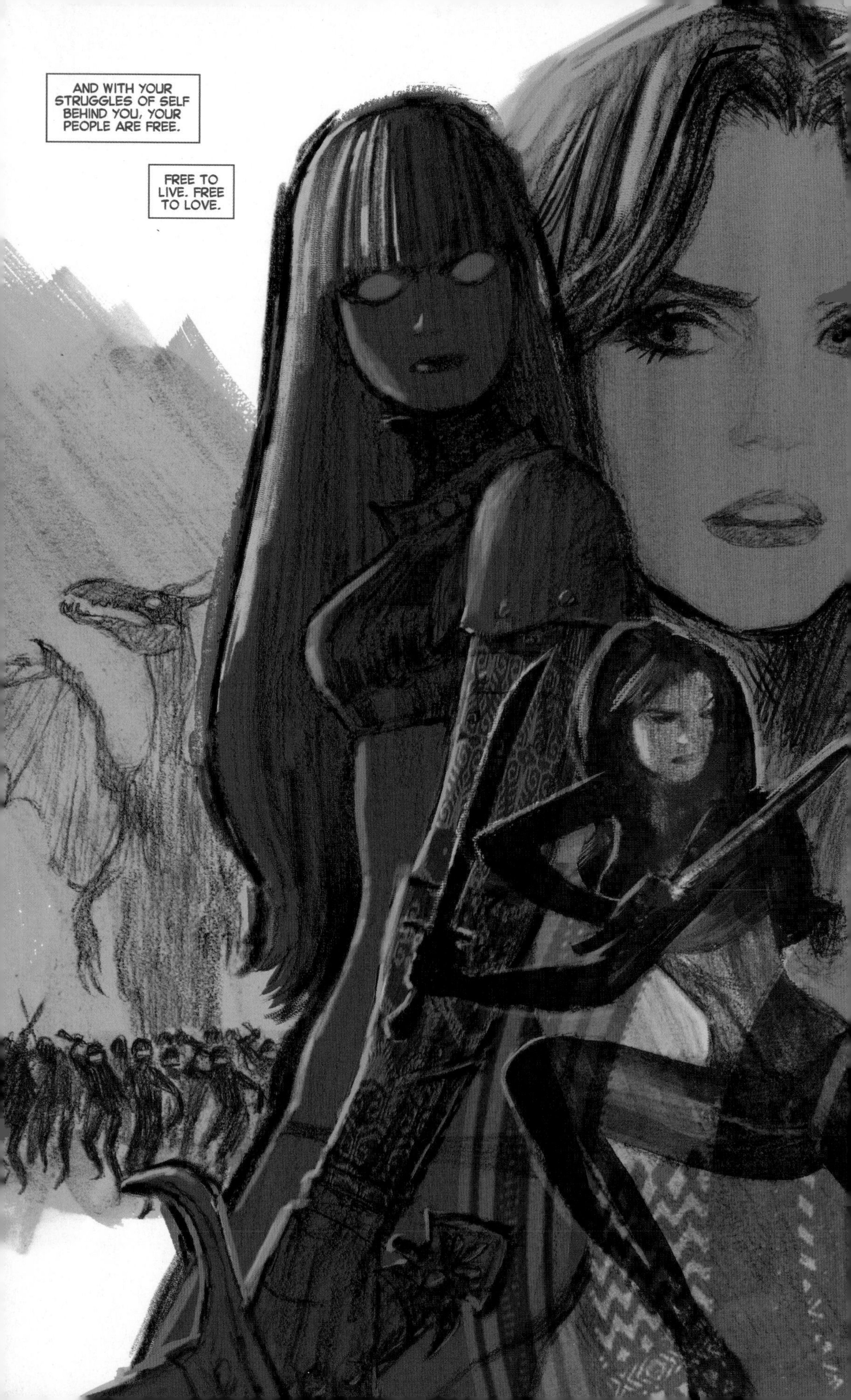
AND WITH YOUR STRUGGLES OF SELF BEHIND YOU, YOUR PEOPLE ARE FREE.
FREE TO LIVE. FREE TO LOVE.

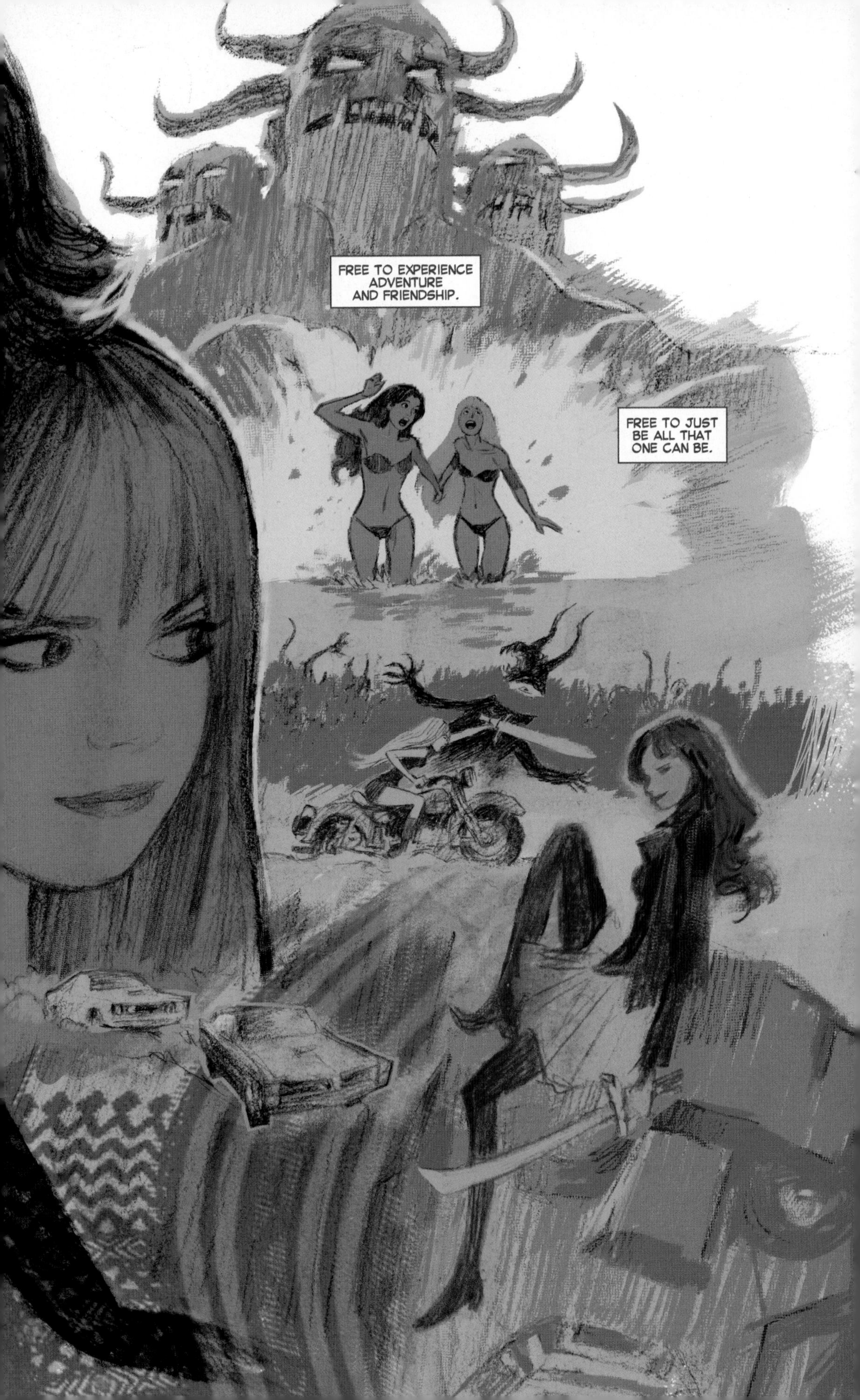
FREE TO EXPERIENCE ADVENTURE AND FRIENDSHIP.
FREE TO JUST BE ALL THAT ONE CAN BE.

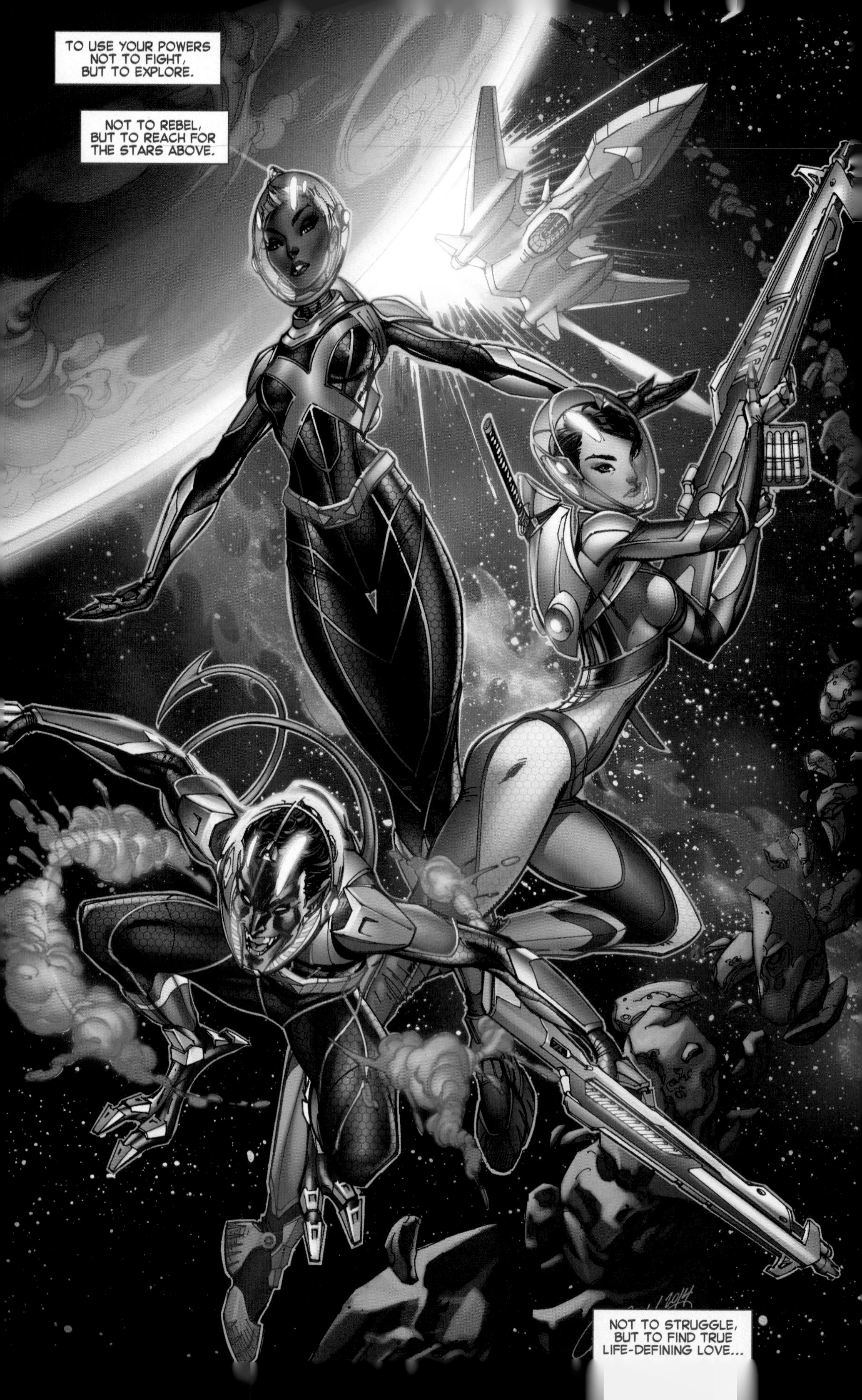
TO USE YOUR POWERS NOT TO FIGHT, BUT TO EXPLORE.
NOT TO REBEL, BUT TO REACH FOR THE STARS ABOVE.
NOT TO STRUGGLE, BUT TO FIND TRUE LIFE-DEFINING LOVE...

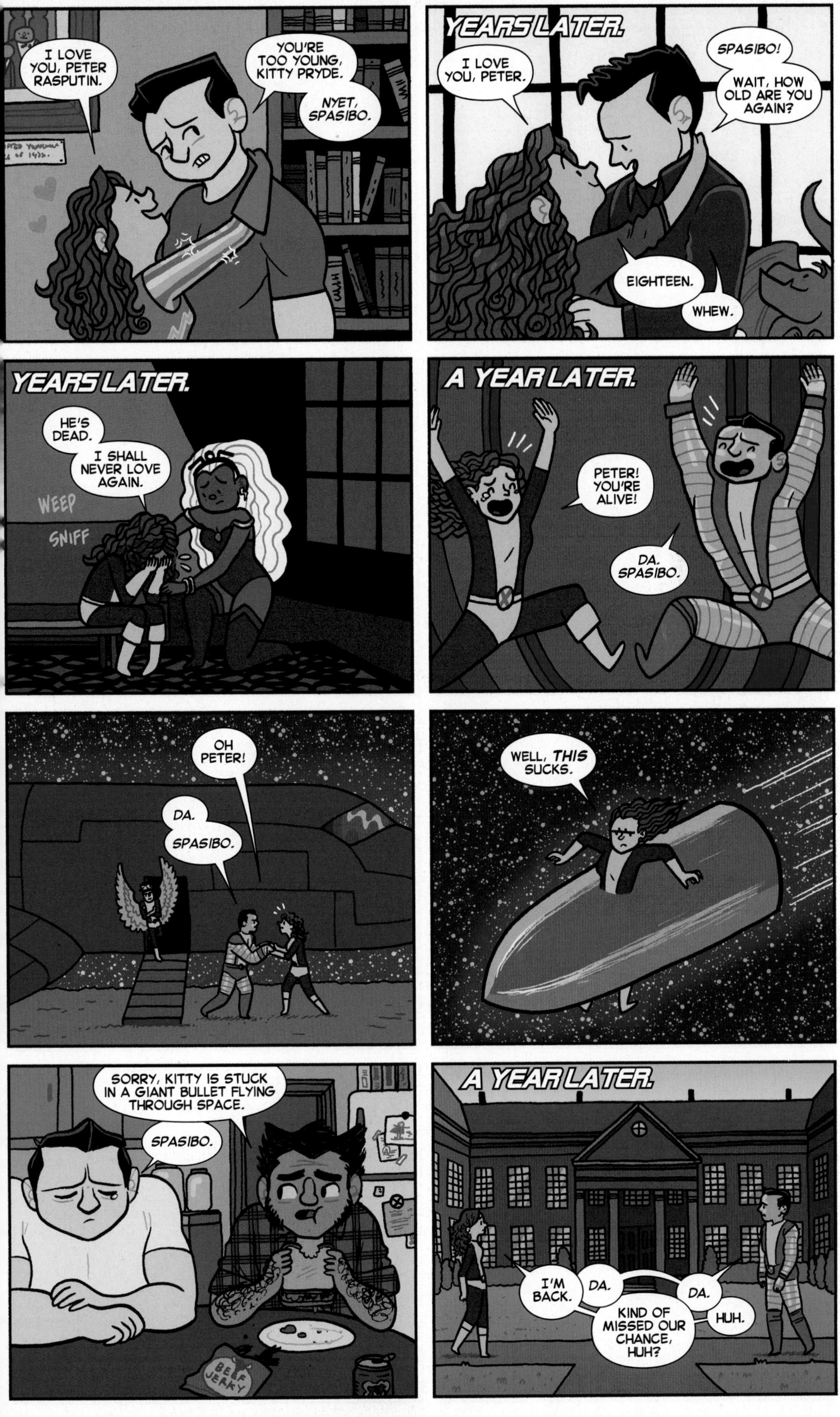
I LOVE YOU, PETER RASPUTIN.
YOU'RE TOO YOUNG, KITTY PRYDE.
NYET, SPASIBO.
YEARS LATER.
I LOVE YOU, PETER.
SPASIBO!
WAIT, HOW OLD ARE YOU AGAIN?
EIGHTEEN.
WHEW.
YEARS LATER.
HE'S DEAD.
I SHALL NEVER LOVE AGAIN.
WEEP
SNIFF
A YEAR LATER.
PETER! YOU'RE ALIVE!
DA. SPASIBO.
OH PETER!
DA.
SPASIBO.
WELL, THIS SUCKS.
SORRY, KITTY IS STUCK IN A GIANT BULLET FLYING THROUGH SPACE.
SPASIBO.
BEEF JERKY
A YEAR LATER.
I'M BACK.
DA.
KIND OF MISSED OUR CHANCE, HUH?
DA.
HUH.

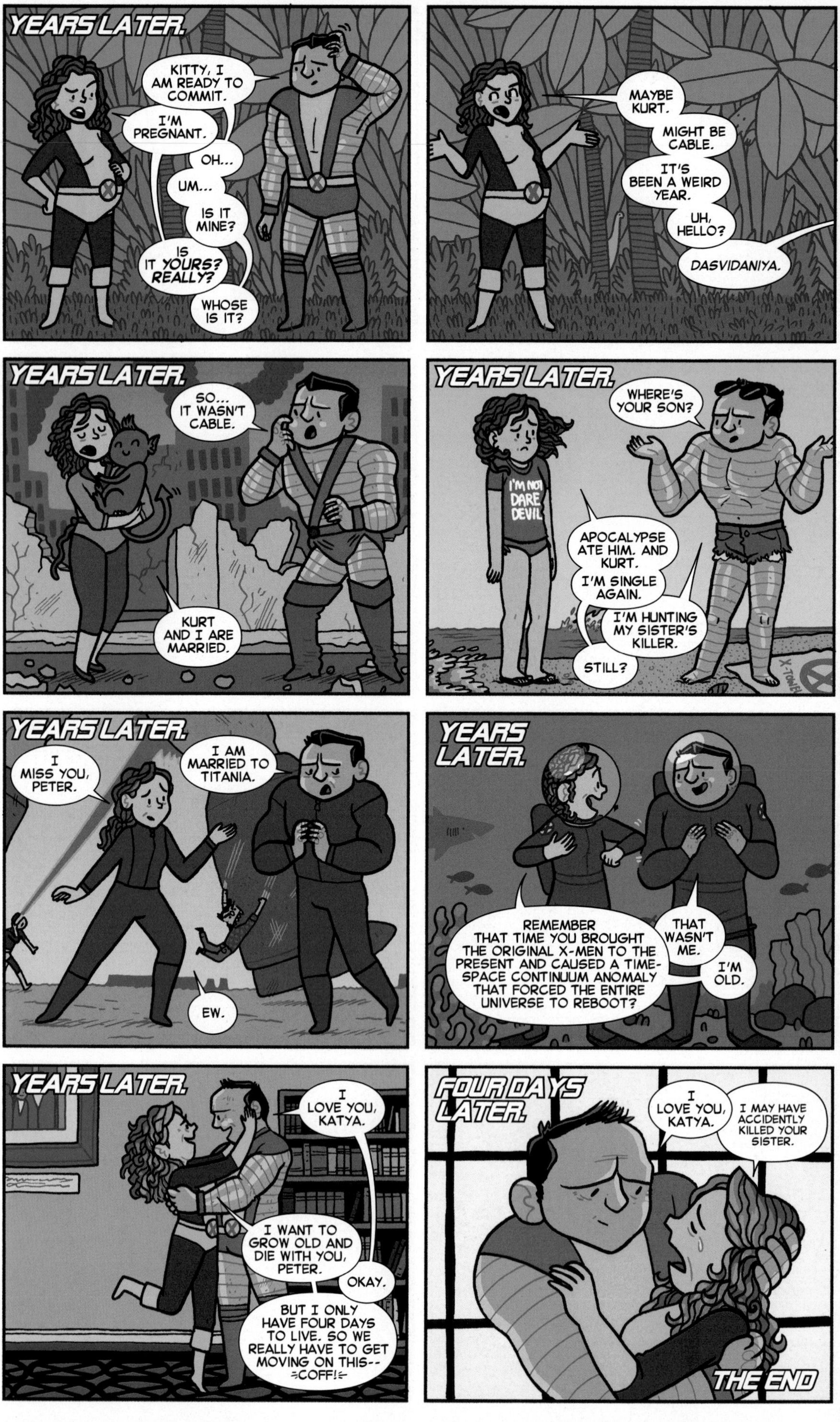
YEARS LATER.
KITTY, I AM READY TO COMMIT.
I'M PREGNANT.
OH...
UM...
IS IT MINE?
IS IT YOURS? REALLY?
WHOSE IS IT?
MAYBE KURT.
MIGHT BE CABLE.
IT'S BEEN A WEIRD YEAR.
UH, HELLO?
DASVIDANIYA.
YEARS LATER.
SO... IT WASN'T CABLE.
KURT AND I ARE MARRIED.
YEARS LATER.
WHERE'S YOUR SON?
I'M NOT DARE DEVIL
APOCALYPSE ATE HIM. AND KURT.
I'M SINGLE AGAIN.
I'M HUNTING MY SISTER'S KILLER.
STILL?
YEARS LATER.
I MISS YOU, PETER.
I AM MARRIED TO TITANIA.
EW.
YEARS LATER.
REMEMBER THAT TIME YOU BROUGHT THE ORIGINAL X-MEN TO THE PRESENT AND CAUSED A TIME-SPACE CONTINUUM ANOMALY THAT FORCED THE ENTIRE UNIVERSE TO REBOOT?
THAT WASN'T ME.
I'M OLD.
YEARS LATER.
I LOVE YOU, KATYA.
I WANT TO GROW OLD AND DIE WITH YOU, PETER.
OKAY.
BUT I ONLY HAVE FOUR DAYS TO LIVE. SO WE REALLY HAVE TO GET MOVING ON THIS-- COFF!
FOUR DAYS LATER.
I LOVE YOU, KATYA.
I MAY HAVE ACCIDENTLY KILLED YOUR SISTER.
THE END

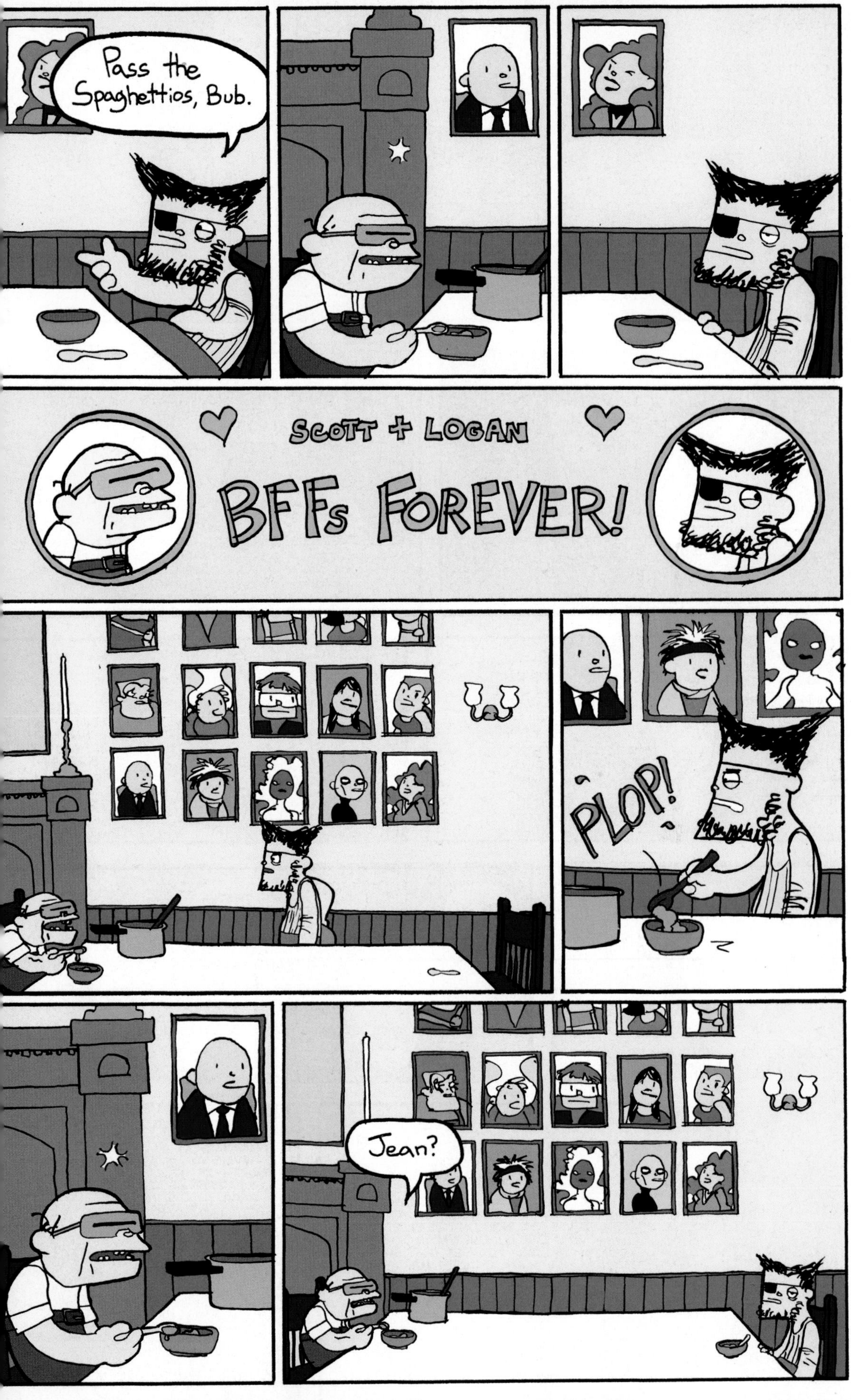

Pass the Spaghettios, Bub.
SCOTT + LOGAN
BFFs FOREVER!
PLOP!
Jean?

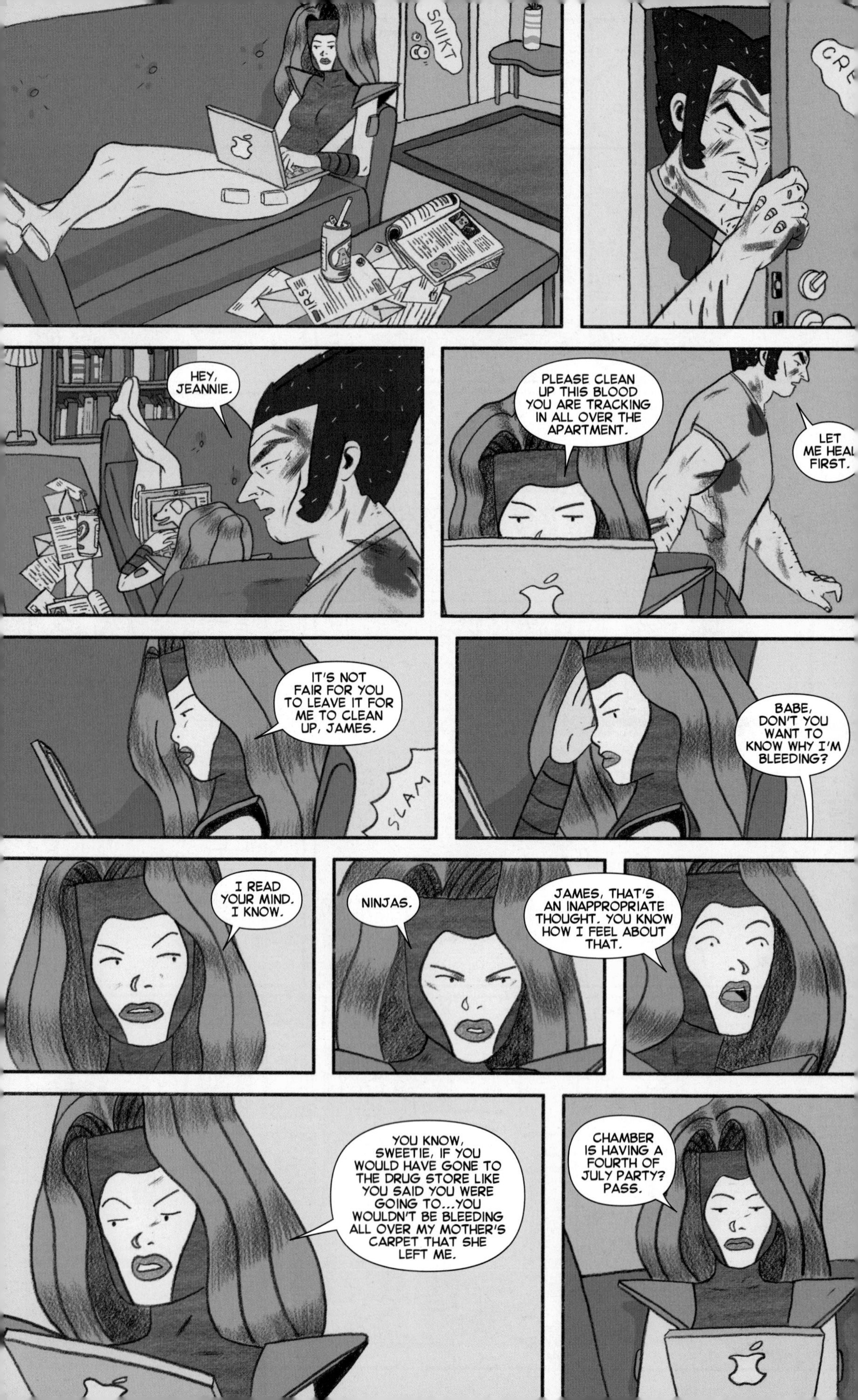
SNIKT
CRE
HEY, JEANNIE.
PLEASE CLEAN UP THIS BLOOD YOU ARE TRACKING IN ALL OVER THE APARTMENT.
LET ME HEAL FIRST.
IT'S NOT FAIR FOR YOU TO LEAVE IT FOR ME TO CLEAN UP, JAMES.
SLAM
BABE, DON'T YOU WANT TO KNOW WHY I'M BLEEDING?
I READ YOUR MIND. I KNOW.
NINJAS.
JAMES, THAT'S AN INAPPROPRIATE THOUGHT. YOU KNOW HOW I FEEL ABOUT THAT.
YOU KNOW, SWEETIE, IF YOU WOULD HAVE GONE TO THE DRUG STORE LIKE YOU SAID YOU WERE GOING TO...YOU WOULDN'T BE BLEEDING ALL OVER MY MOTHER'S CARPET THAT SHE LEFT ME.
CHAMBER IS HAVING A FOURTH OF JULY PARTY? PASS.

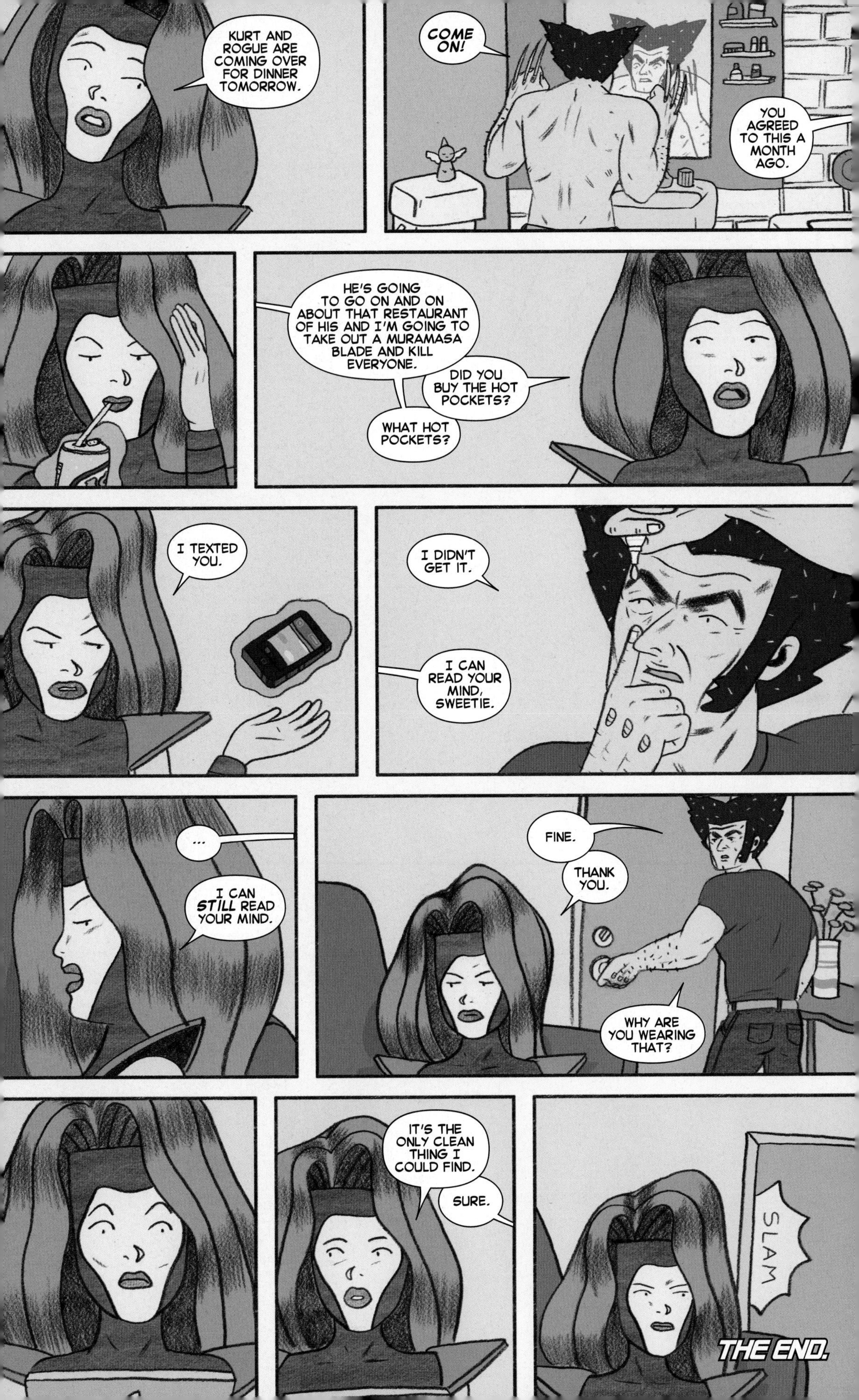
KURT AND ROGUE ARE COMING OVER FOR DINNER TOMORROW.
COME ON!
YOU AGREED TO THIS A MONTH AGO.
HE'S GOING TO GO ON AND ON ABOUT THAT RESTAURANT OF HIS AND I'M GOING TO TAKE OUT A MURAMASA BLADE AND KILL EVERYONE.
DID YOU BUY THE HOT POCKETS?
WHAT HOT POCKETS?
I TEXTED YOU.
I DIDN'T GET IT.
I CAN READ YOUR MIND, SWEETIE.
...
I CAN STILL READ YOUR MIND.
FINE.
THANK YOU.
WHY ARE YOU WEARING THAT?
IT'S THE ONLY CLEAN THING I COULD FIND.
SURE.
SLAM
THE END.

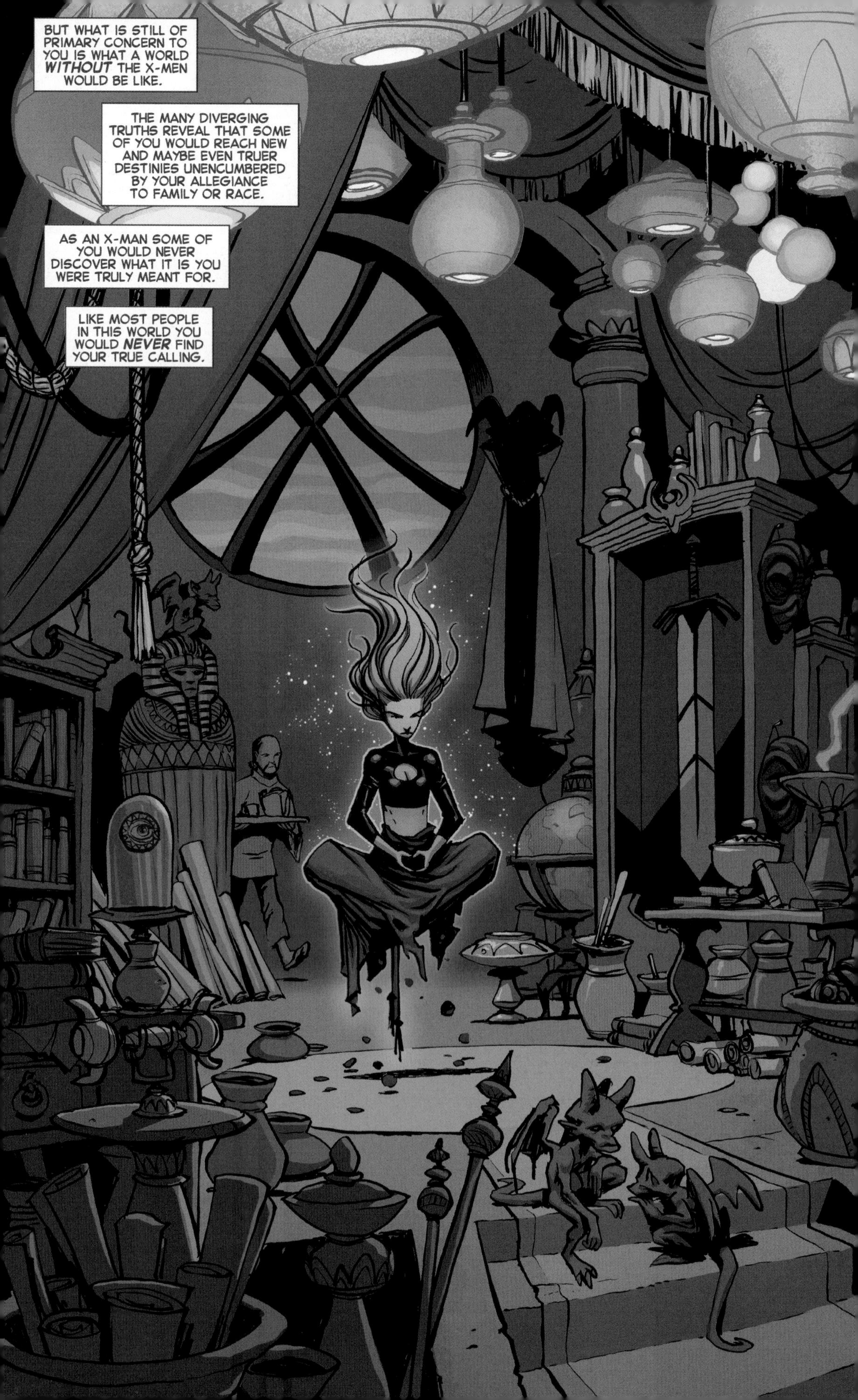
BUT WHAT IS STILL OF PRIMARY CONCERN TO YOU IS WHAT A WORLD *WITHOUT* THE X-MEN WOULD BE LIKE.
THE MANY DIVERGING TRUTHS REVEAL THAT SOME OF YOU WOULD REACH NEW AND MAYBE EVEN TRUER DESTINIES UNENCUMBERED BY YOUR ALLEGIANCE TO FAMILY OR RACE.
AS AN X-MAN SOME OF YOU WOULD NEVER DISCOVER WHAT IT IS YOU WERE TRULY MEANT FOR.
LIKE MOST PEOPLE IN THIS WORLD YOU WOULD *NEVER* FIND YOUR TRUE CALLING.

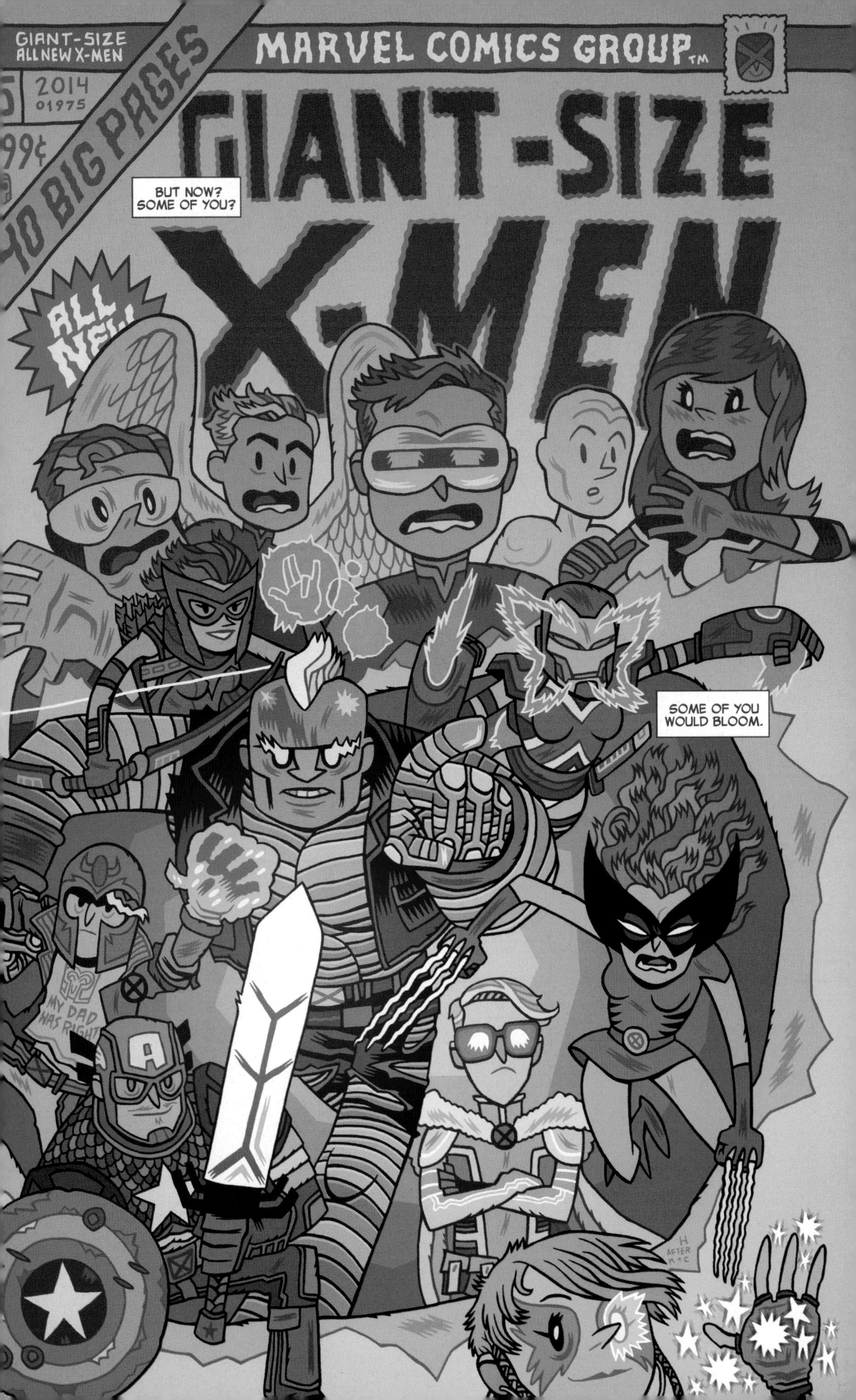
GIANT-SIZE
ALL NEW X-MEN
MARVEL COMICS GROUP
TM
2014
01975
99¢
40 BIG PAGES
GIANT-SIZE
X-MEN
ALL NEW
BUT NOW?
SOME OF YOU?
SOME OF YOU
WOULD BLOOM.
MY DAD
WAS RIGHT
H
AFTER
K+C

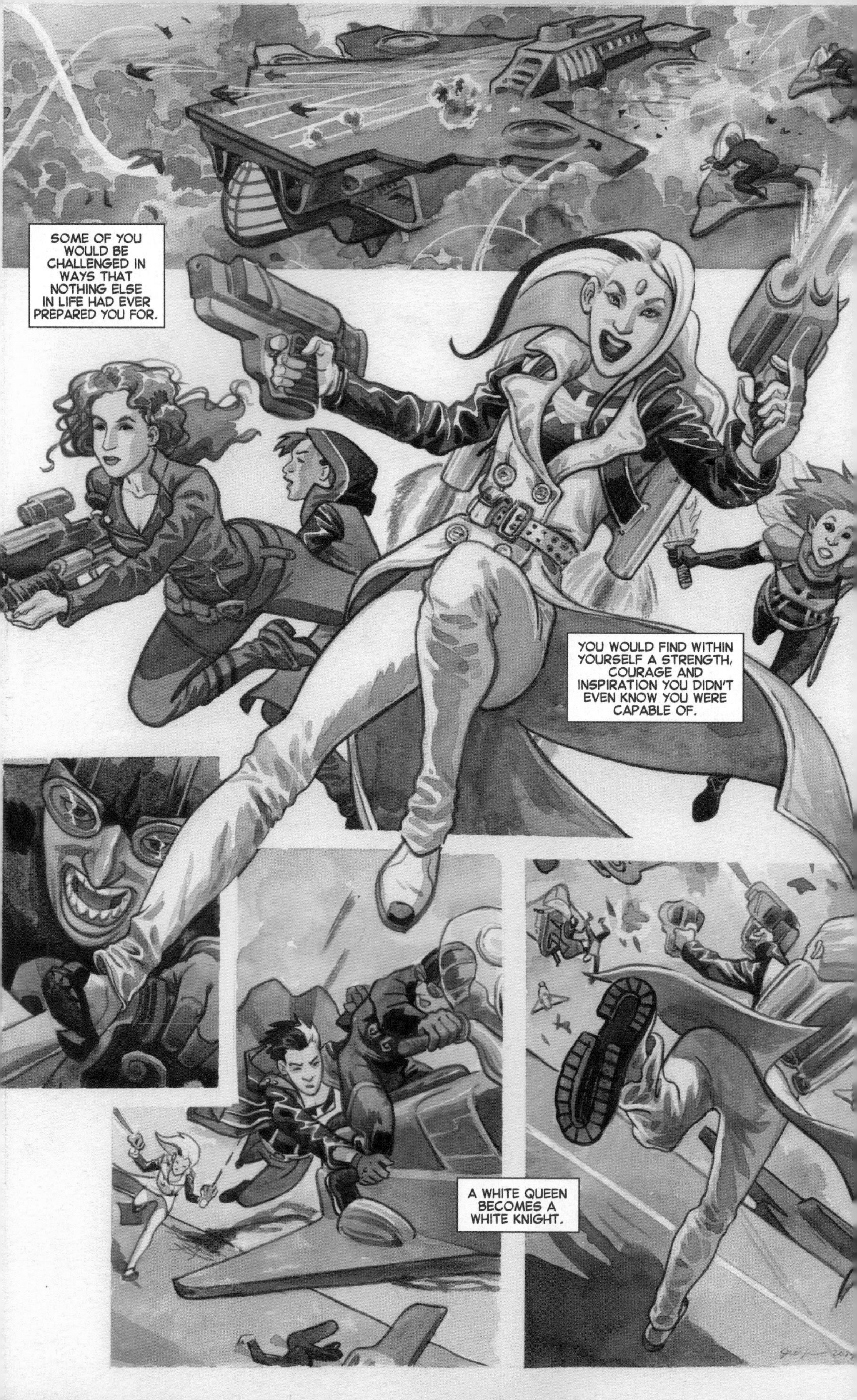
SOME OF YOU WOULD BE CHALLENGED IN WAYS THAT NOTHING ELSE IN LIFE HAD EVER PREPARED YOU FOR.
YOU WOULD FIND WITHIN YOURSELF A STRENGTH, COURAGE AND INSPIRATION YOU DIDN'T EVEN KNOW YOU WERE CAPABLE OF.
A WHITE QUEEN BECOMES A WHITE KNIGHT.

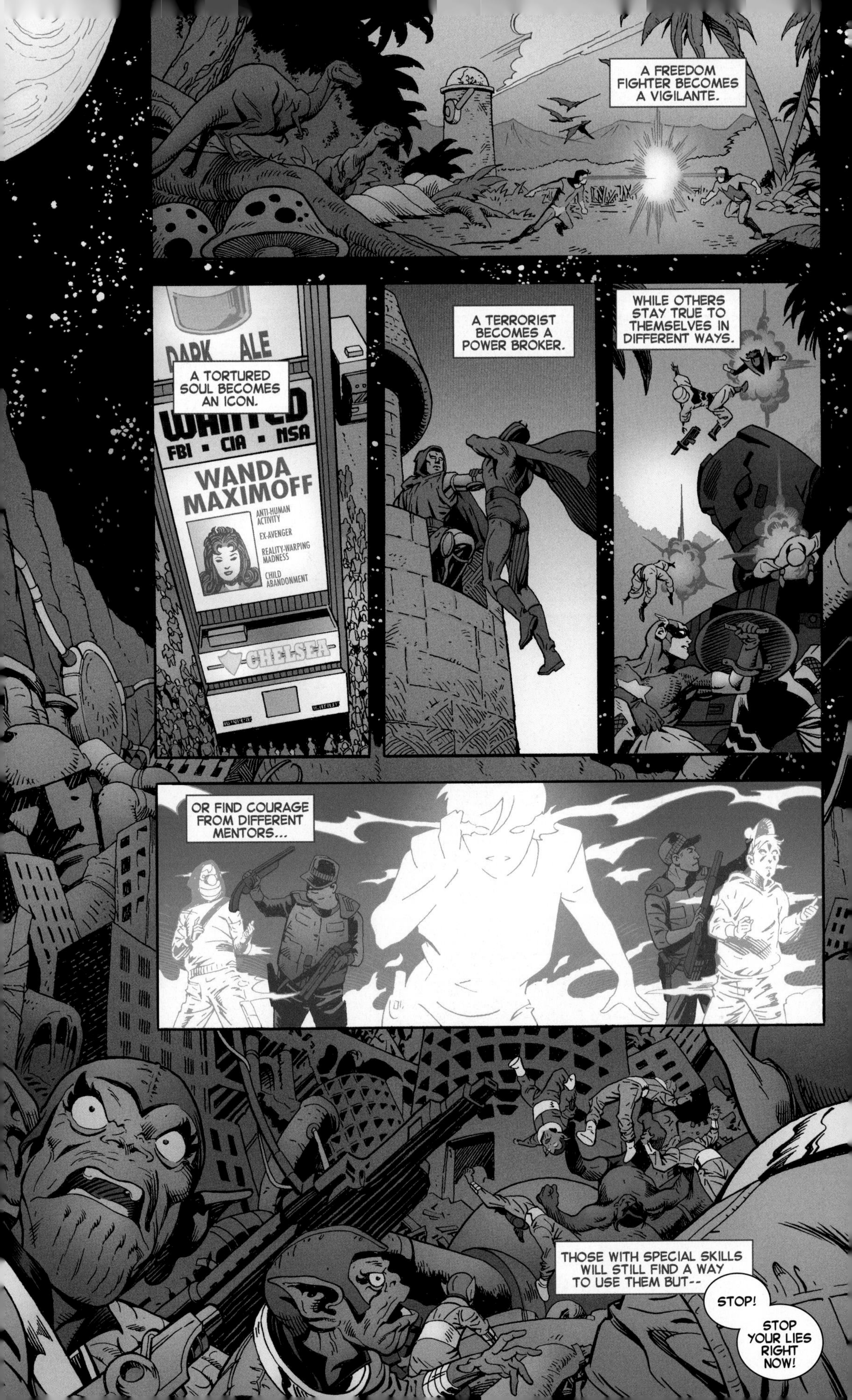
A FREEDOM FIGHTER BECOMES A VIGILANTE.
DARK ALE
A TORTURED SOUL BECOMES AN ICON.
WANTED
FBI • CIA • NSA
WANDA MAXIMOFF
ANTI-HUMAN ACTIVITY
EX-AVENGER
REALITY-WARPING MADNESS
CHILD ABANDONMENT
CHELSEA
A TERRORIST BECOMES A POWER BROKER.
WHILE OTHERS STAY TRUE TO THEMSELVES IN DIFFERENT WAYS.
OR FIND COURAGE FROM DIFFERENT MENTORS...
THOSE WITH SPECIAL SKILLS WILL STILL FIND A WAY TO USE THEM BUT--
STOP!
STOP YOUR LIES RIGHT NOW!

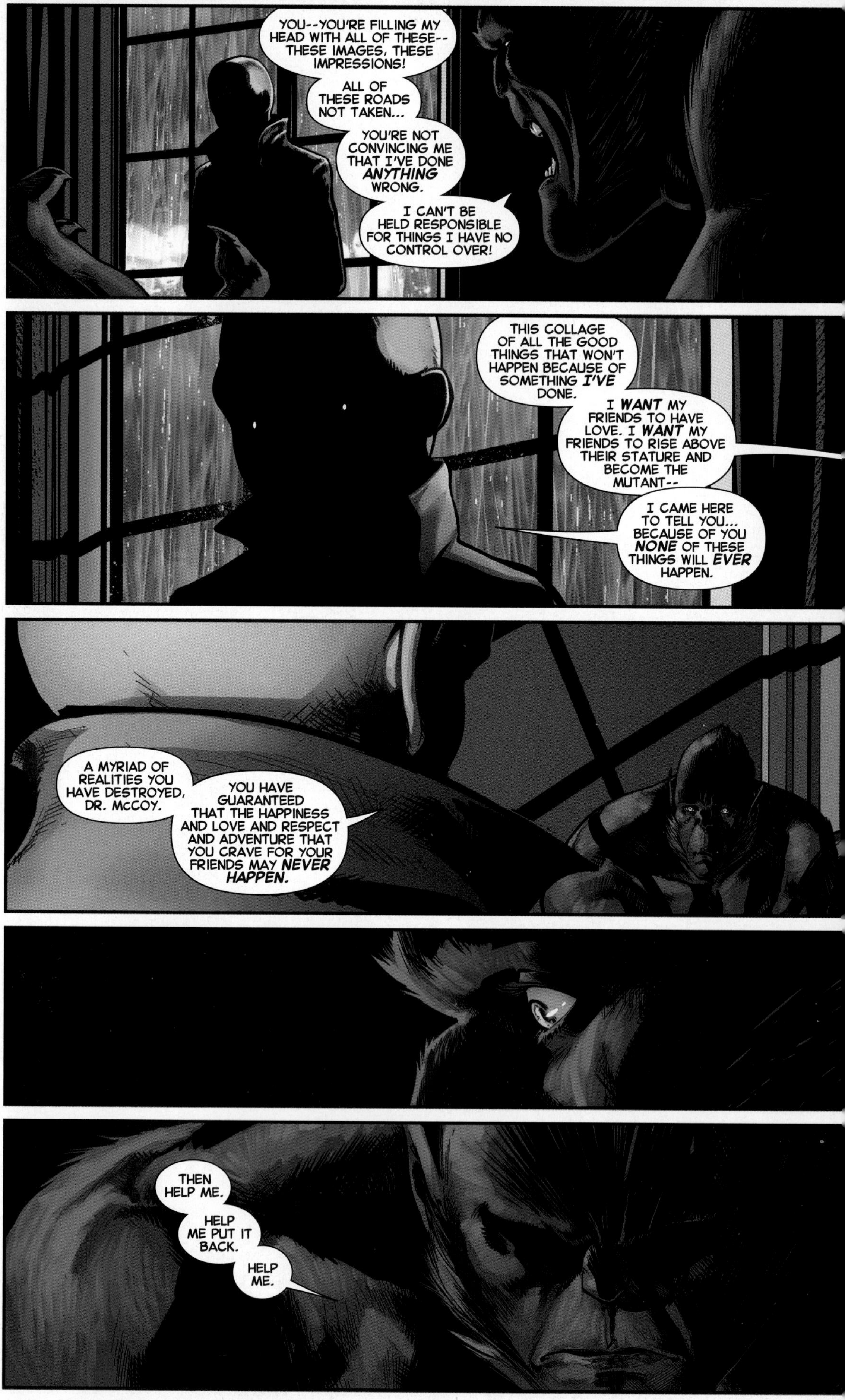
YOU--YOU'RE FILLING MY HEAD WITH ALL OF THESE--THESE IMAGES, THESE IMPRESSIONS!
ALL OF THESE ROADS NOT TAKEN...
YOU'RE NOT CONVINCING ME THAT I'VE DONE ANYTHING WRONG.
I CAN'T BE HELD RESPONSIBLE FOR THINGS I HAVE NO CONTROL OVER!
THIS COLLAGE OF ALL THE GOOD THINGS THAT WON'T HAPPEN BECAUSE OF SOMETHING I'VE DONE.
I WANT MY FRIENDS TO HAVE LOVE. I WANT MY FRIENDS TO RISE ABOVE THEIR STATURE AND BECOME THE MUTANT--
I CAME HERE TO TELL YOU... BECAUSE OF YOU NONE OF THESE THINGS WILL EVER HAPPEN.
A MYRIAD OF REALITIES YOU HAVE DESTROYED, DR. McCOY.
YOU HAVE GUARANTEED THAT THE HAPPINESS AND LOVE AND RESPECT AND ADVENTURE THAT YOU CRAVE FOR YOUR FRIENDS MAY NEVER HAPPEN.
THEN HELP ME.
HELP ME PUT IT BACK.
HELP ME.

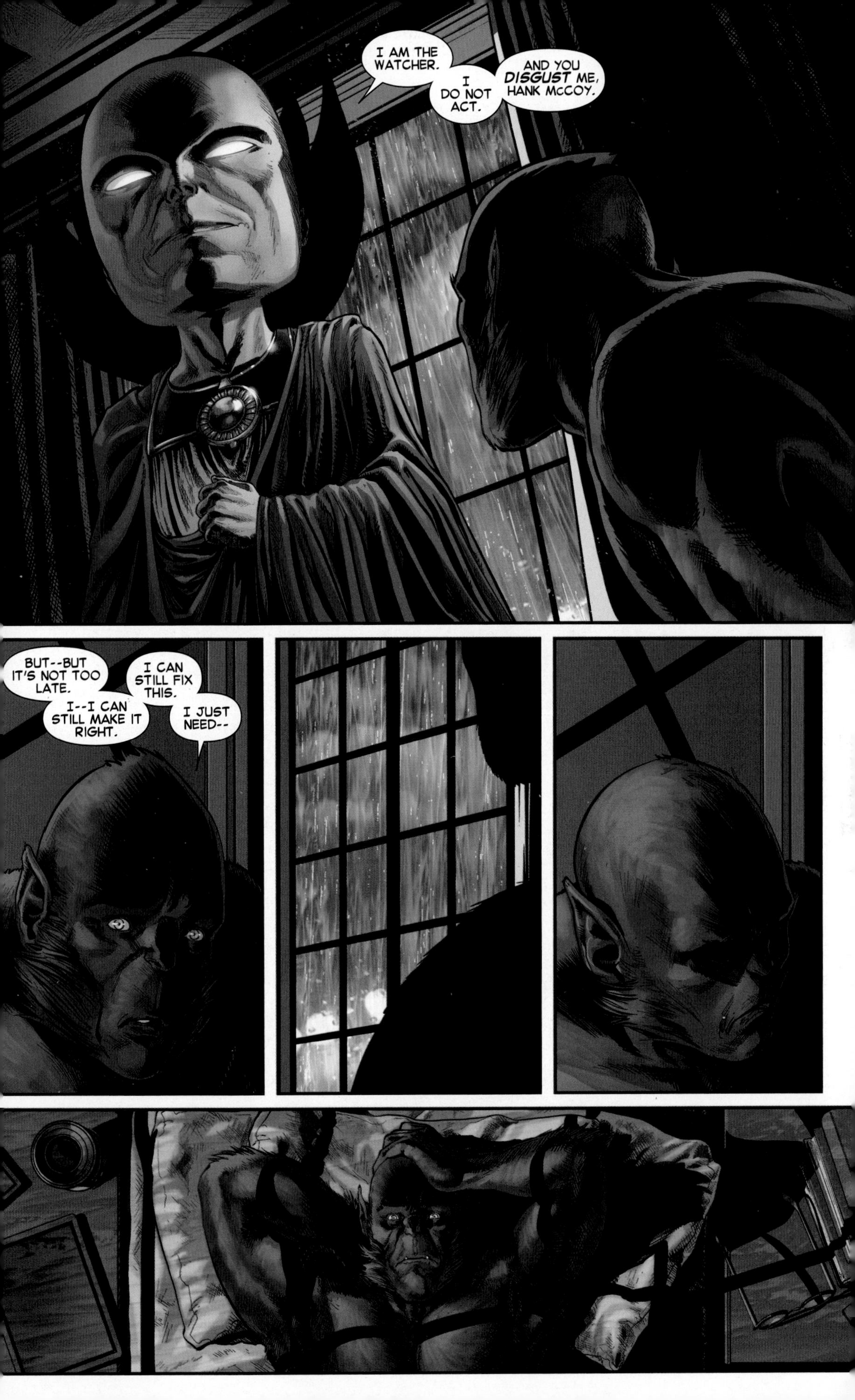
I AM THE WATCHER.
I DO NOT ACT.
AND YOU DISGUST ME, HANK McCOY.
BUT--BUT IT'S NOT TOO LATE.
I--I CAN STILL MAKE IT RIGHT.
I CAN STILL FIX THIS.
I JUST NEED--

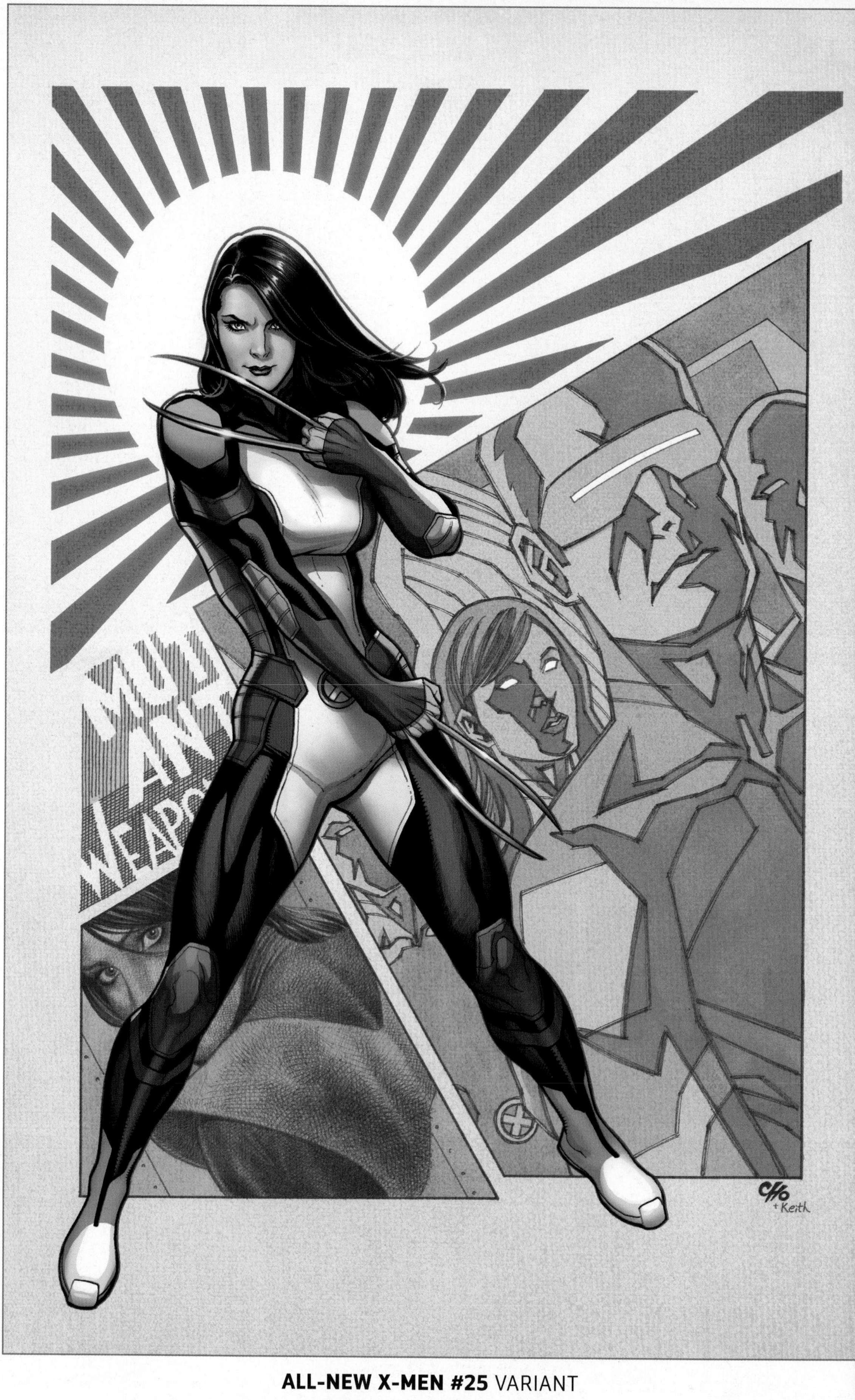
CHO
+ Keith

ALL-NEW X-MEN #25 VARIANT
BY FRANK CHO & JASON KEITH

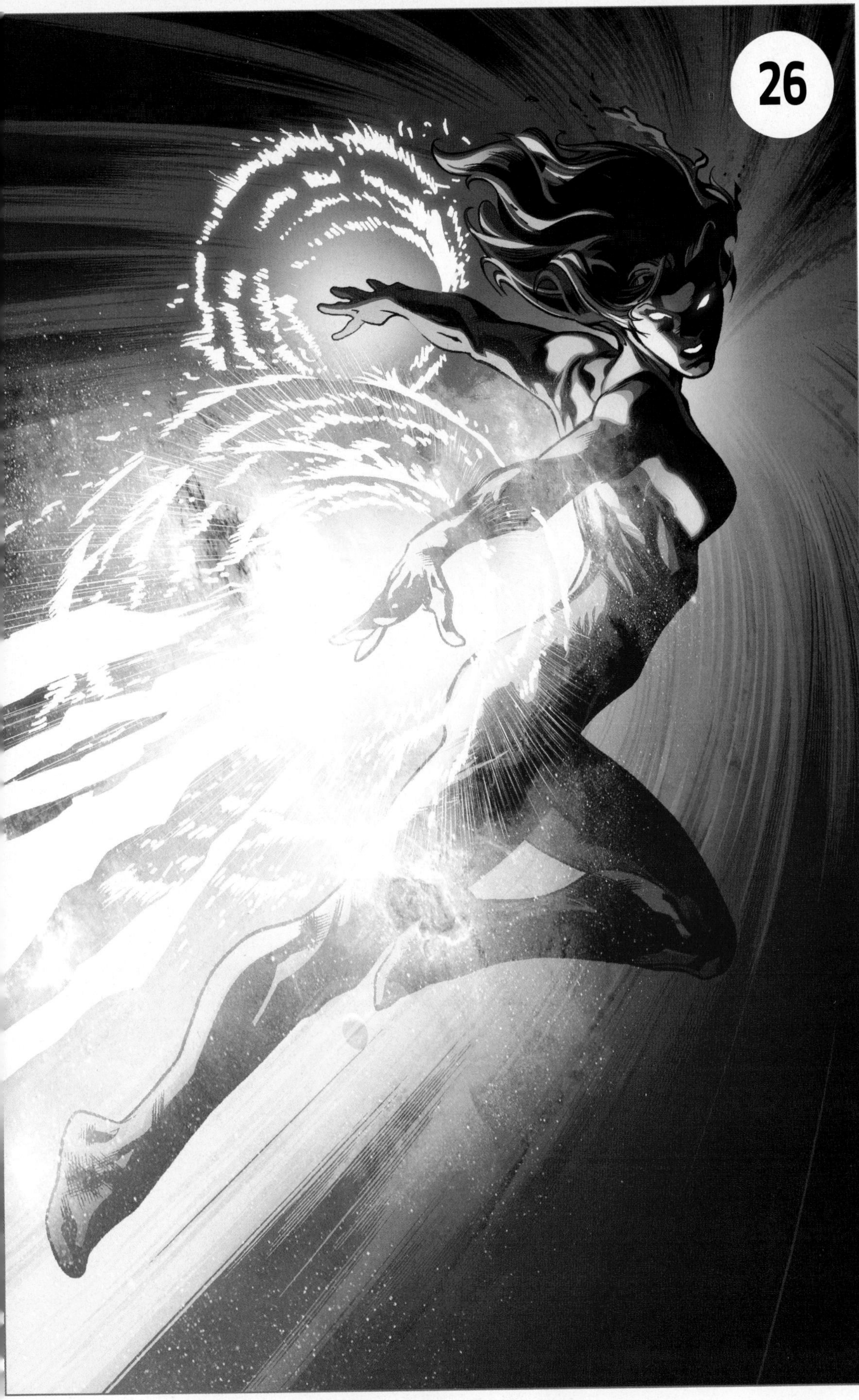
26

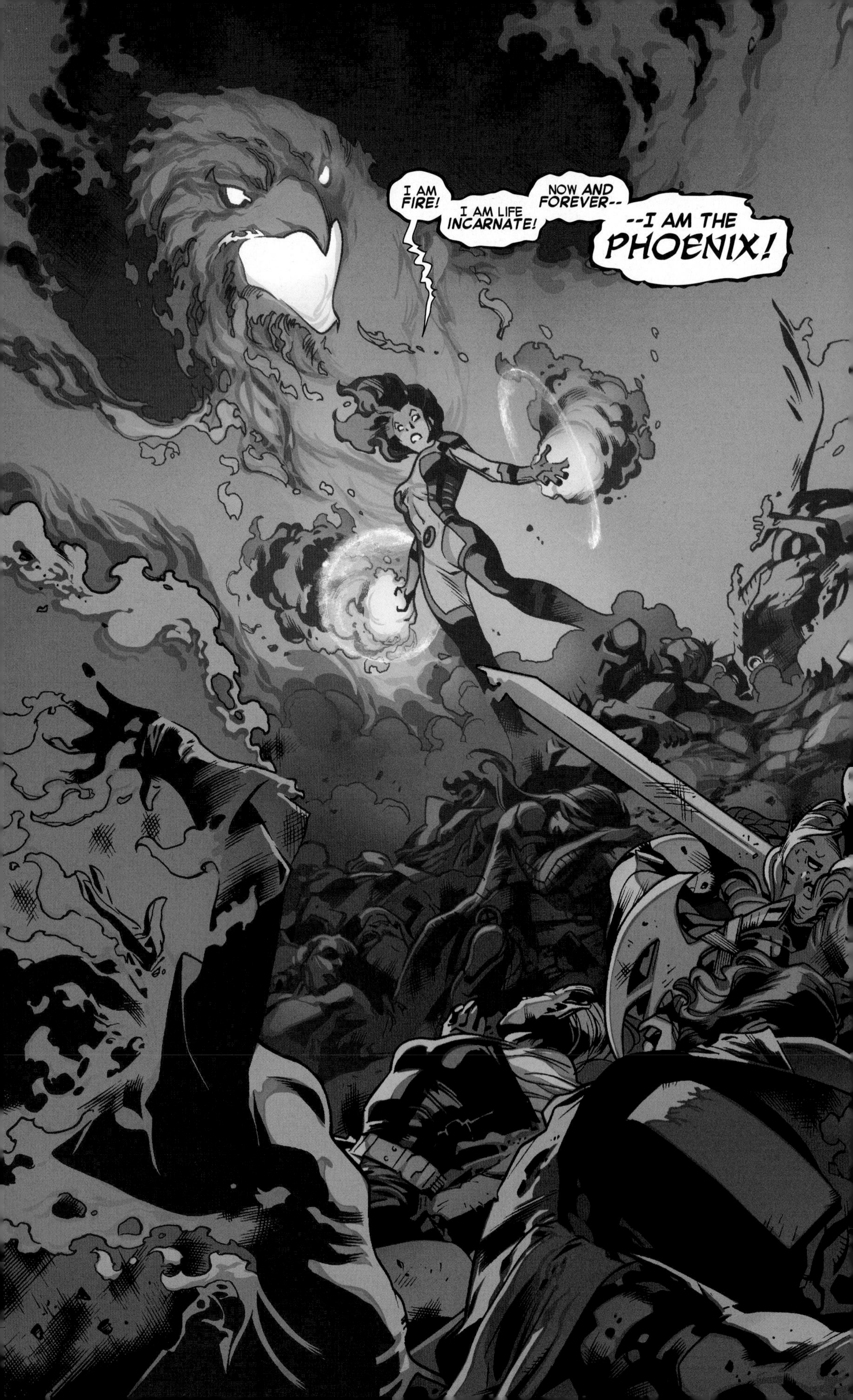
I AM FIRE!
I AM LIFE INCARNATE!
NOW AND FOREVER--
--I AM THE PHOENIX!

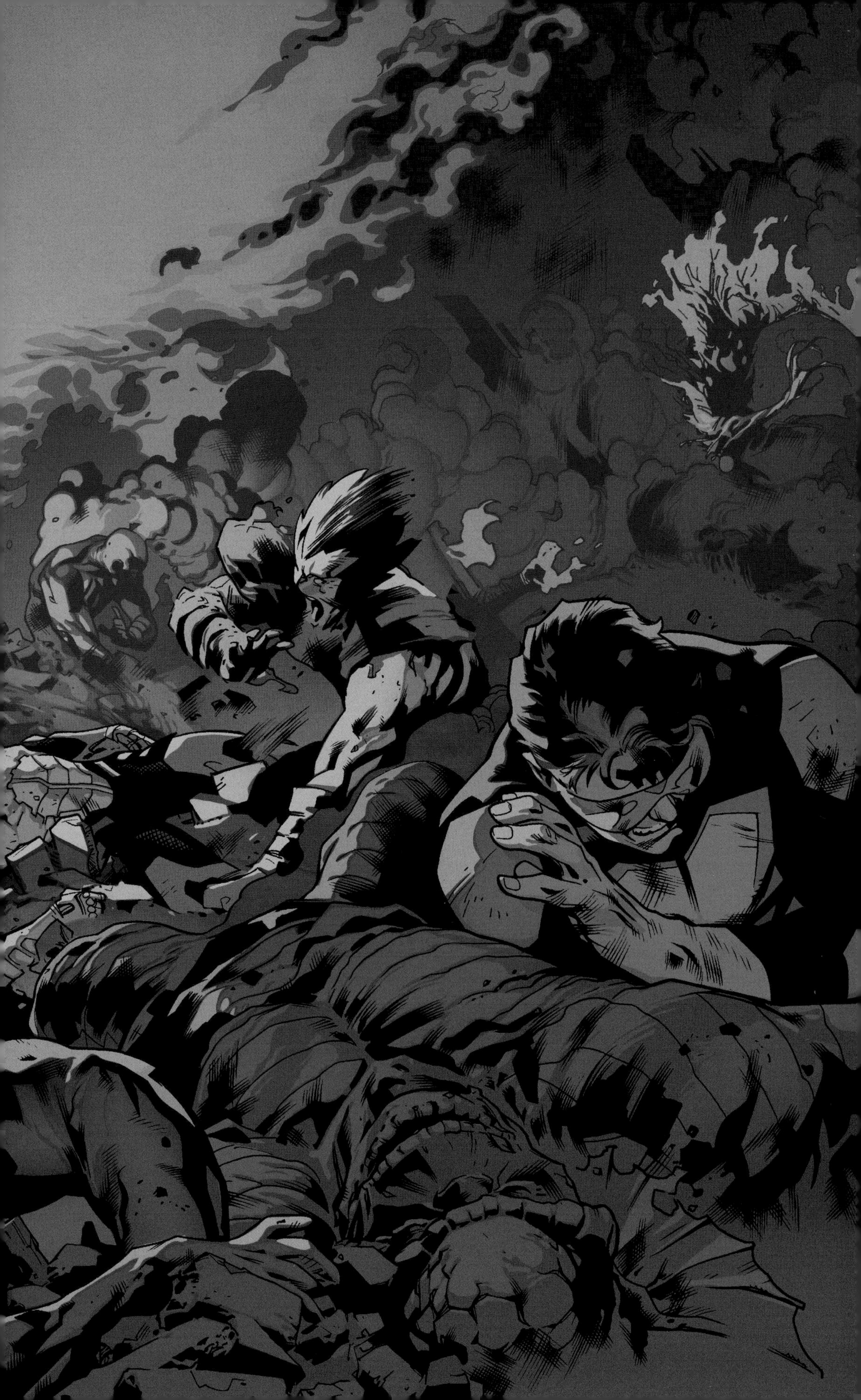

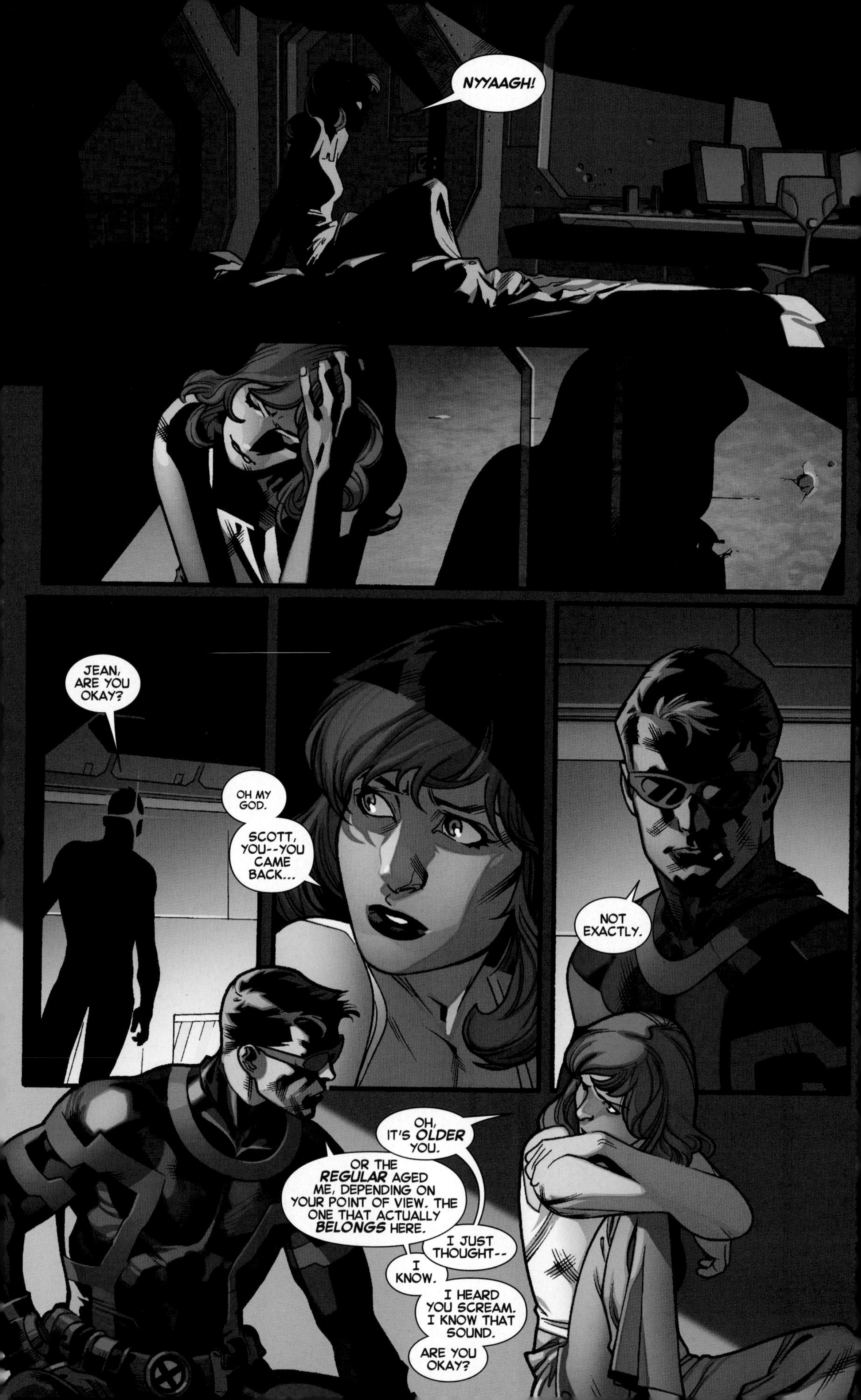
NYYAAGH!
JEAN, ARE YOU OKAY?
OH MY GOD.
SCOTT, YOU--YOU CAME BACK...
NOT EXACTLY.
OH, IT'S OLDER YOU.
OR THE REGULAR AGED ME, DEPENDING ON YOUR POINT OF VIEW. THE ONE THAT ACTUALLY BELONGS HERE.
I JUST THOUGHT--
I KNOW.
I HEARD YOU SCREAM. I KNOW THAT SOUND.
ARE YOU OKAY?

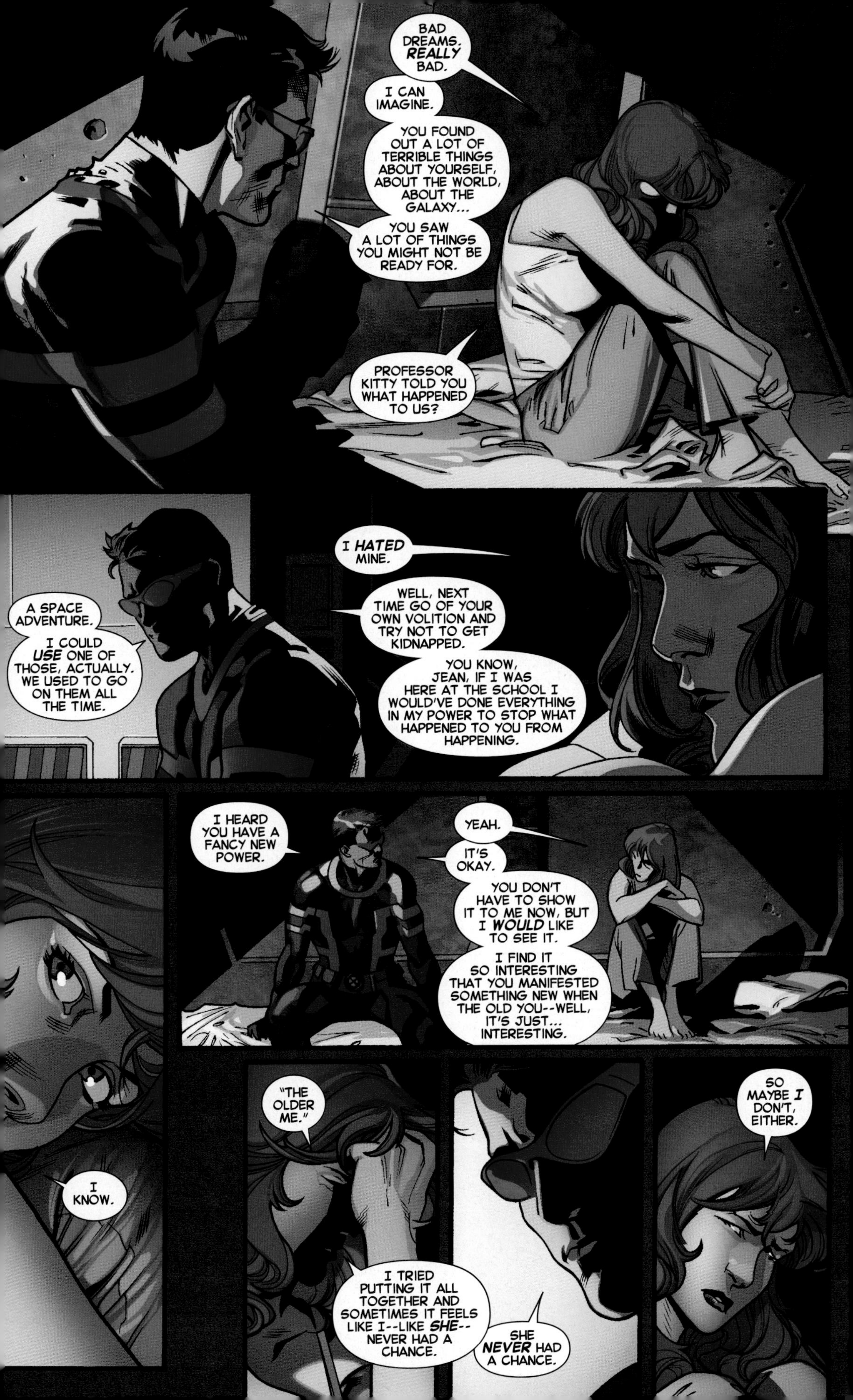

BAD DREAMS. REALLY BAD.
I CAN IMAGINE.
YOU FOUND OUT A LOT OF TERRIBLE THINGS ABOUT YOURSELF, ABOUT THE WORLD, ABOUT THE GALAXY...
YOU SAW A LOT OF THINGS YOU MIGHT NOT BE READY FOR.
PROFESSOR KITTY TOLD YOU WHAT HAPPENED TO US?
A SPACE ADVENTURE.
I COULD USE ONE OF THOSE, ACTUALLY. WE USED TO GO ON THEM ALL THE TIME.
I HATED MINE.
WELL, NEXT TIME GO OF YOUR OWN VOLITION AND TRY NOT TO GET KIDNAPPED.
YOU KNOW, JEAN, IF I WAS HERE AT THE SCHOOL I WOULD'VE DONE EVERYTHING IN MY POWER TO STOP WHAT HAPPENED TO YOU FROM HAPPENING.
I HEARD YOU HAVE A FANCY NEW POWER.
YEAH.
IT'S OKAY.
YOU DON'T HAVE TO SHOW IT TO ME NOW, BUT I WOULD LIKE TO SEE IT.
I FIND IT SO INTERESTING THAT YOU MANIFESTED SOMETHING NEW WHEN THE OLD YOU--WELL, IT'S JUST... INTERESTING.
I KNOW.
"THE OLDER ME."
I TRIED PUTTING IT ALL TOGETHER AND SOMETIMES IT FEELS LIKE I--LIKE SHE--NEVER HAD A CHANCE.
SHE NEVER HAD A CHANCE.
SO MAYBE I DON'T, EITHER.

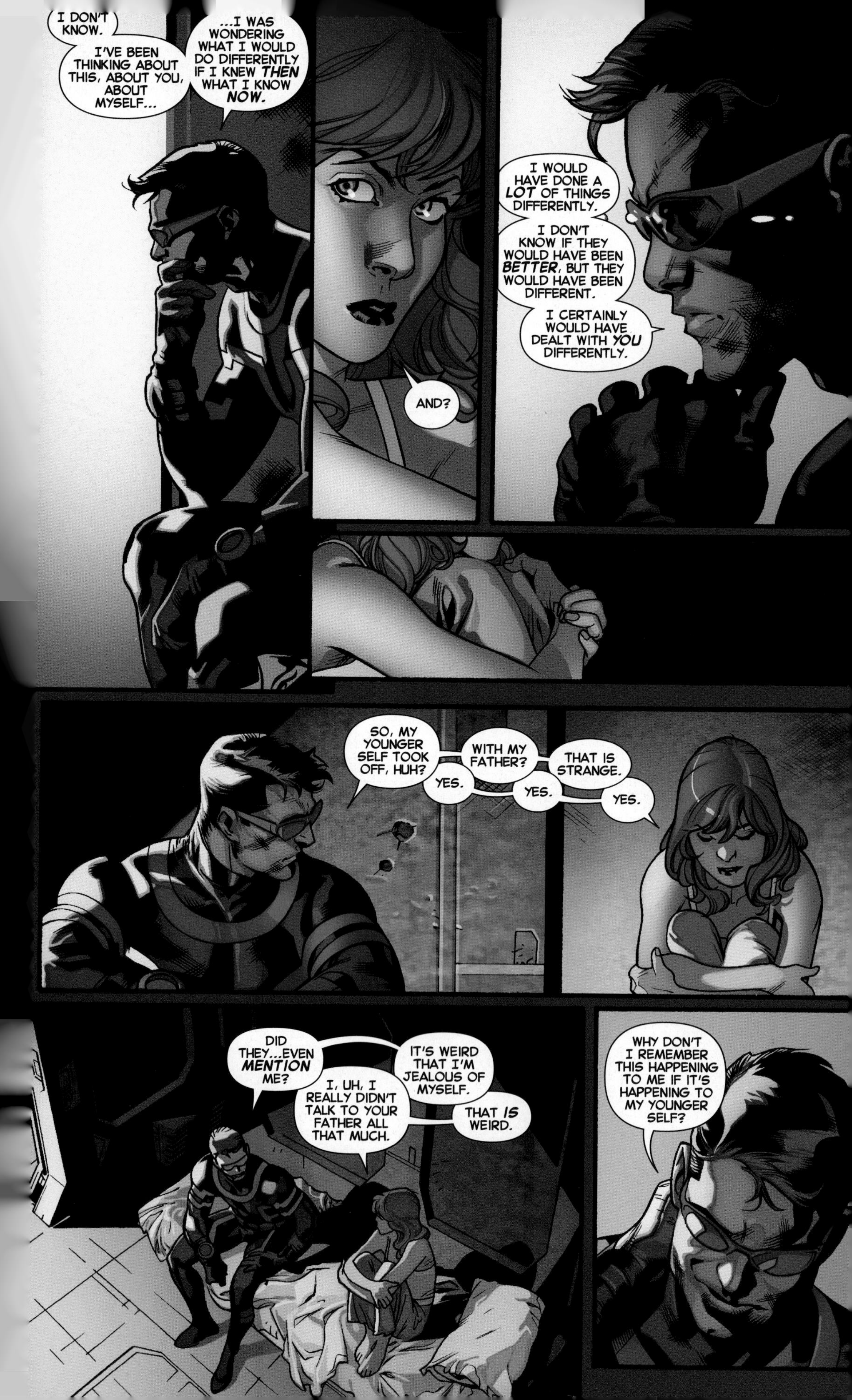
I DON'T KNOW.
I'VE BEEN THINKING ABOUT THIS, ABOUT YOU, ABOUT MYSELF...
...I WAS WONDERING WHAT I WOULD DO DIFFERENTLY IF I KNEW *THEN* WHAT I KNOW *NOW.*
AND?
I WOULD HAVE DONE A *LOT* OF THINGS DIFFERENTLY.
I DON'T KNOW IF THEY WOULD HAVE BEEN *BETTER*, BUT THEY WOULD HAVE BEEN DIFFERENT.
I CERTAINLY WOULD HAVE DEALT WITH *YOU* DIFFERENTLY.
SO, MY YOUNGER SELF TOOK OFF, HUH?
YES.
WITH MY FATHER?
YES.
THAT IS STRANGE.
YES.
DID THEY...EVEN *MENTION* ME?
I, UH, I REALLY DIDN'T TALK TO YOUR FATHER ALL THAT MUCH.
IT'S WEIRD THAT I'M JEALOUS OF MYSELF.
THAT *IS* WEIRD.
WHY DON'T I REMEMBER THIS HAPPENING TO ME IF IT'S HAPPENING TO MY YOUNGER SELF?

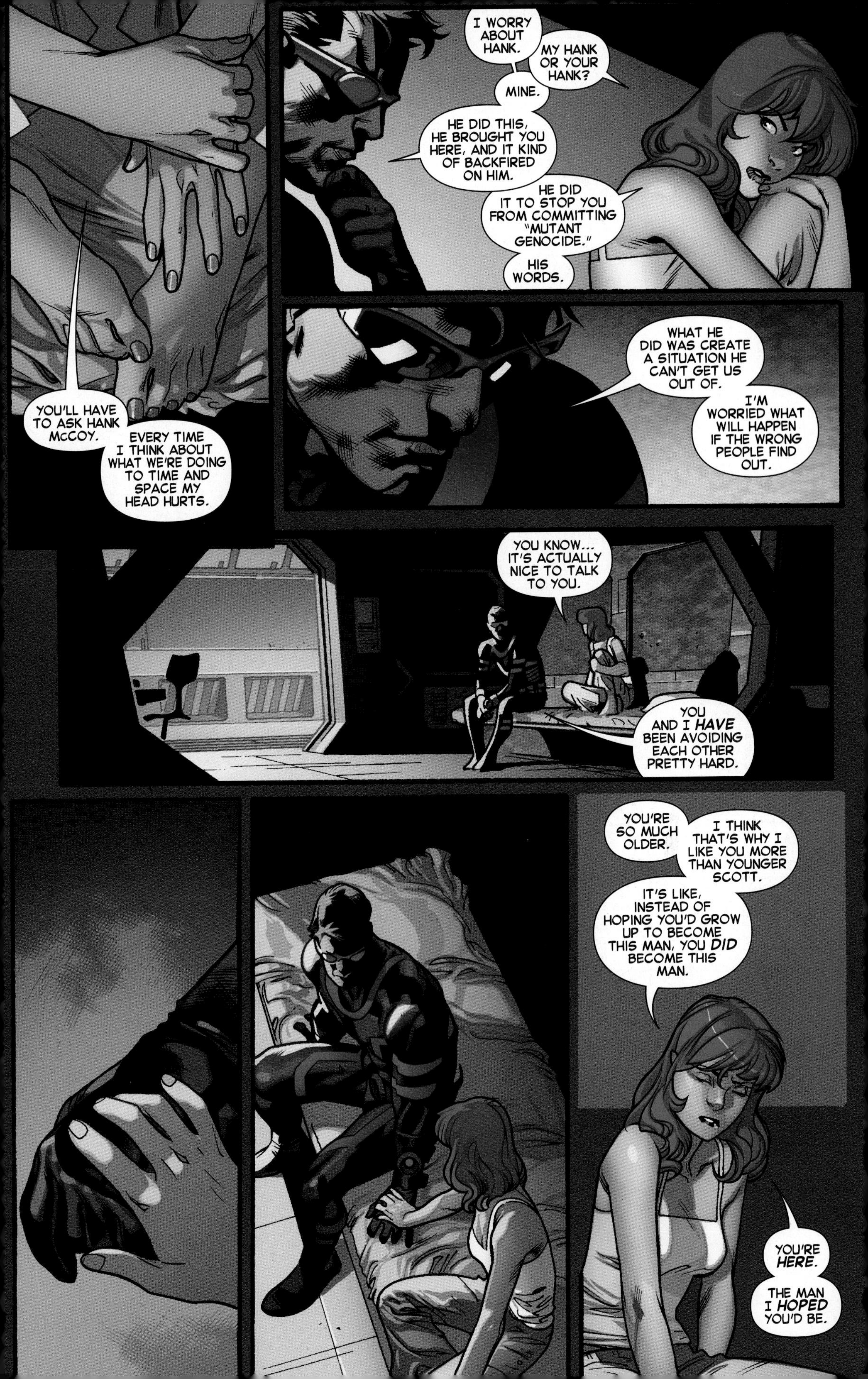
I WORRY ABOUT HANK.
MY HANK OR YOUR HANK?
MINE.
HE DID THIS, HE BROUGHT YOU HERE, AND IT KIND OF BACKFIRED ON HIM.
HE DID IT TO STOP YOU FROM COMMITTING "MUTANT GENOCIDE."
HIS WORDS.
YOU'LL HAVE TO ASK HANK McCOY.
EVERY TIME I THINK ABOUT WHAT WE'RE DOING TO TIME AND SPACE MY HEAD HURTS.
WHAT HE DID WAS CREATE A SITUATION HE CAN'T GET US OUT OF.
I'M WORRIED WHAT WILL HAPPEN IF THE WRONG PEOPLE FIND OUT.
YOU KNOW... IT'S ACTUALLY NICE TO TALK TO YOU.
YOU AND I *HAVE* BEEN AVOIDING EACH OTHER PRETTY HARD.
YOU'RE SO MUCH OLDER.
I THINK THAT'S WHY I LIKE YOU MORE THAN YOUNGER SCOTT.
IT'S LIKE, INSTEAD OF HOPING YOU'D GROW UP TO BECOME THIS MAN, YOU *DID* BECOME THIS MAN.
YOU'RE *HERE*.
THE MAN I *HOPED* YOU'D BE.

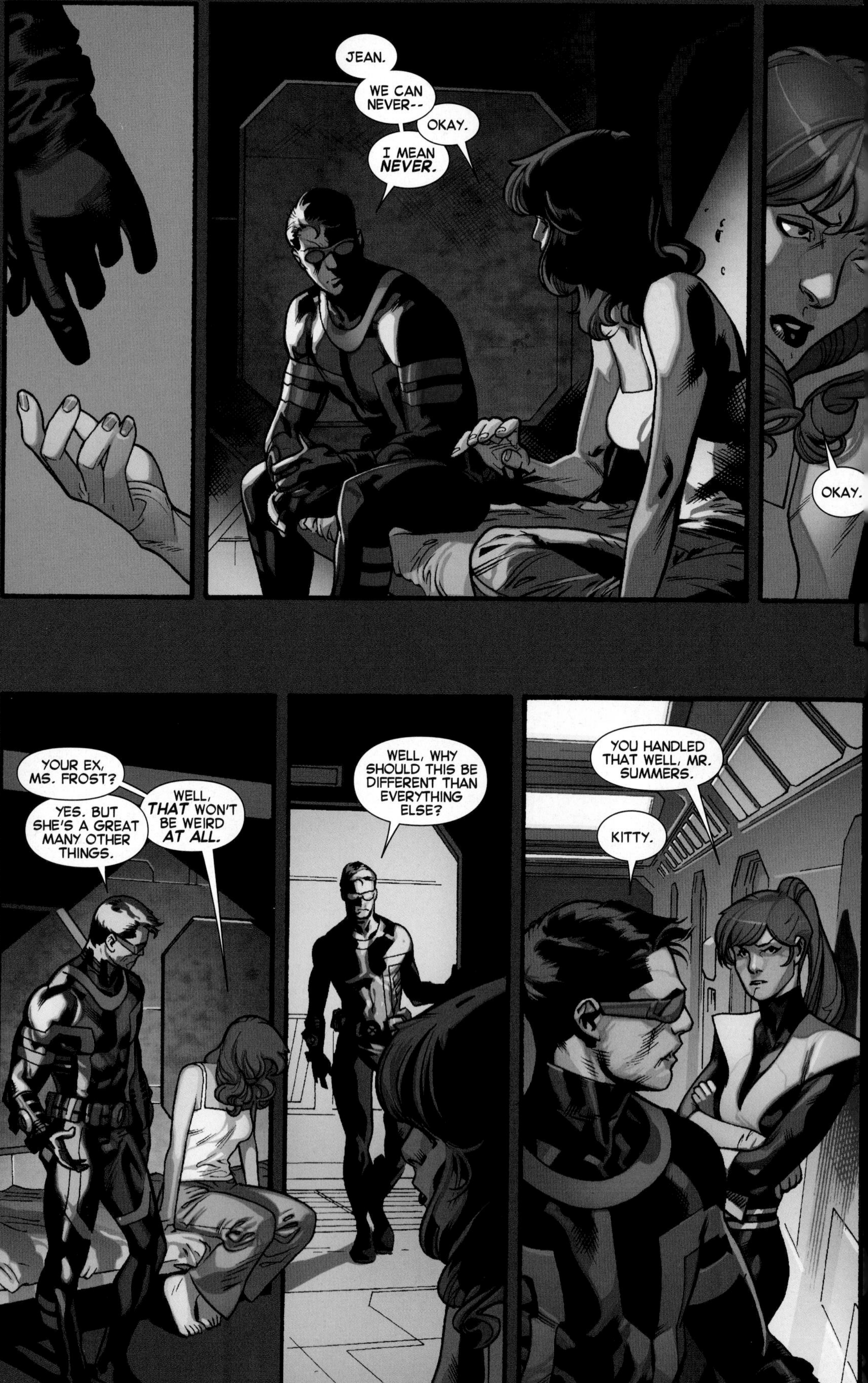
JEAN.
WE CAN NEVER--
OKAY.
I MEAN NEVER.
OKAY.
YOUR EX, MS. FROST?
YES. BUT SHE'S A GREAT MANY OTHER THINGS.
WELL, THAT WON'T BE WEIRD AT ALL.
WELL, WHY SHOULD THIS BE DIFFERENT THAN EVERYTHING ELSE?
YOU HANDLED THAT WELL, MR. SUMMERS.
KITTY.

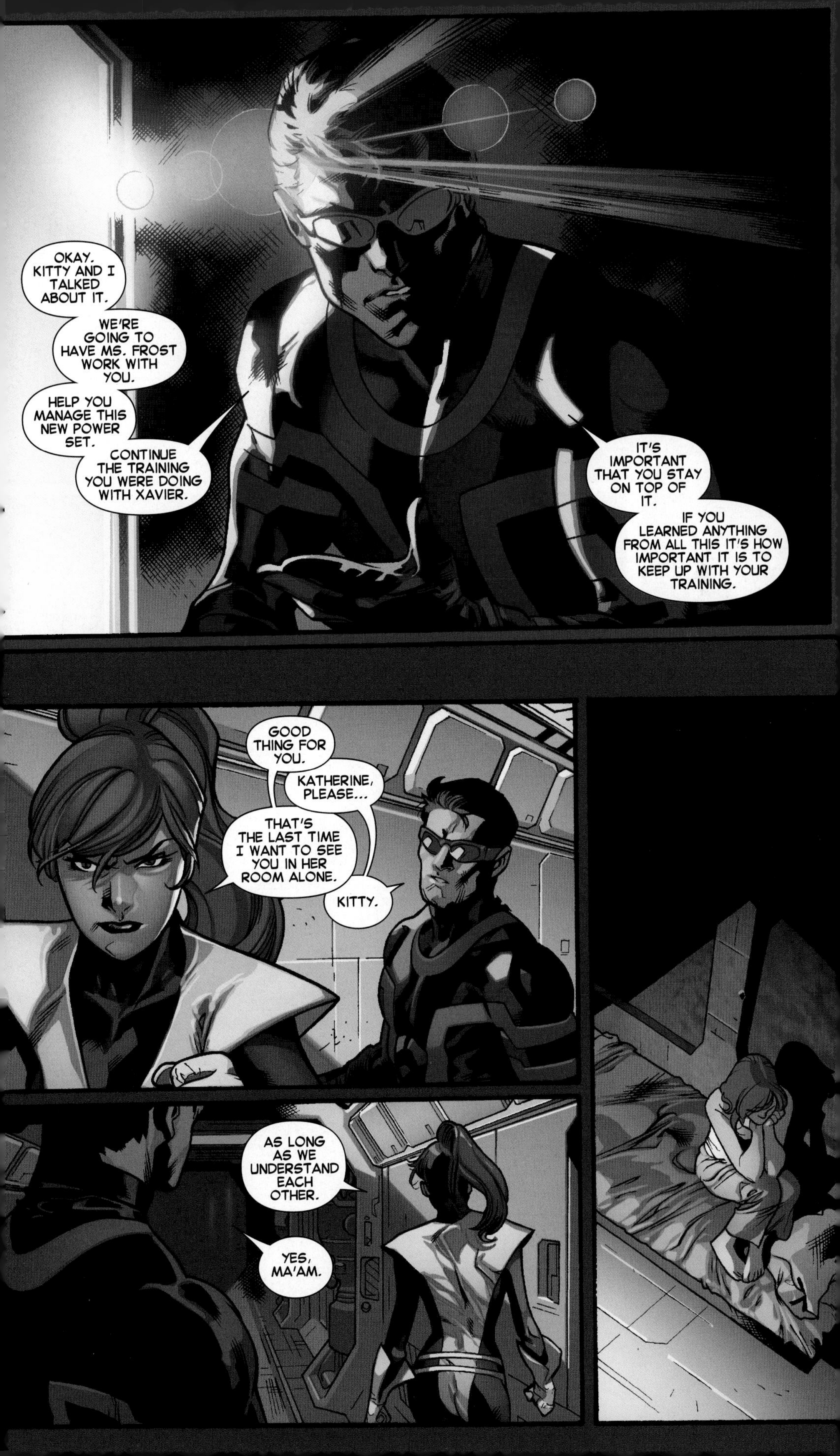
OKAY. KITTY AND I TALKED ABOUT IT.
WE'RE GOING TO HAVE MS. FROST WORK WITH YOU.
HELP YOU MANAGE THIS NEW POWER SET.
CONTINUE THE TRAINING YOU WERE DOING WITH XAVIER.
IT'S IMPORTANT THAT YOU STAY ON TOP OF IT.
IF YOU LEARNED ANYTHING FROM ALL THIS IT'S HOW IMPORTANT IT IS TO KEEP UP WITH YOUR TRAINING.
GOOD THING FOR YOU.
KATHERINE, PLEASE...
THAT'S THE LAST TIME I WANT TO SEE YOU IN HER ROOM ALONE.
KITTY.
AS LONG AS WE UNDERSTAND EACH OTHER.
YES, MA'AM.

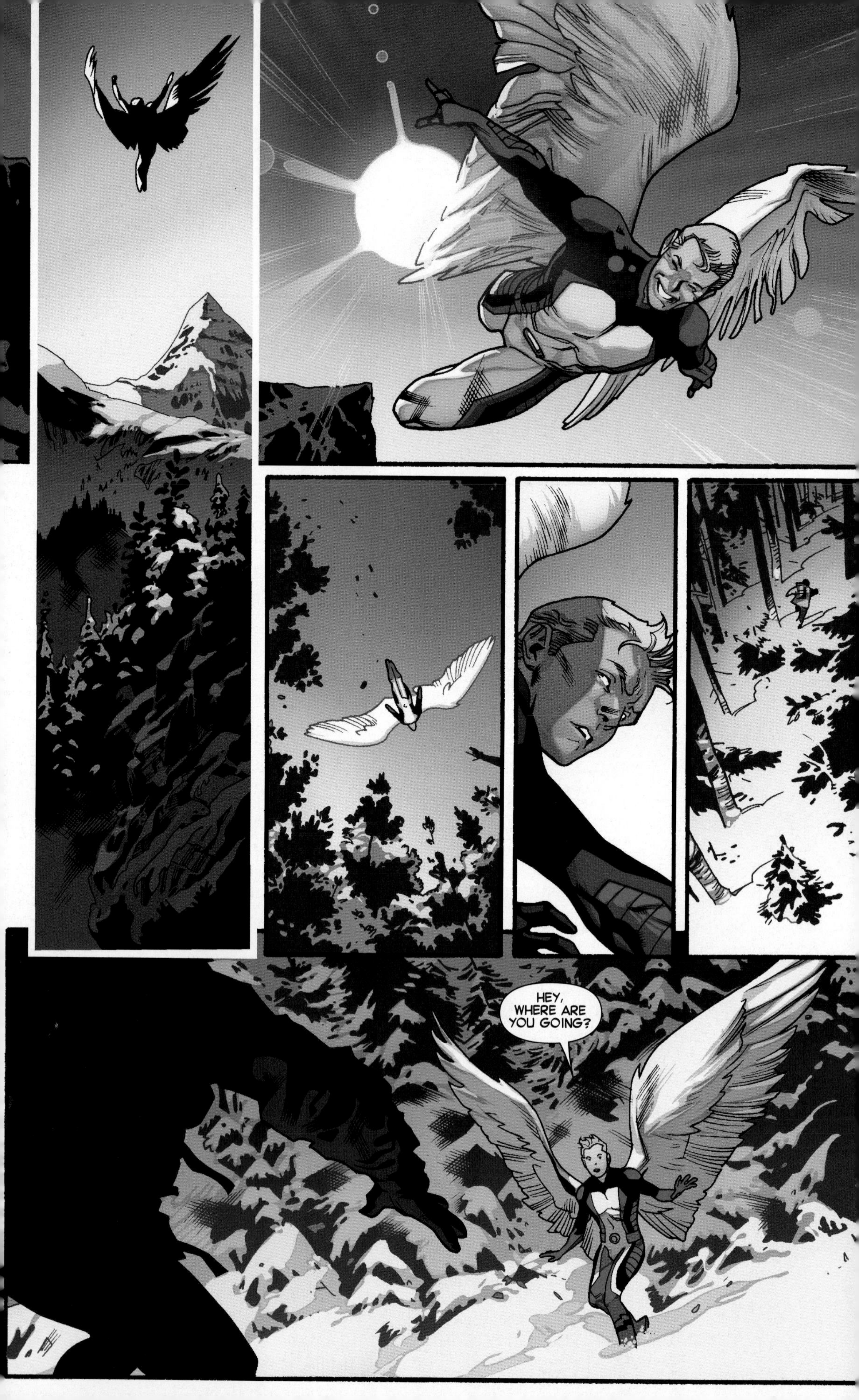
HEY, WHERE ARE YOU GOING?

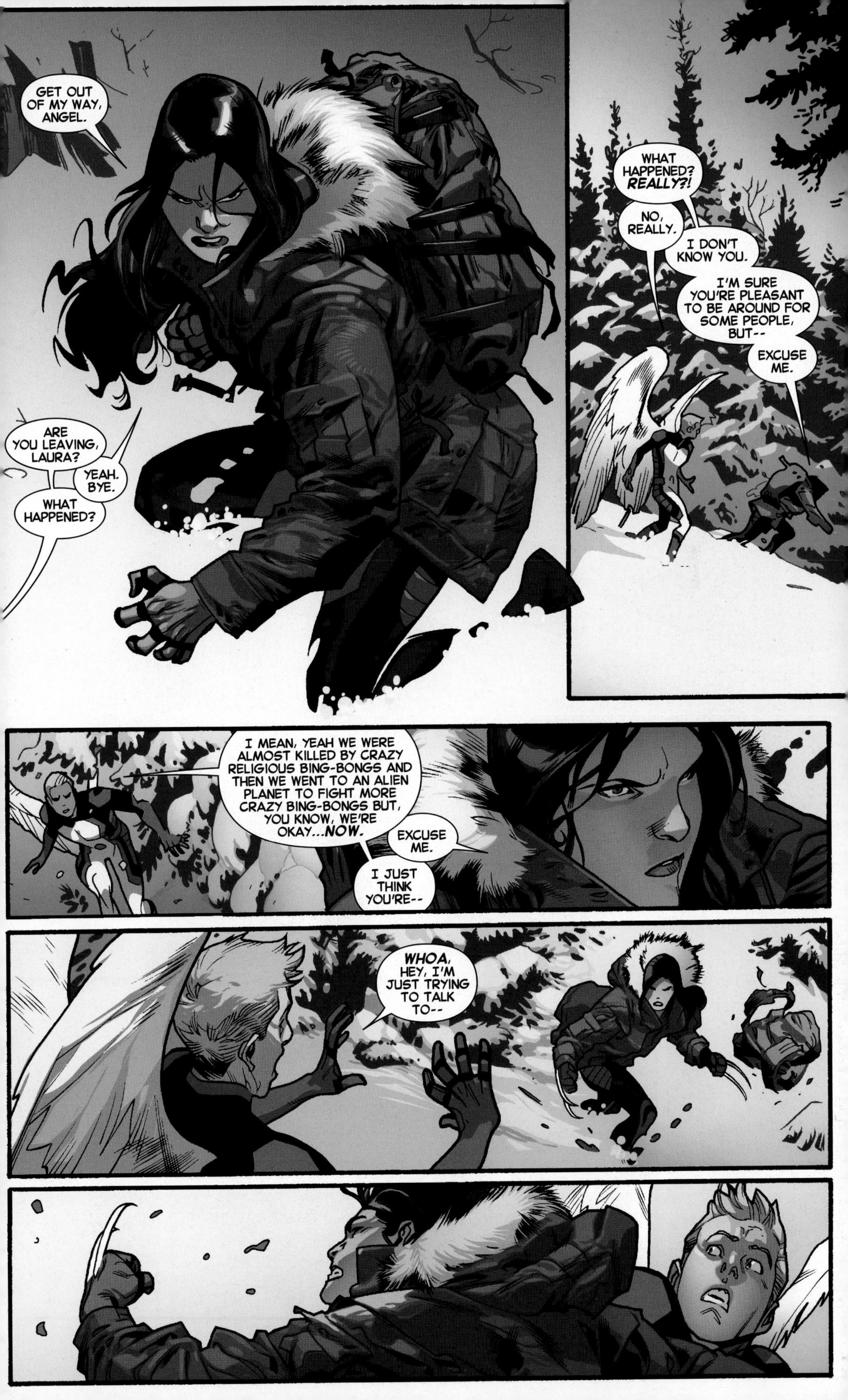
GET OUT OF MY WAY, ANGEL.
ARE YOU LEAVING, LAURA?
YEAH. BYE.
WHAT HAPPENED?
WHAT HAPPENED? REALLY?!
NO, REALLY.
I DON'T KNOW YOU.
I'M SURE YOU'RE PLEASANT TO BE AROUND FOR SOME PEOPLE, BUT--
EXCUSE ME.
I MEAN, YEAH WE WERE ALMOST KILLED BY CRAZY RELIGIOUS BING-BONGS AND THEN WE WENT TO AN ALIEN PLANET TO FIGHT MORE CRAZY BING-BONGS BUT, YOU KNOW, WE'RE OKAY...NOW.
EXCUSE ME.
I JUST THINK YOU'RE--
WHOA, HEY, I'M JUST TRYING TO TALK TO--

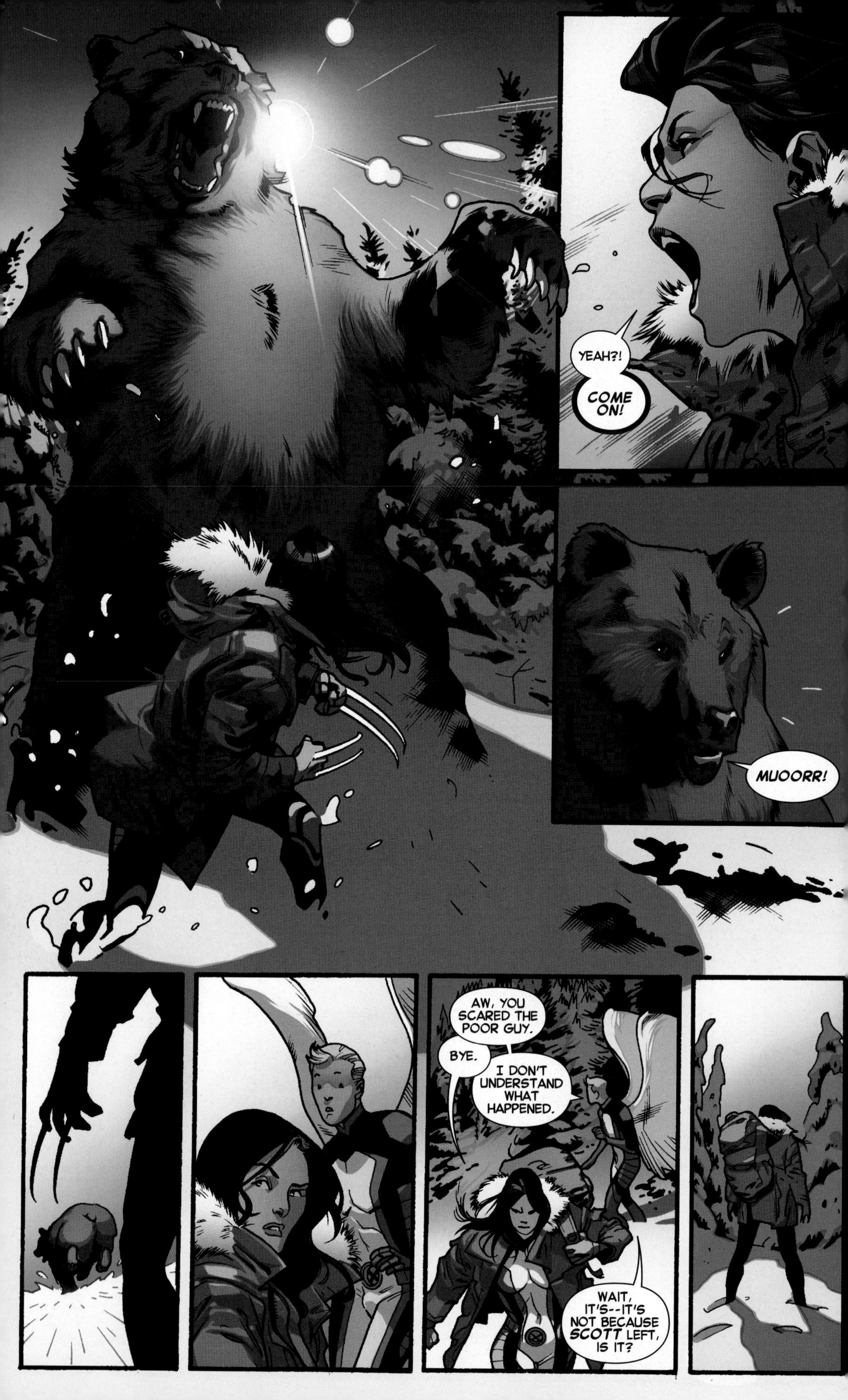
YEAH?!
COME ON!
MUOORR!
AW, YOU SCARED THE POOR GUY.
BYE.
I DON'T UNDERSTAND WHAT HAPPENED.
WAIT, IT'S--IT'S NOT BECAUSE SCOTT LEFT, IS IT?

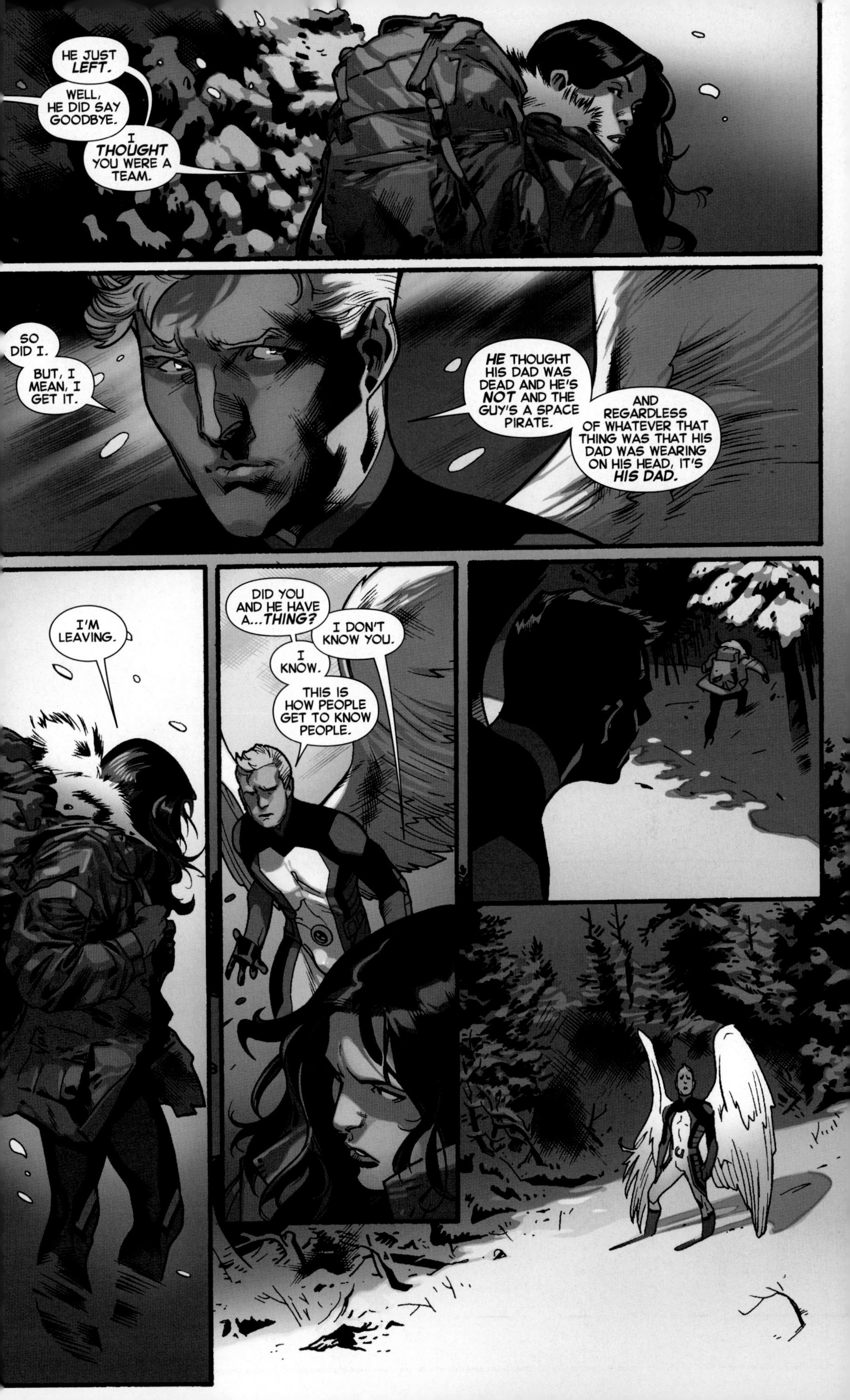
HE JUST LEFT.
WELL, HE DID SAY GOODBYE.
I THOUGHT YOU WERE A TEAM.
SO DID I.
BUT, I MEAN, I GET IT.
HE THOUGHT HIS DAD WAS DEAD AND HE'S NOT AND THE GUY'S A SPACE PIRATE.
AND REGARDLESS OF WHATEVER THAT THING WAS THAT HIS DAD WAS WEARING ON HIS HEAD, IT'S HIS DAD.
I'M LEAVING.
DID YOU AND HE HAVE A...THING?
I DON'T KNOW YOU.
I KNOW.
THIS IS HOW PEOPLE GET TO KNOW PEOPLE.

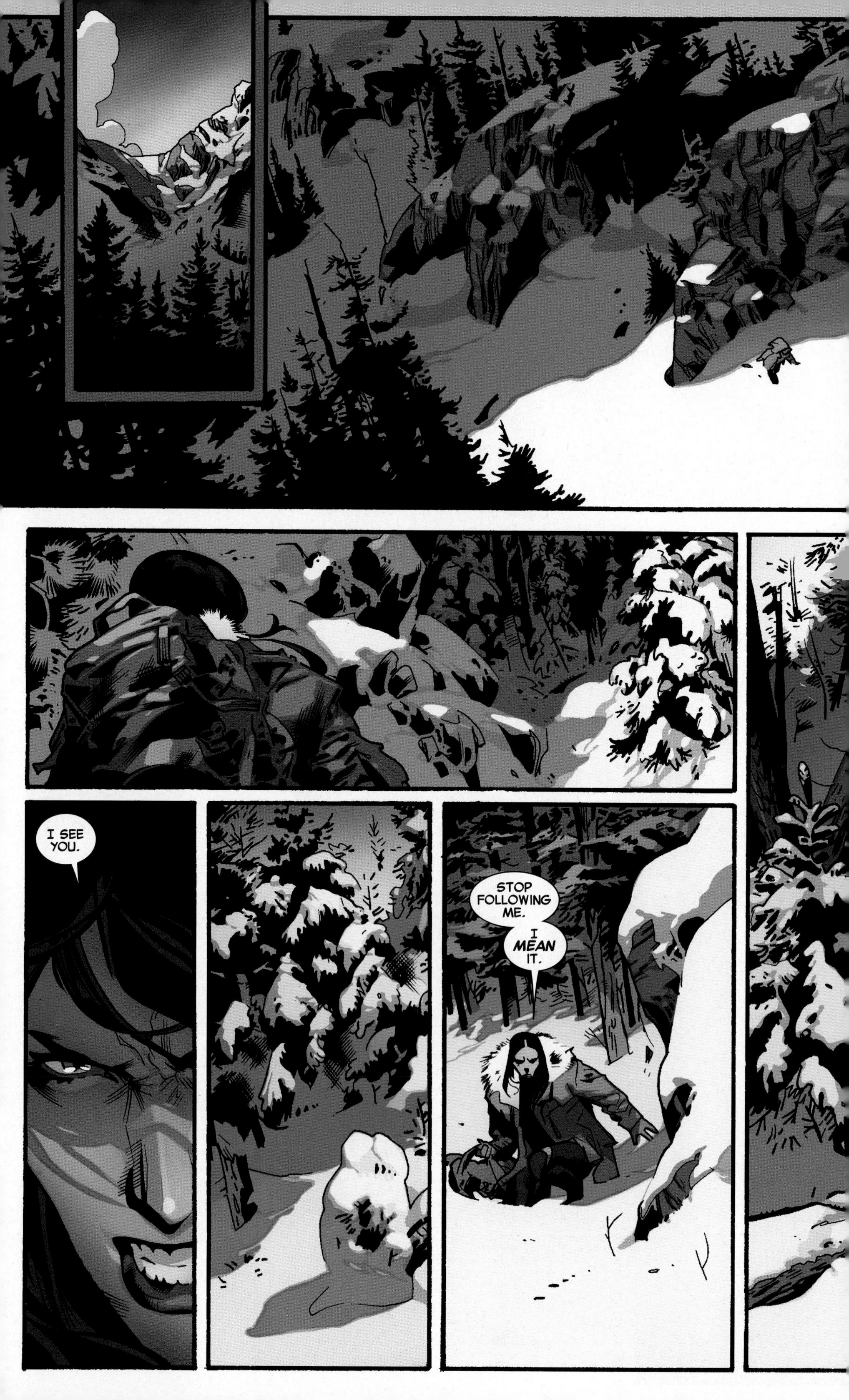
I SEE YOU.
STOP FOLLOWING ME.
I MEAN IT.

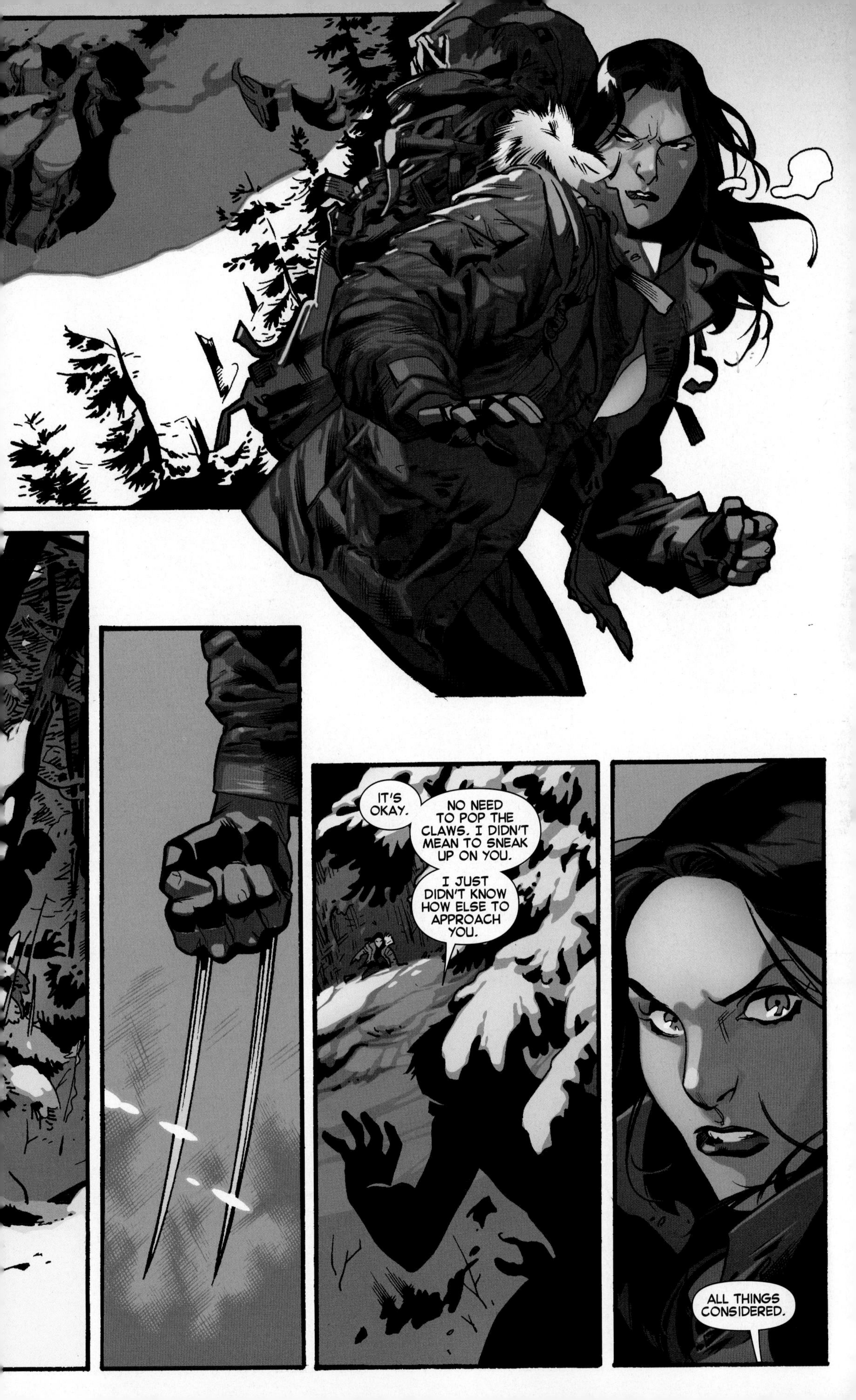
IT'S OKAY.
NO NEED TO POP THE CLAWS. I DIDN'T MEAN TO SNEAK UP ON YOU.
I JUST DIDN'T KNOW HOW ELSE TO APPROACH YOU.
ALL THINGS CONSIDERED.

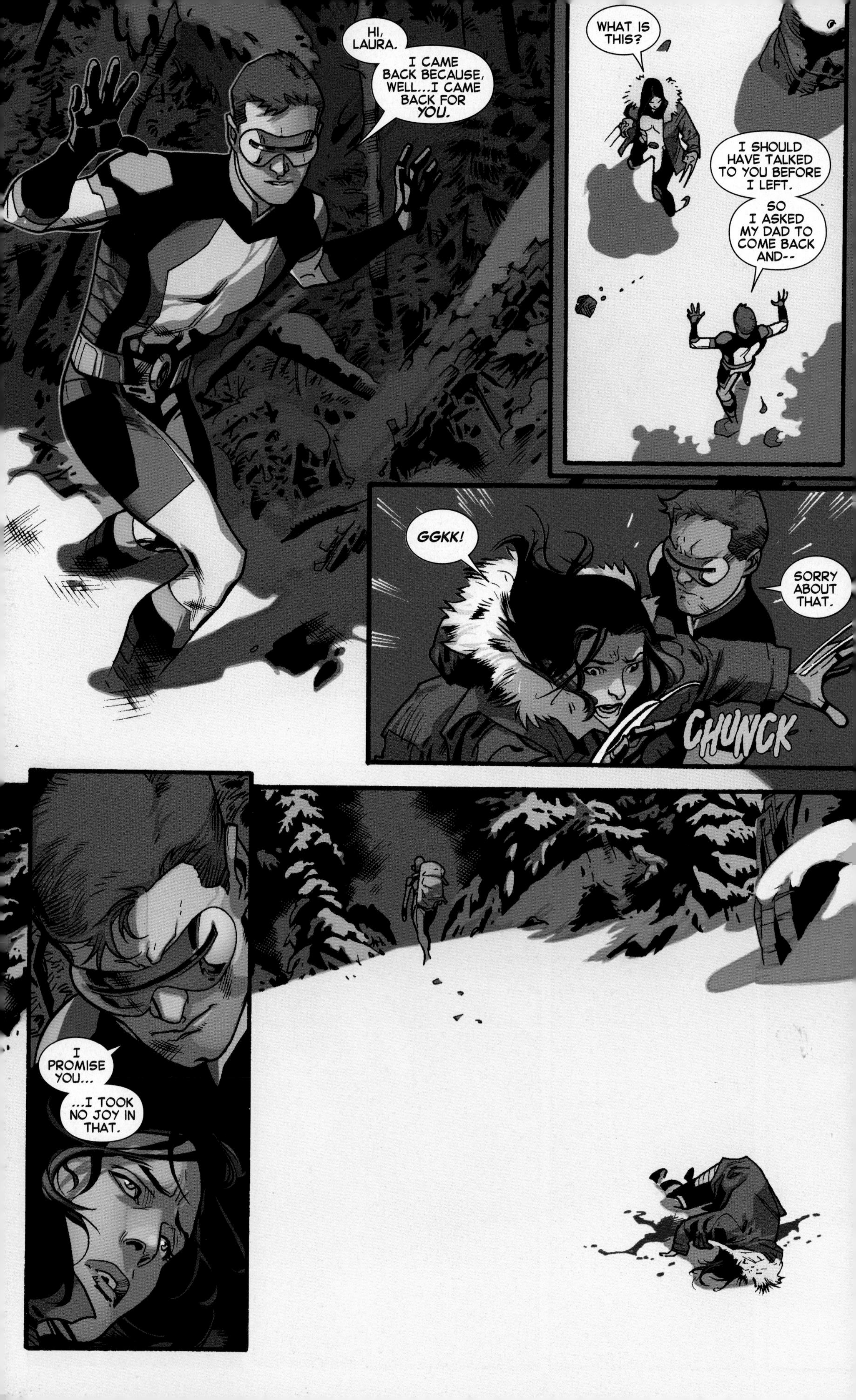
HI, LAURA.
I CAME BACK BECAUSE, WELL...I CAME BACK FOR YOU.
WHAT IS THIS?
I SHOULD HAVE TALKED TO YOU BEFORE I LEFT.
SO I ASKED MY DAD TO COME BACK AND--
GGKK!
SORRY ABOUT THAT.
CHUNCK
I PROMISE YOU...
...I TOOK NO JOY IN THAT.

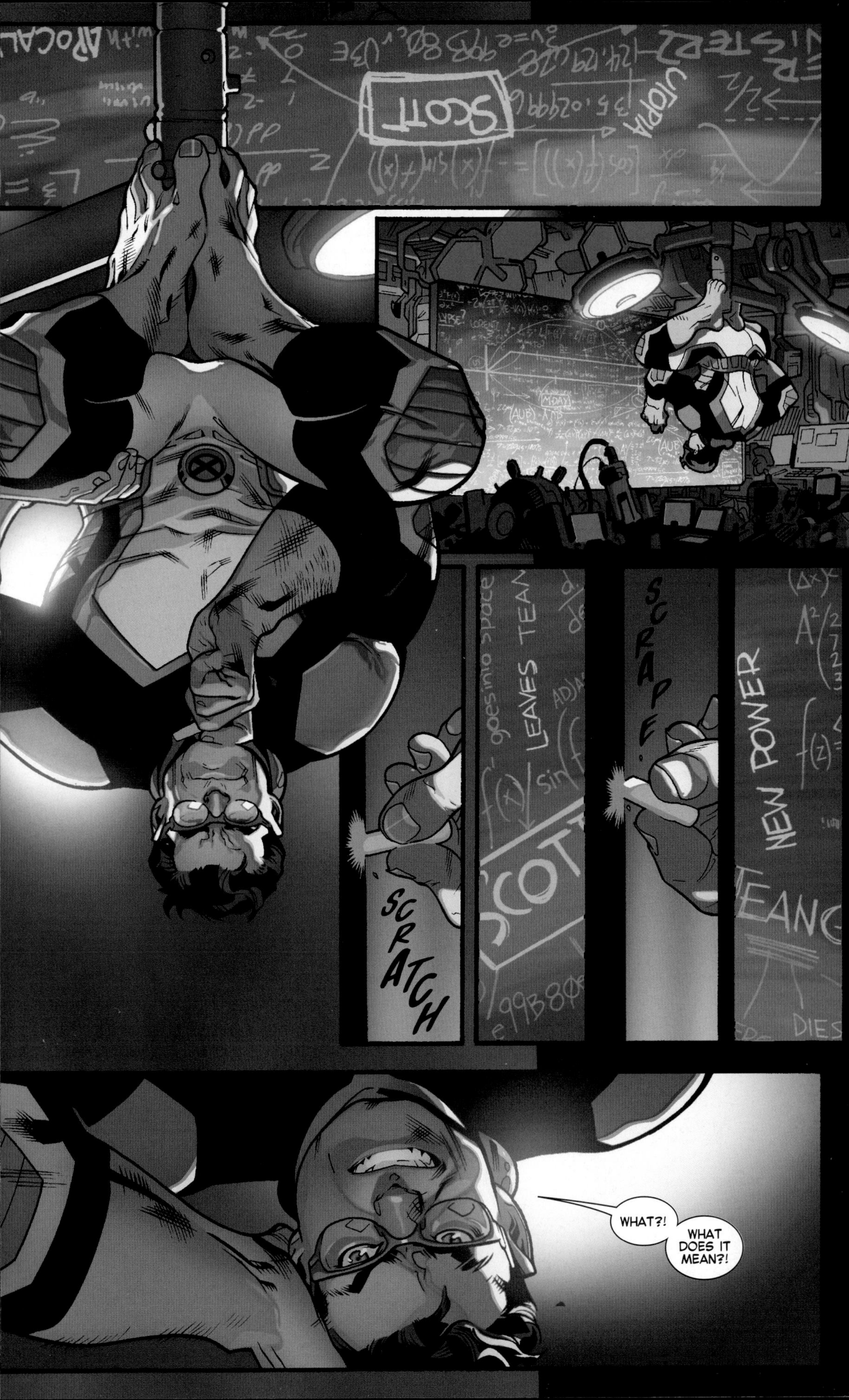
SCOTT
UTOPIA
goes into space
LEAVES TEAM
SCOTT
SCRATCH
SCRAPE
NEW POWER
WHAT?!
WHAT DOES IT MEAN?!

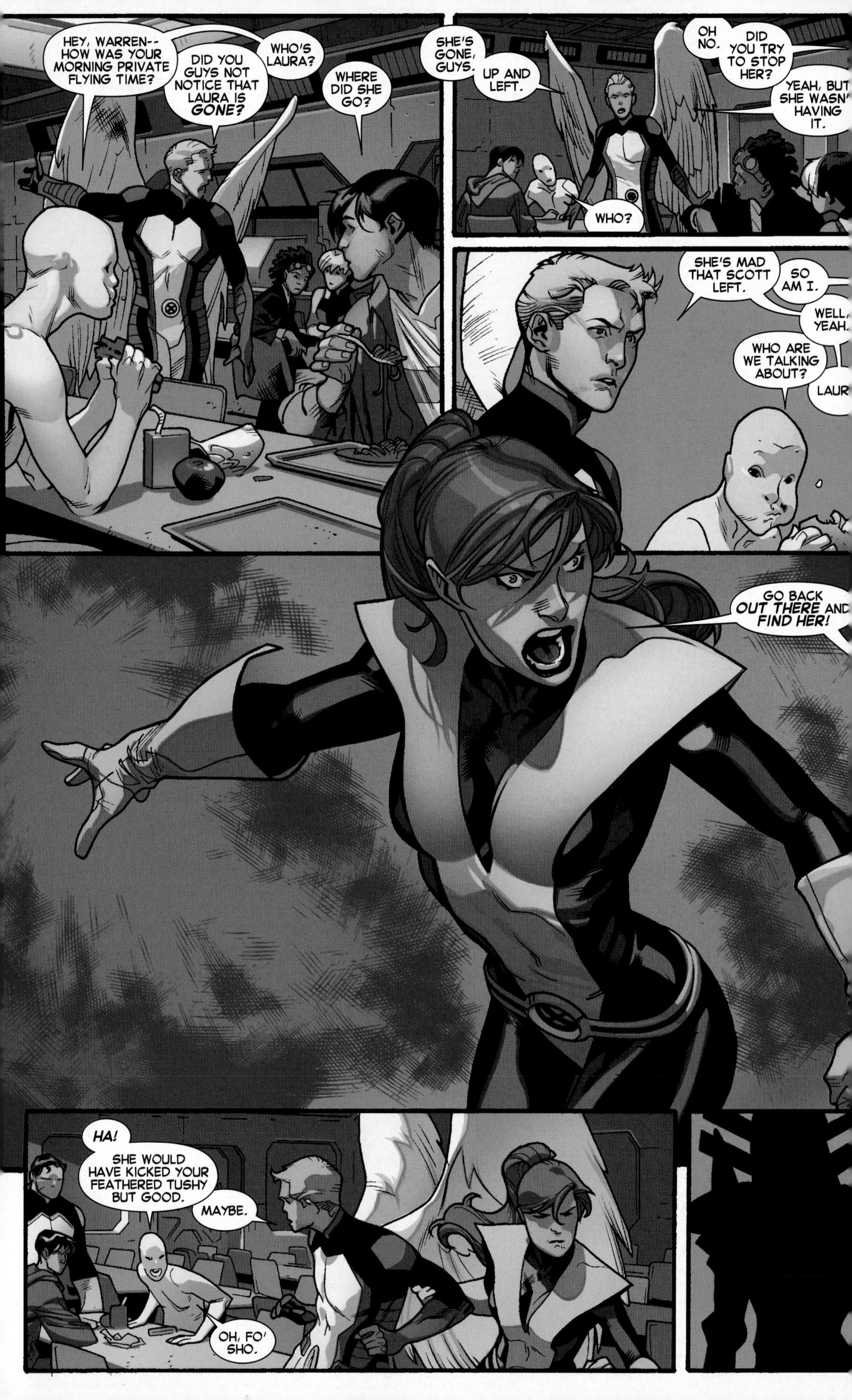
HEY, WARREN-- HOW WAS YOUR MORNING PRIVATE FLYING TIME?
DID YOU GUYS NOT NOTICE THAT LAURA IS GONE?
WHO'S LAURA?
WHERE DID SHE GO?
SHE'S GONE, GUYS.
UP AND LEFT.
OH NO.
DID YOU TRY TO STOP HER?
YEAH, BUT SHE WASN' HAVING IT.
WHO?
SHE'S MAD THAT SCOTT LEFT.
SO AM I.
WELL, YEAH.
WHO ARE WE TALKING ABOUT?
LAUR
GO BACK OUT THERE AND FIND HER!
HA!
SHE WOULD HAVE KICKED YOUR FEATHERED TUSHY BUT GOOD.
MAYBE.
OH, FO' SHO.

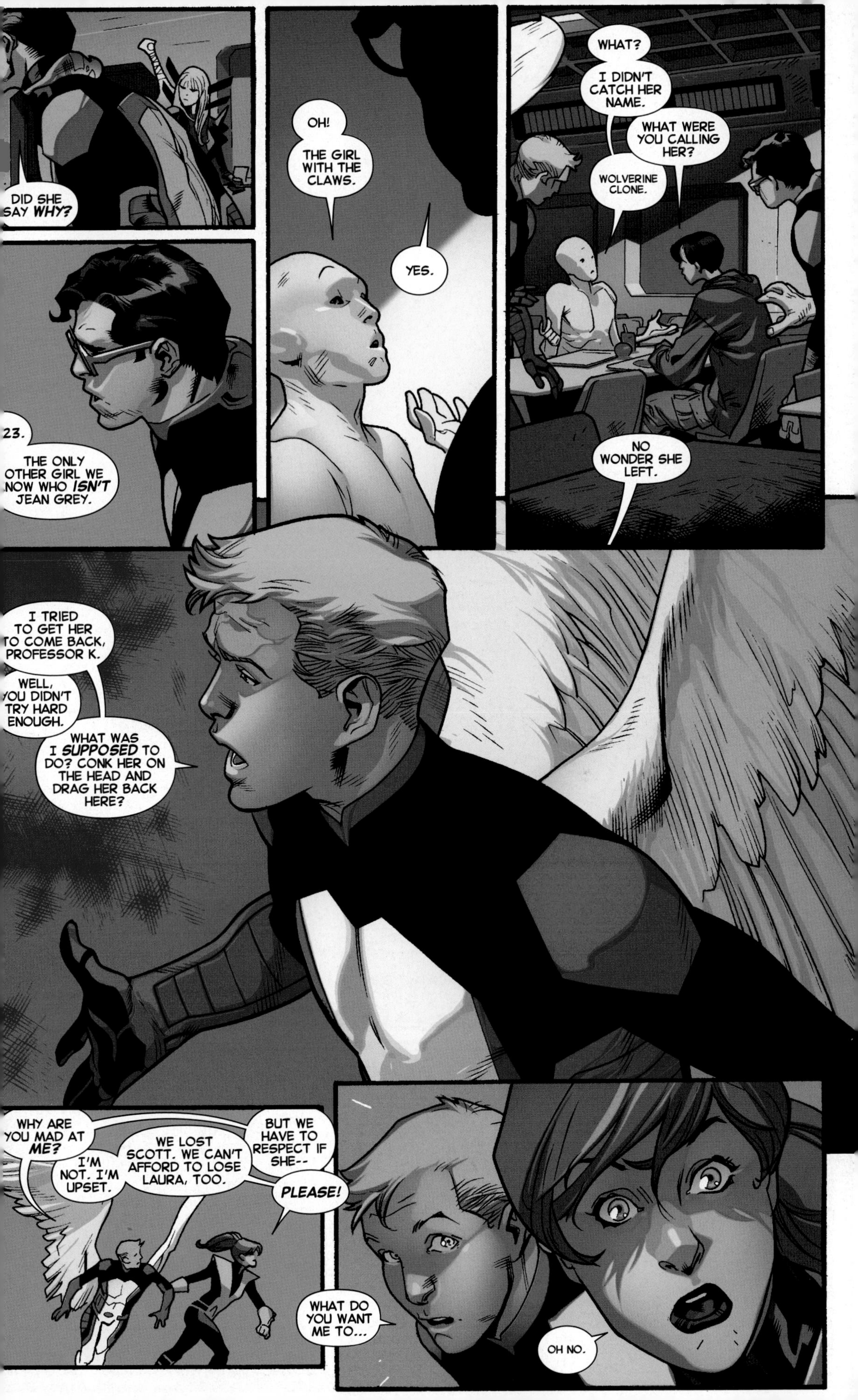

DID SHE SAY WHY?
23.
THE ONLY OTHER GIRL WE KNOW WHO ISN'T JEAN GREY.
OH!
THE GIRL WITH THE CLAWS.
YES.
WHAT?
I DIDN'T CATCH HER NAME.
WHAT WERE YOU CALLING HER?
WOLVERINE CLONE.
NO WONDER SHE LEFT.
I TRIED TO GET HER TO COME BACK, PROFESSOR K.
WELL, YOU DIDN'T TRY HARD ENOUGH.
WHAT WAS I SUPPOSED TO DO? CONK HER ON THE HEAD AND DRAG HER BACK HERE?
WHY ARE YOU MAD AT ME?
I'M NOT. I'M UPSET.
WE LOST SCOTT. WE CAN'T AFFORD TO LOSE LAURA, TOO.
BUT WE HAVE TO RESPECT IF SHE--
PLEASE!
WHAT DO YOU WANT ME TO...
OH NO.

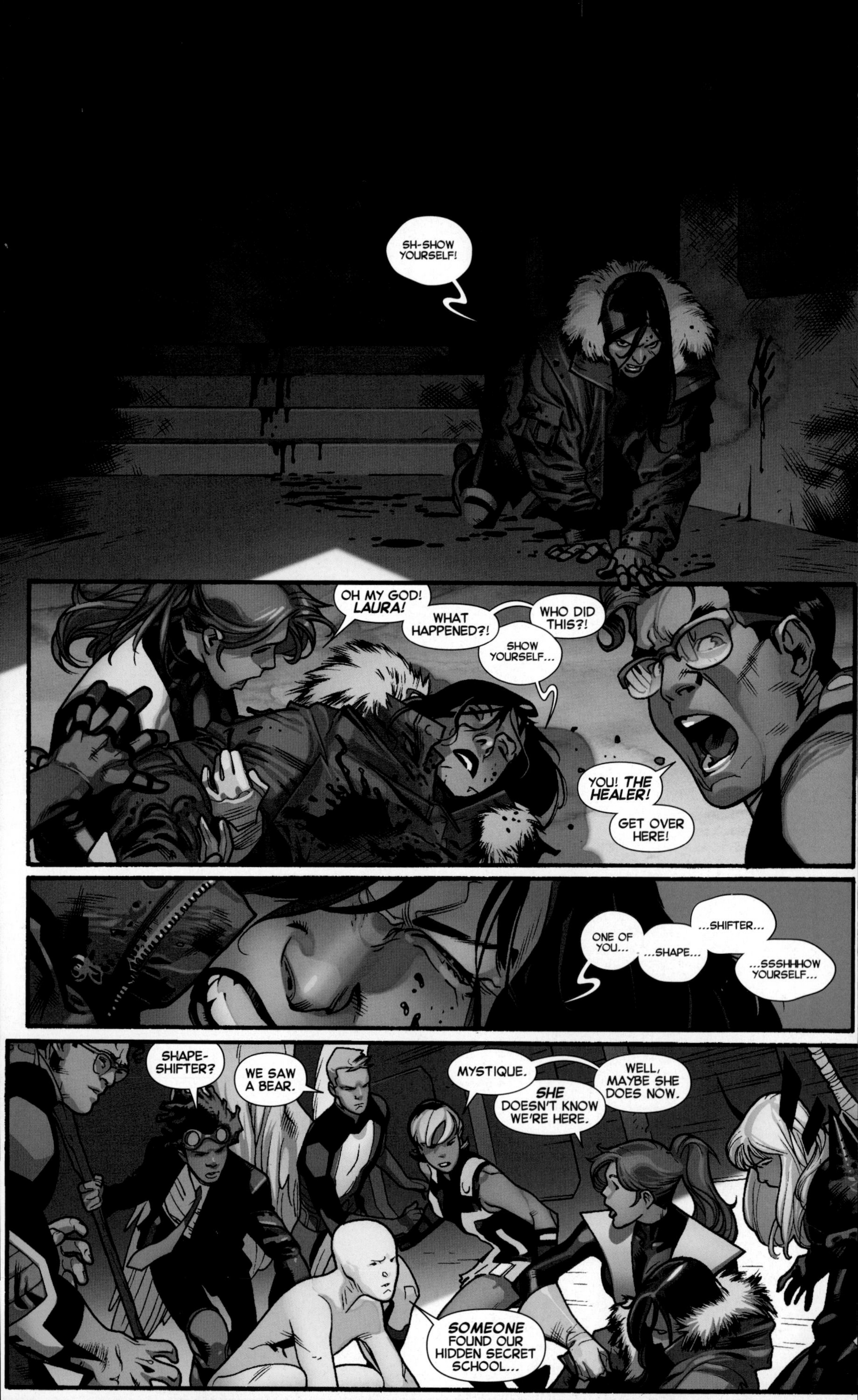
SH-SHOW YOURSELF!
OH MY GOD! LAURA!
WHAT HAPPENED?!
WHO DID THIS?!
SHOW YOURSELF...
YOU! THE HEALER!
GET OVER HERE!
ONE OF YOU...
...SHAPE...
...SHIFTER...
...SSSHHHOW YOURSELF...
SHAPE-SHIFTER?
WE SAW A BEAR.
MYSTIQUE.
SHE DOESN'T KNOW WE'RE HERE.
WELL, MAYBE SHE DOES NOW.
SOMEONE FOUND OUR HIDDEN SECRET SCHOOL...

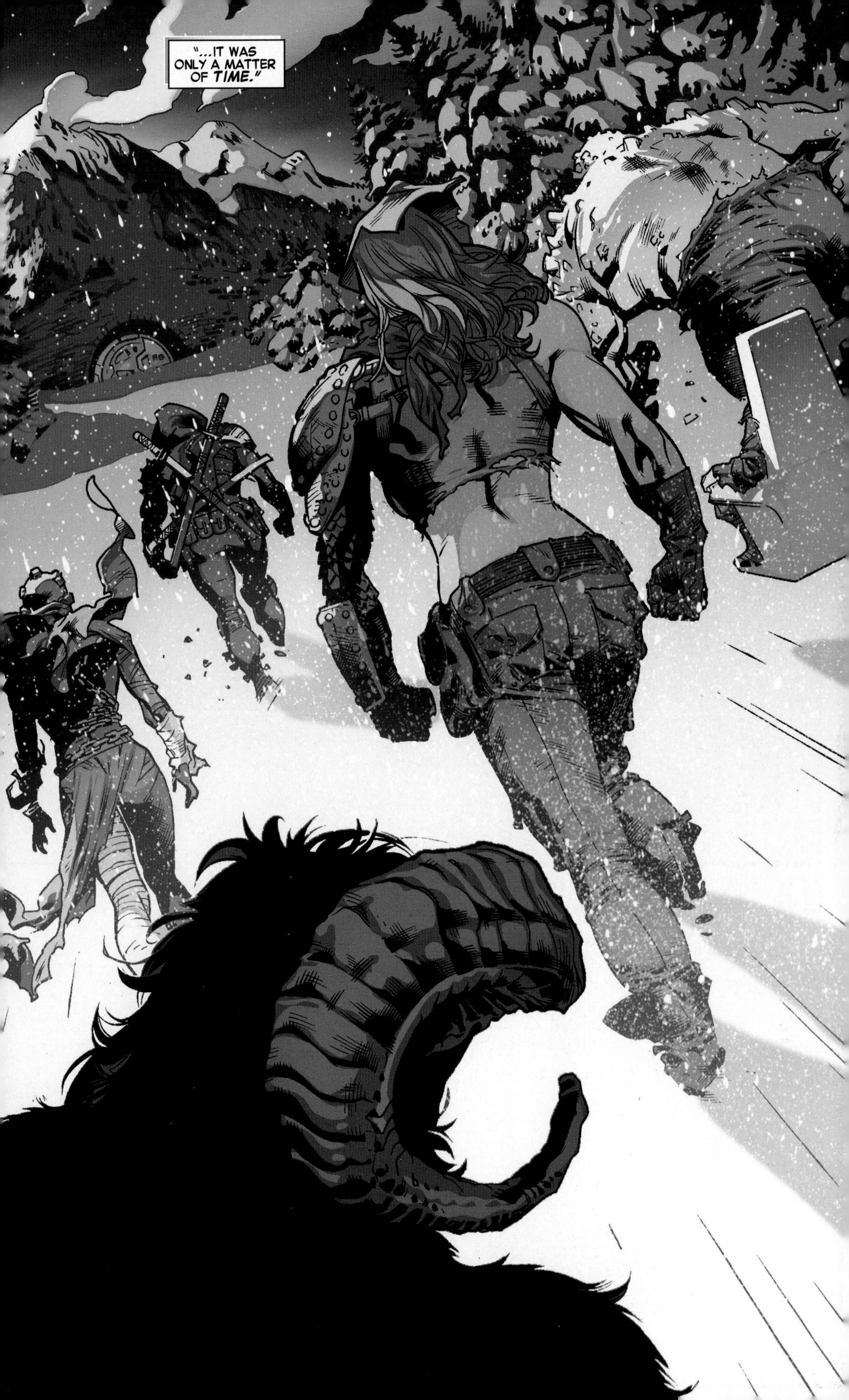
"...IT WAS ONLY A MATTER OF TIME."

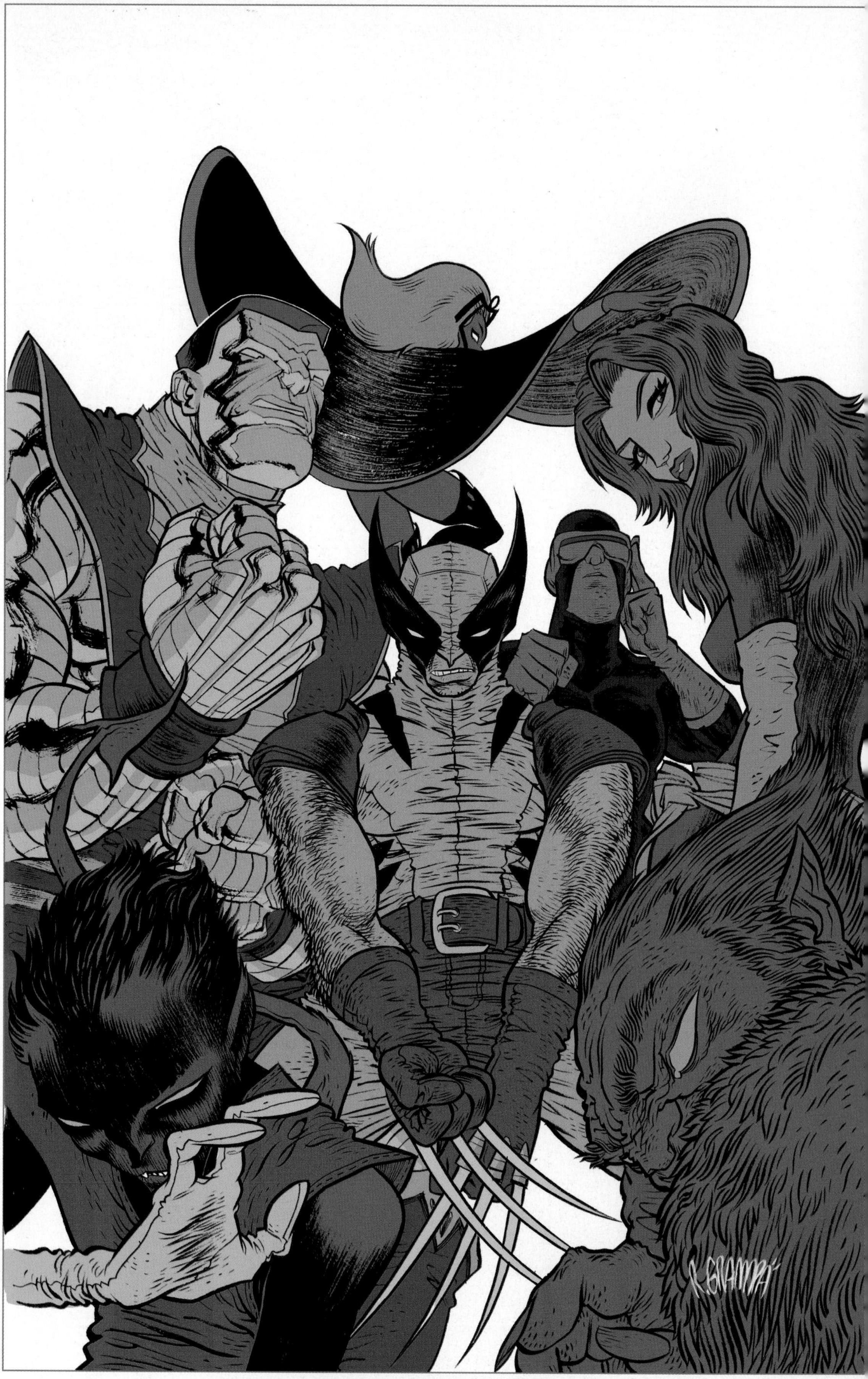

ALL-NEW X-MEN #25 VARIANT
BY RAFAEL GRAMPÁ

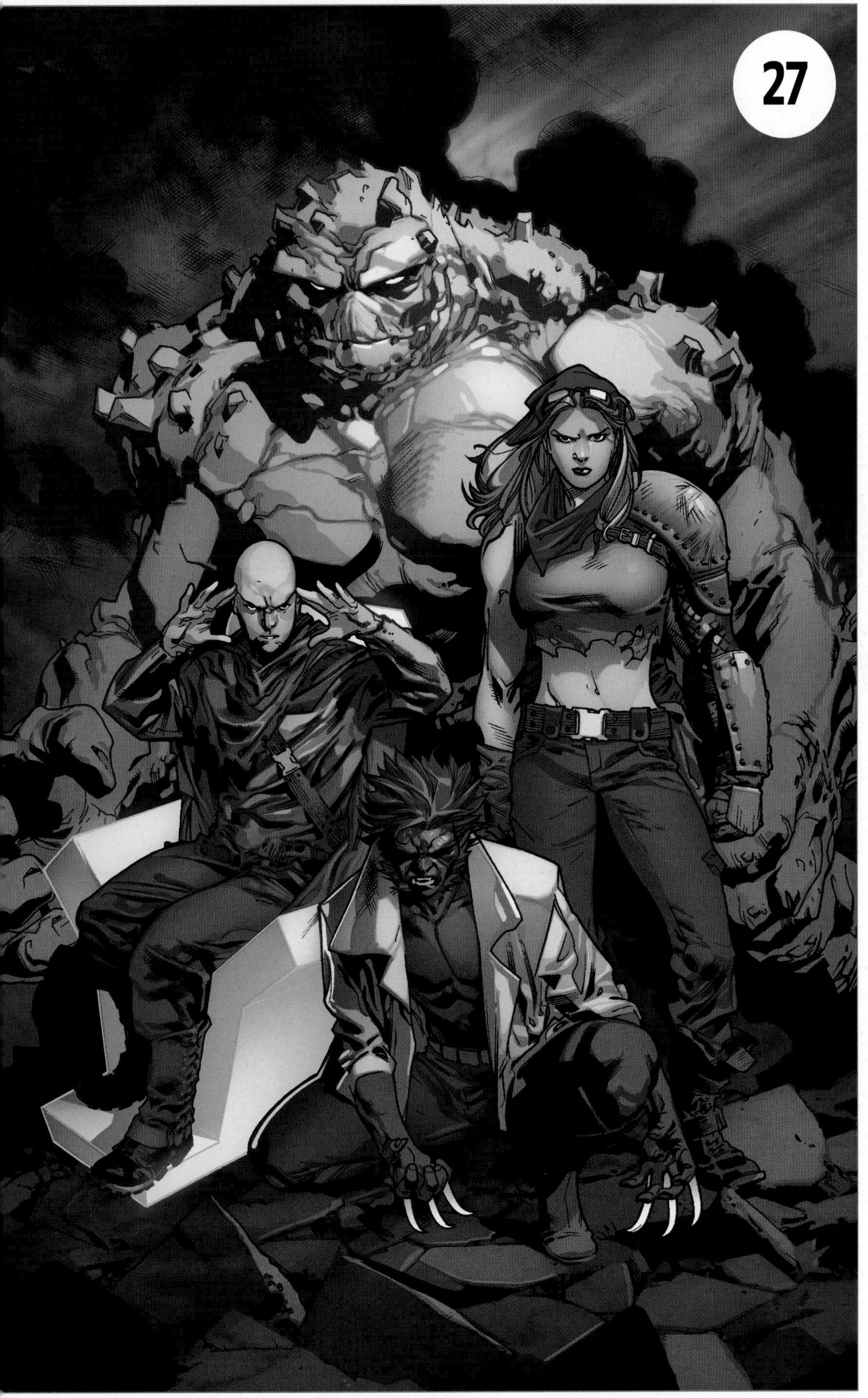
27

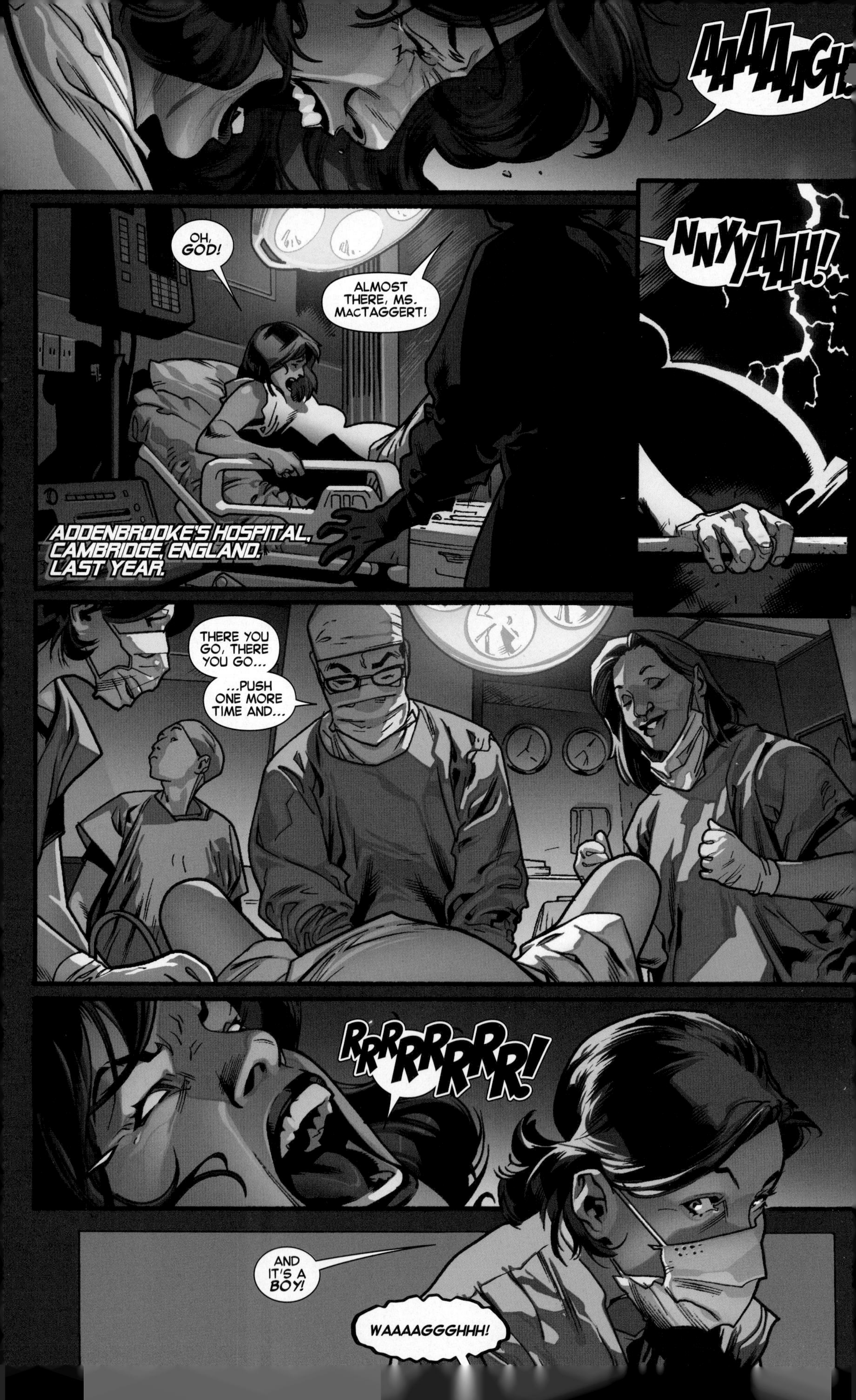
AAAAAAGH!
OH, GOD!
ALMOST THERE, MS. MACTAGGERT!
ADDENBROOKE'S HOSPITAL, CAMBRIDGE, ENGLAND. LAST YEAR.
NNYYAAAH!
THERE YOU GO, THERE YOU GO...
...PUSH ONE MORE TIME AND...
RRRRRRRR!
AND IT'S A BOY!
WAAAAGGGHHH!

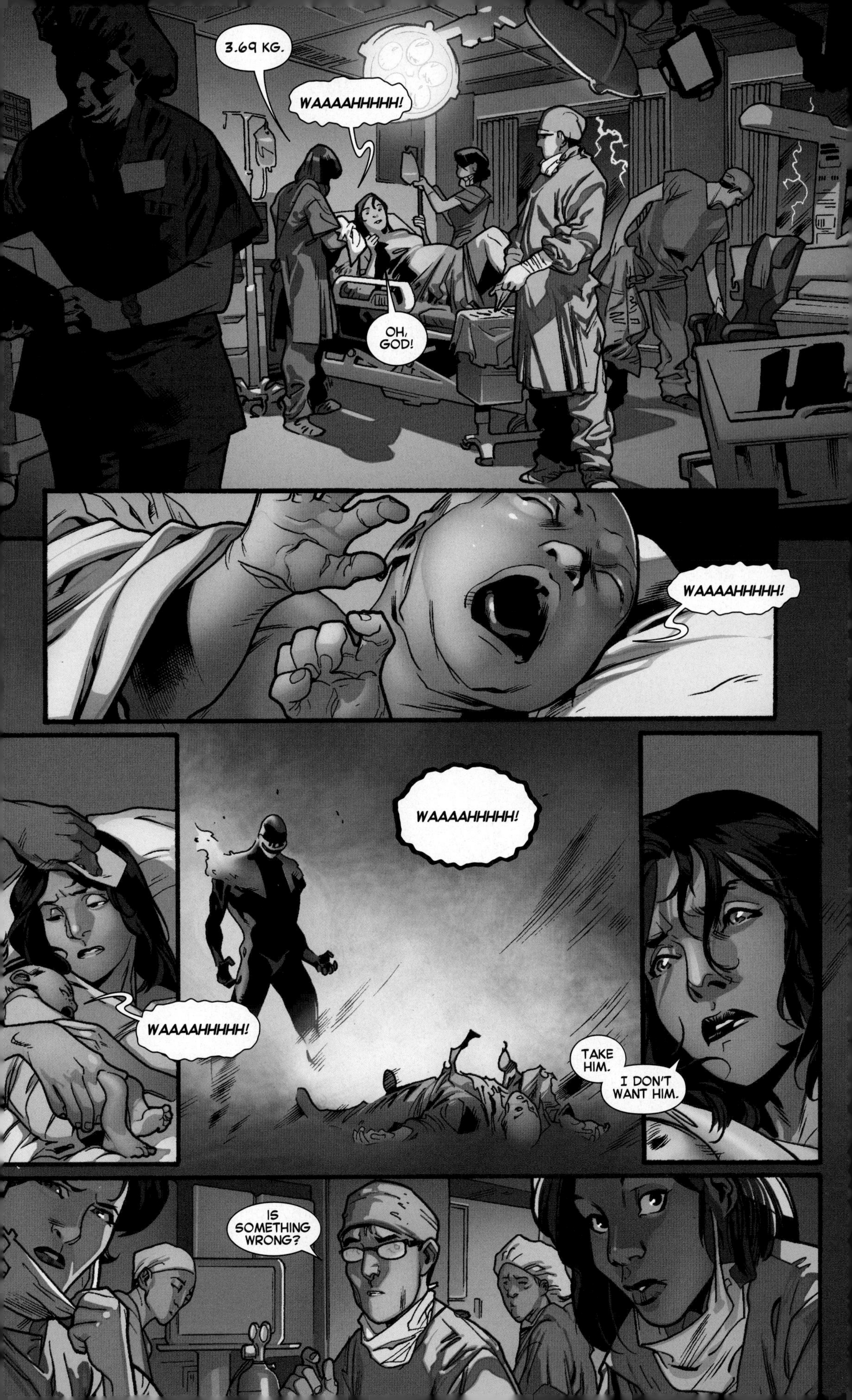
3.69 KG.
WAAAAHHHHH!
OH, GOD!
WAAAAHHHHH!
WAAAAHHHHH!
WAAAAHHHHH!
TAKE HIM.
I DON'T WANT HIM.
IS SOMETHING WRONG?

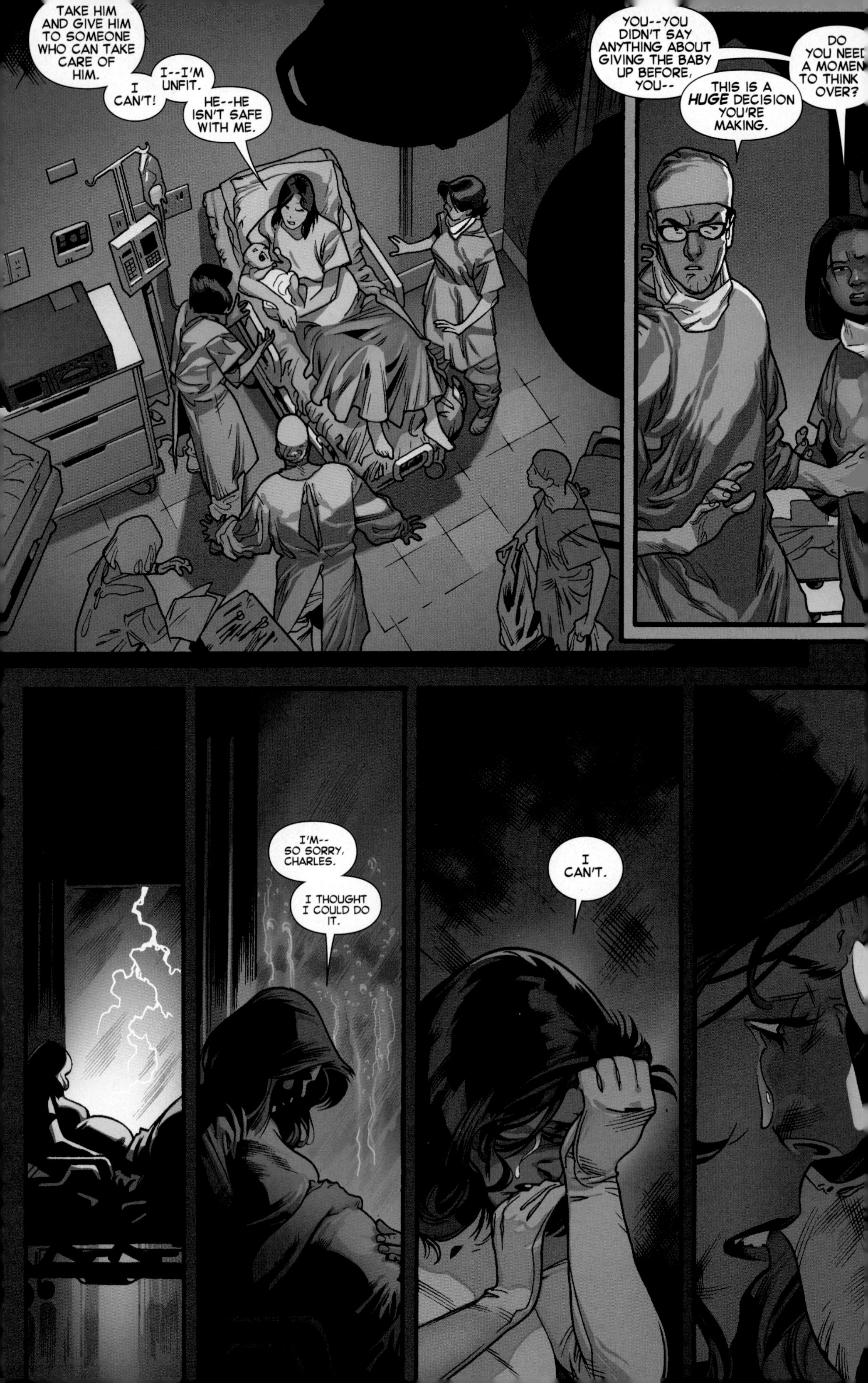
TAKE HIM AND GIVE HIM TO SOMEONE WHO CAN TAKE CARE OF HIM.
I CAN'T!
I--I'M UNFIT.
HE--HE ISN'T SAFE WITH ME.
YOU--YOU DIDN'T SAY ANYTHING ABOUT GIVING THE BABY UP BEFORE, YOU--
THIS IS A HUGE DECISION YOU'RE MAKING.
DO YOU NEED A MOMEN TO THINK OVER?
I'M-- SO SORRY, CHARLES.
I THOUGHT I COULD DO IT.
I CAN'T.

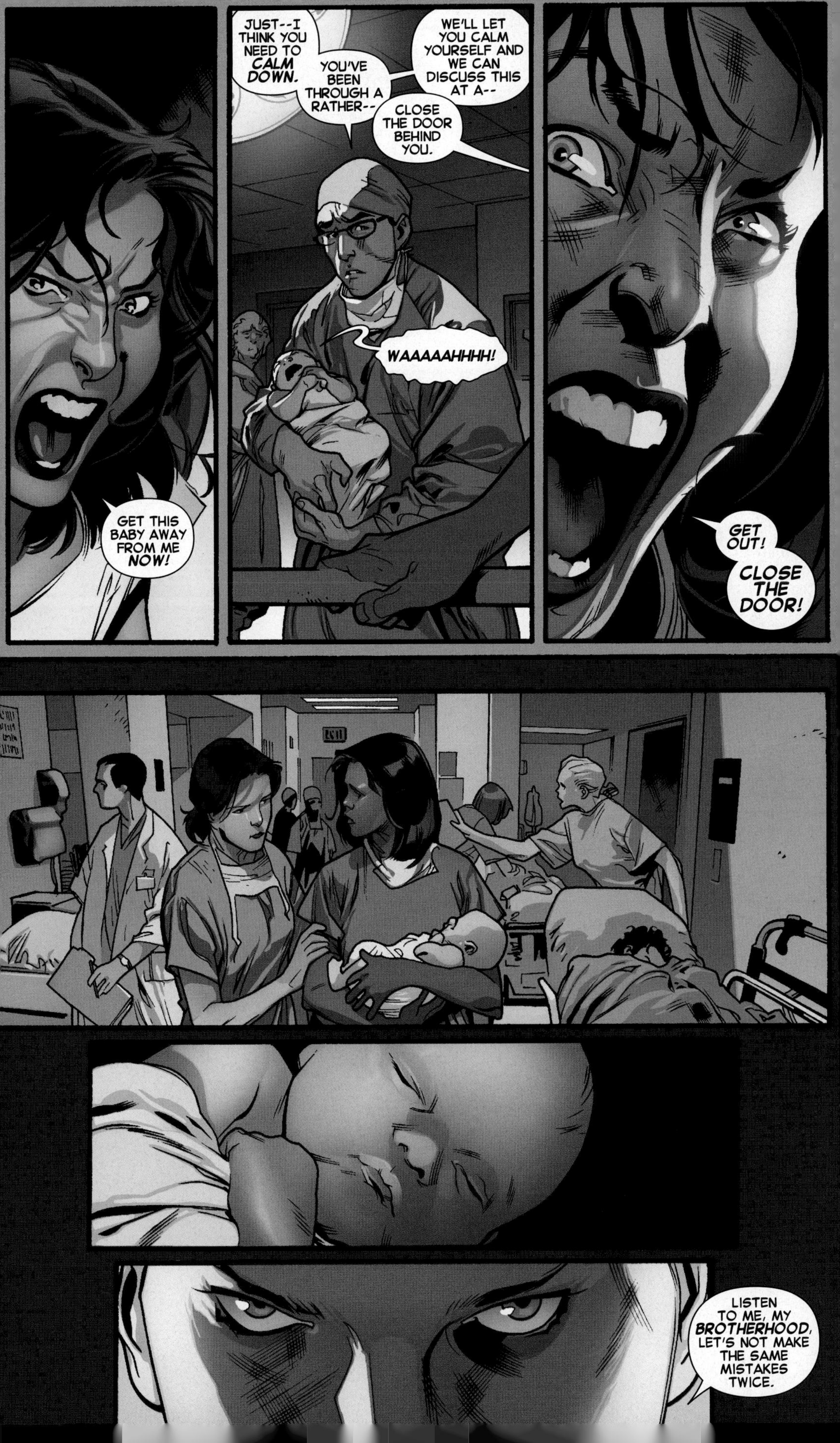
GET THIS BABY AWAY FROM ME NOW!
JUST--I THINK YOU NEED TO CALM DOWN.
YOU'VE BEEN THROUGH A RATHER--
WE'LL LET YOU CALM YOURSELF AND WE CAN DISCUSS THIS AT A--
CLOSE THE DOOR BEHIND YOU.
WAAAAAHHHH!
GET OUT!
CLOSE THE DOOR!
LISTEN TO ME, MY BROTHERHOOD, LET'S NOT MAKE THE SAME MISTAKES TWICE.

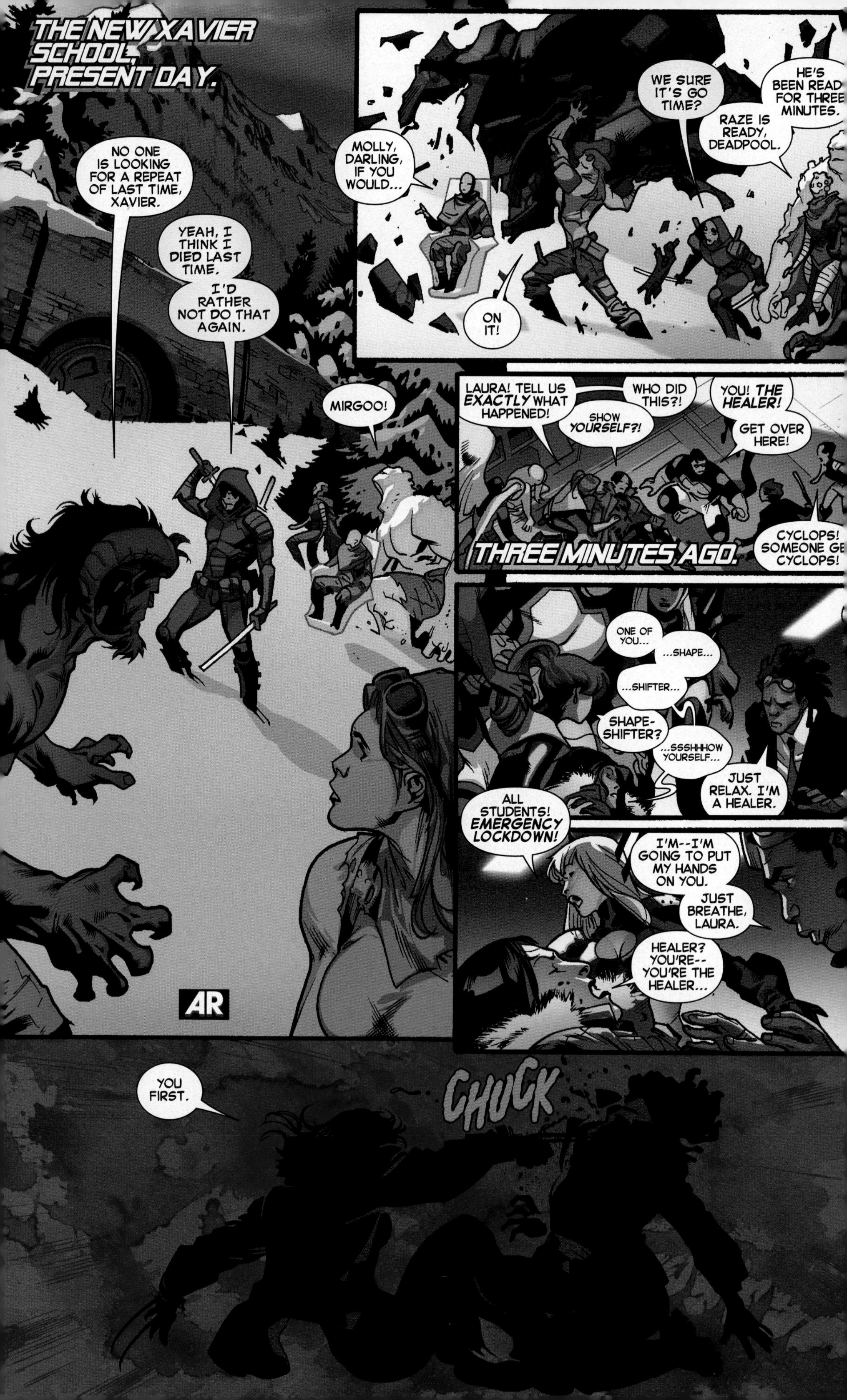
THE NEW XAVIER SCHOOL, PRESENT DAY.
MOLLY, DARLING, IF YOU WOULD...
ON IT!
WE SURE IT'S GO TIME?
HE'S BEEN READ FOR THREE MINUTES.
RAZE IS READY, DEADPOOL.
NO ONE IS LOOKING FOR A REPEAT OF LAST TIME, XAVIER.
YEAH, I THINK I DIED LAST TIME.
I'D RATHER NOT DO THAT AGAIN.
MIRGOO!
LAURA! TELL US EXACTLY WHAT HAPPENED!
SHOW YOURSELF?!
WHO DID THIS?!
YOU! THE HEALER!
GET OVER HERE!
THREE MINUTES AGO.
CYCLOPS! SOMEONE GE CYCLOPS!
ONE OF YOU...
...SHAPE...
...SHIFTER...
SHAPE-SHIFTER?
...SSSHHHOW YOURSELF...
JUST RELAX. I'M A HEALER.
ALL STUDENTS! EMERGENCY LOCKDOWN!
I'M--I'M GOING TO PUT MY HANDS ON YOU.
JUST BREATHE, LAURA.
HEALER? YOU'RE--YOU'RE THE HEALER...
AR
YOU FIRST.
CHUCK

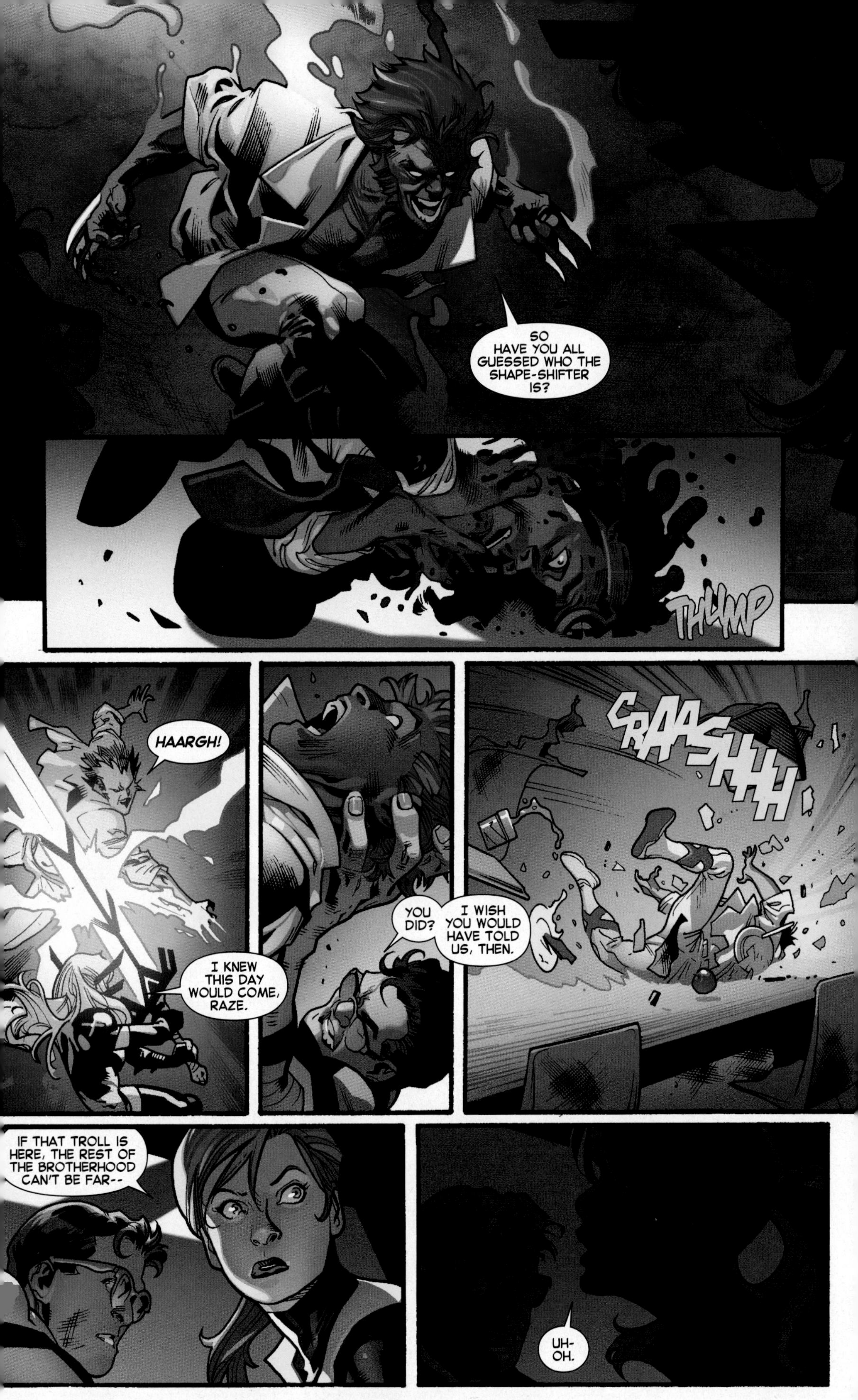
SO HAVE YOU ALL GUESSED WHO THE SHAPE-SHIFTER IS?
THUMP
HAARGH!
I KNEW THIS DAY WOULD COME, RAZE.
YOU DID?
I WISH YOU WOULD HAVE TOLD US, THEN.
CRAASHHH
IF THAT TROLL IS HERE, THE REST OF THE BROTHERHOOD CAN'T BE FAR--
UH-OH.

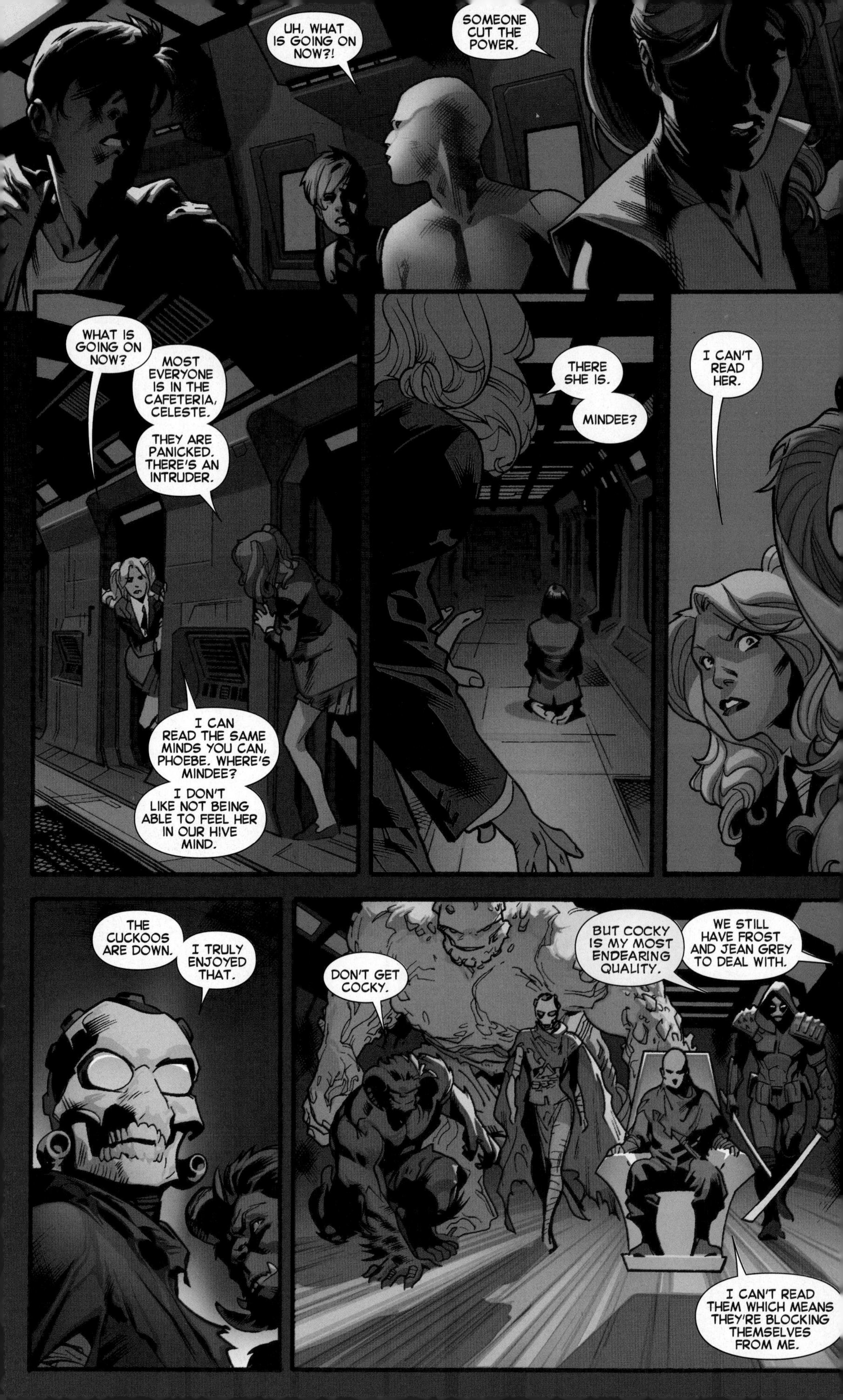
UH, WHAT IS GOING ON NOW?!
SOMEONE CUT THE POWER.
WHAT IS GOING ON NOW?
MOST EVERYONE IS IN THE CAFETERIA, CELESTE.
THEY ARE PANICKED. THERE'S AN INTRUDER.
I CAN READ THE SAME MINDS YOU CAN, PHOEBE. WHERE'S MINDEE?
I DON'T LIKE NOT BEING ABLE TO FEEL HER IN OUR HIVE MIND.
THERE SHE IS.
MINDEE?
I CAN'T READ HER.
THE CUCKOOS ARE DOWN.
I TRULY ENJOYED THAT.
DON'T GET COCKY.
BUT COCKY IS MY MOST ENDEARING QUALITY.
WE STILL HAVE FROST AND JEAN GREY TO DEAL WITH.
I CAN'T READ THEM WHICH MEANS THEY'RE BLOCKING THEMSELVES FROM ME.

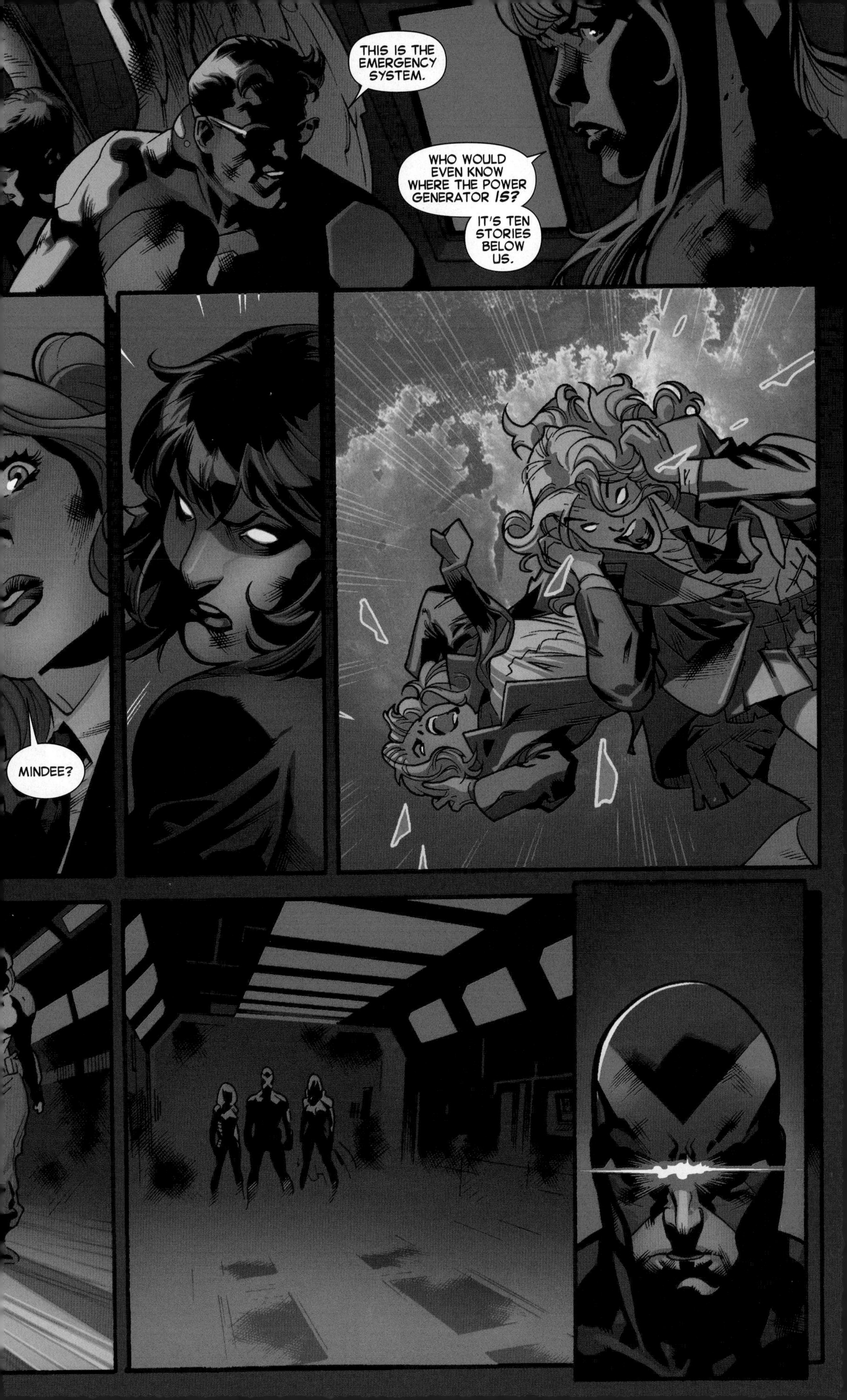
THIS IS THE EMERGENCY SYSTEM.
WHO WOULD EVEN KNOW WHERE THE POWER GENERATOR *IS?*
IT'S TEN STORIES BELOW US.
MINDEE?

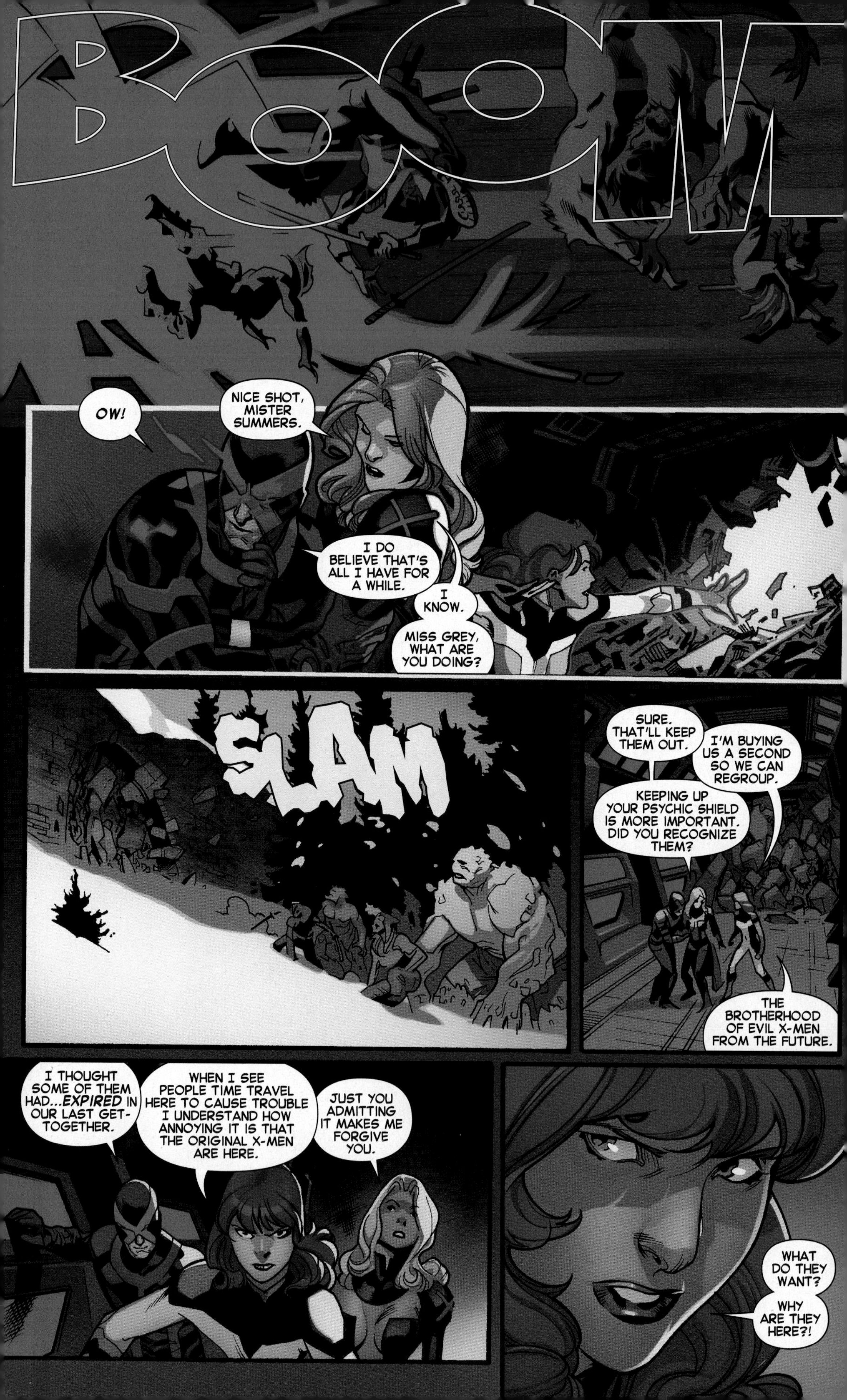
BOOM
OW!
NICE SHOT, MISTER SUMMERS.
I DO BELIEVE THAT'S ALL I HAVE FOR A WHILE.
I KNOW.
MISS GREY, WHAT ARE YOU DOING?
SLAM
SURE. THAT'LL KEEP THEM OUT.
I'M BUYING US A SECOND SO WE CAN REGROUP.
KEEPING UP YOUR PSYCHIC SHIELD IS MORE IMPORTANT. DID YOU RECOGNIZE THEM?
THE BROTHERHOOD OF EVIL X-MEN FROM THE FUTURE.
I THOUGHT SOME OF THEM HAD...*EXPIRED* IN OUR LAST GET-TOGETHER.
WHEN I SEE PEOPLE TIME TRAVEL HERE TO CAUSE TROUBLE I UNDERSTAND HOW ANNOYING IT IS THAT THE ORIGINAL X-MEN ARE HERE.
JUST YOU ADMITTING IT MAKES ME FORGIVE YOU.
WHAT DO THEY WANT?
WHY ARE THEY HERE?!

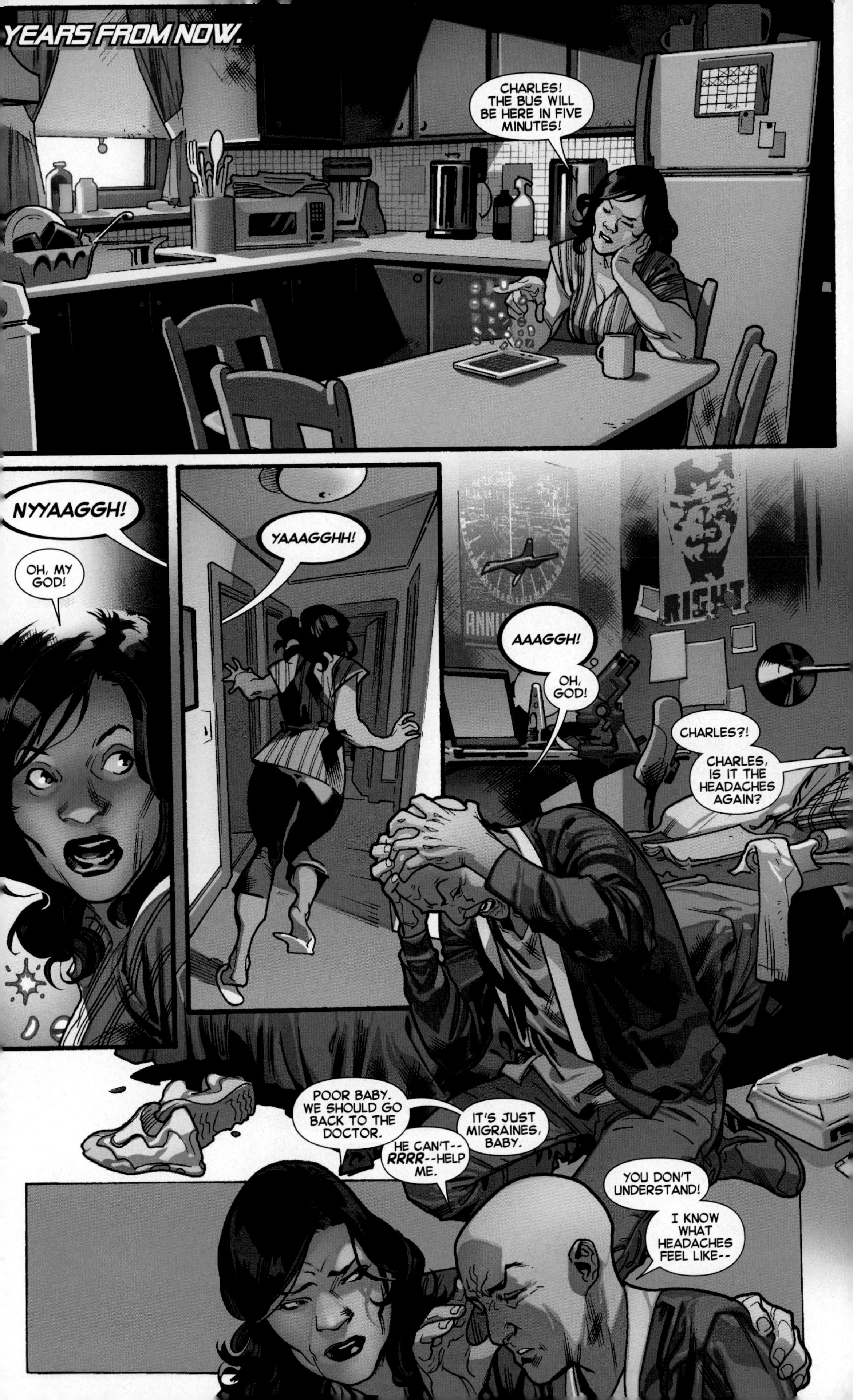
YEARS FROM NOW.
CHARLES! THE BUS WILL BE HERE IN FIVE MINUTES!
NYYAAGGH!
OH, MY GOD!
YAAAGGHH!
AAAGGH!
OH, GOD!
CHARLES?!
CHARLES, IS IT THE HEADACHES AGAIN?
RIGHT
POOR BABY. WE SHOULD GO BACK TO THE DOCTOR.
IT'S JUST MIGRAINES, BABY.
HE CAN'T-- RRRR--HELP ME.
YOU DON'T UNDERSTAND!
I KNOW WHAT HEADACHES FEEL LIKE--

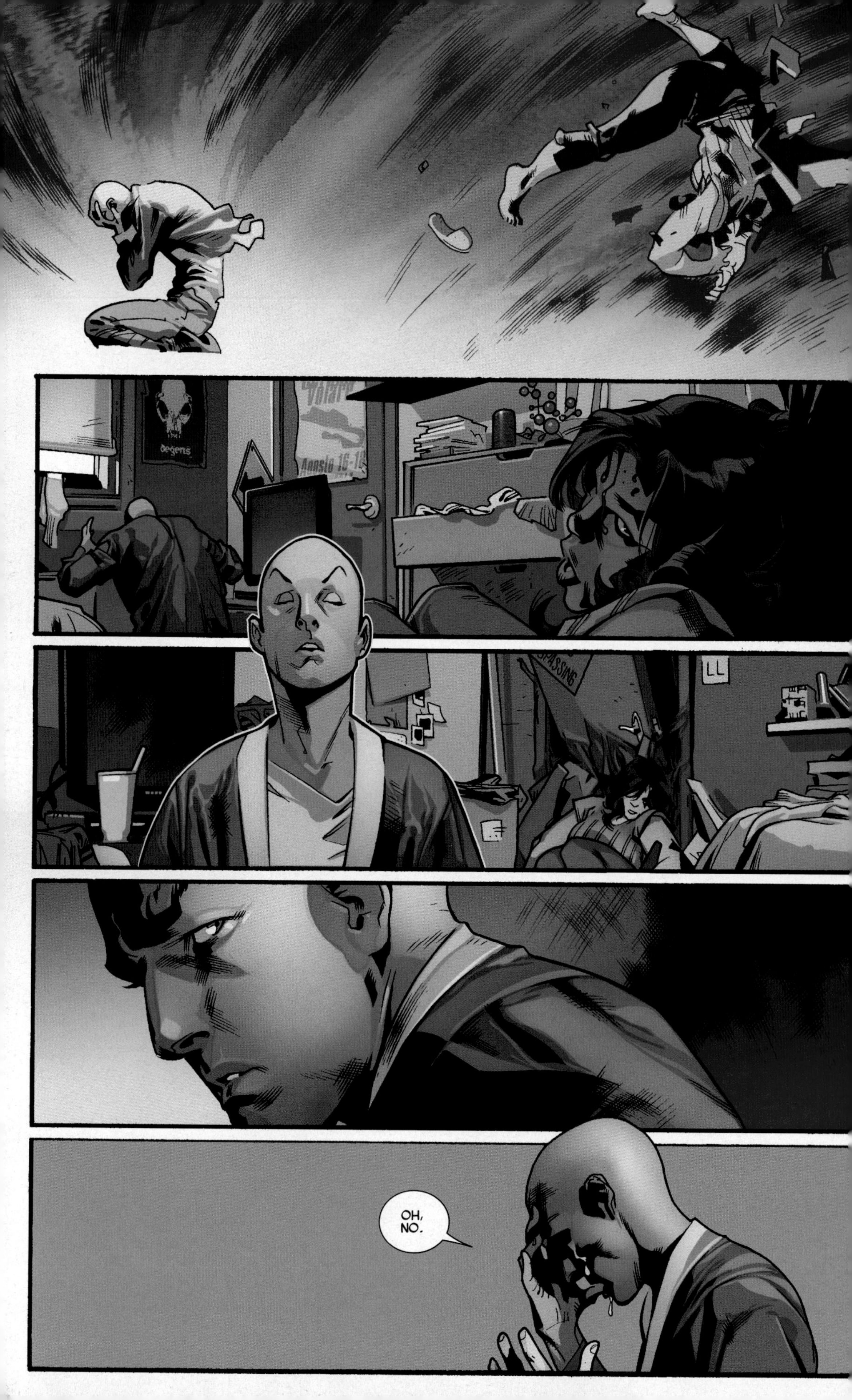
degens
OH, NO.

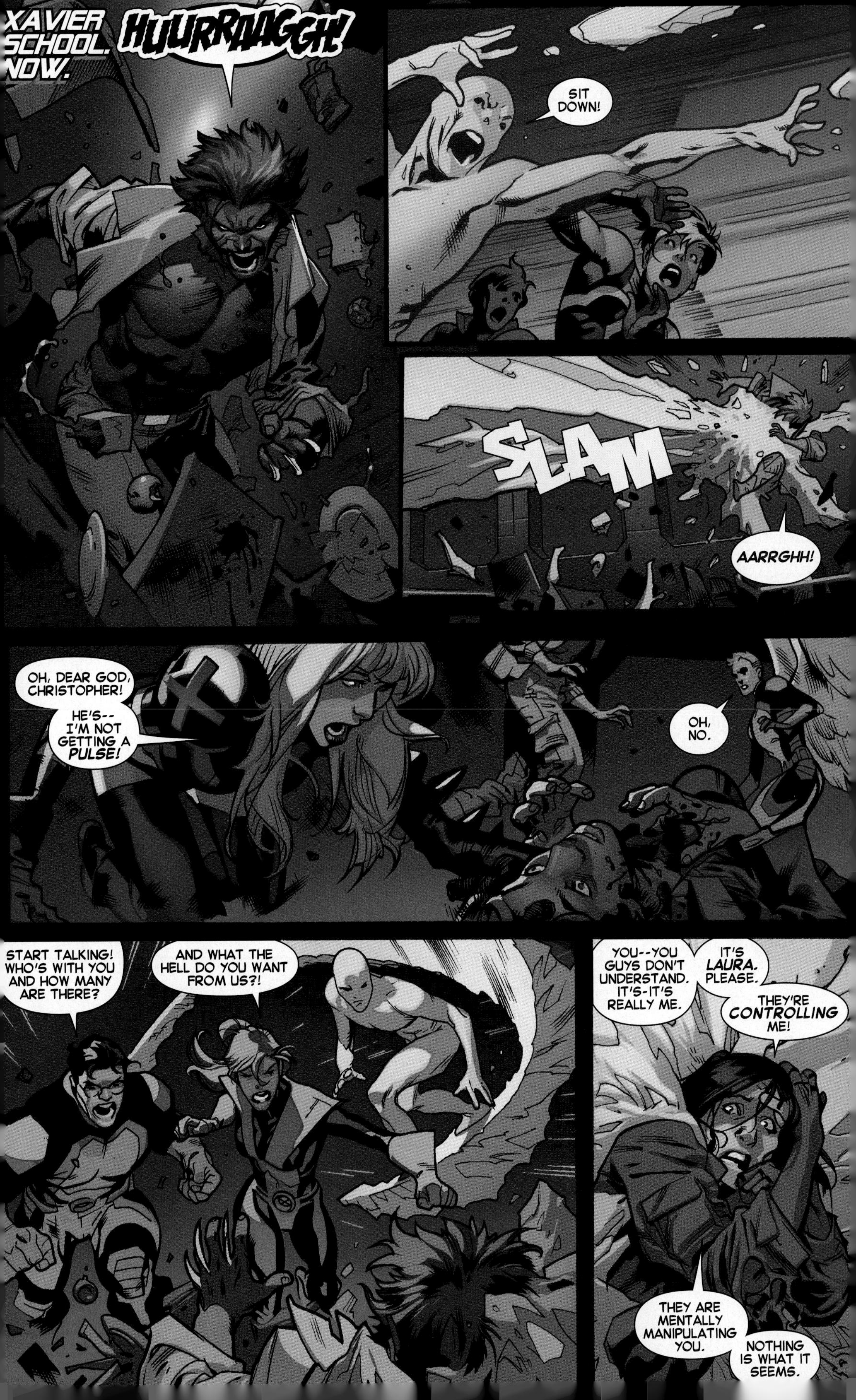
XAVIER SCHOOL. NOW.
HUURRAAGGH!
SIT DOWN!
SLAM
AARRGHH!
OH, DEAR GOD, CHRISTOPHER!
HE'S-- I'M NOT GETTING A PULSE!
OH, NO.
START TALKING! WHO'S WITH YOU AND HOW MANY ARE THERE?
AND WHAT THE HELL DO YOU WANT FROM US?!
YOU--YOU GUYS DON'T UNDERSTAND. IT'S-IT'S REALLY ME.
IT'S LAURA. PLEASE.
THEY'RE CONTROLLING ME!
THEY ARE MENTALLY MANIPULATING YOU.
NOTHING IS WHAT IT SEEMS.

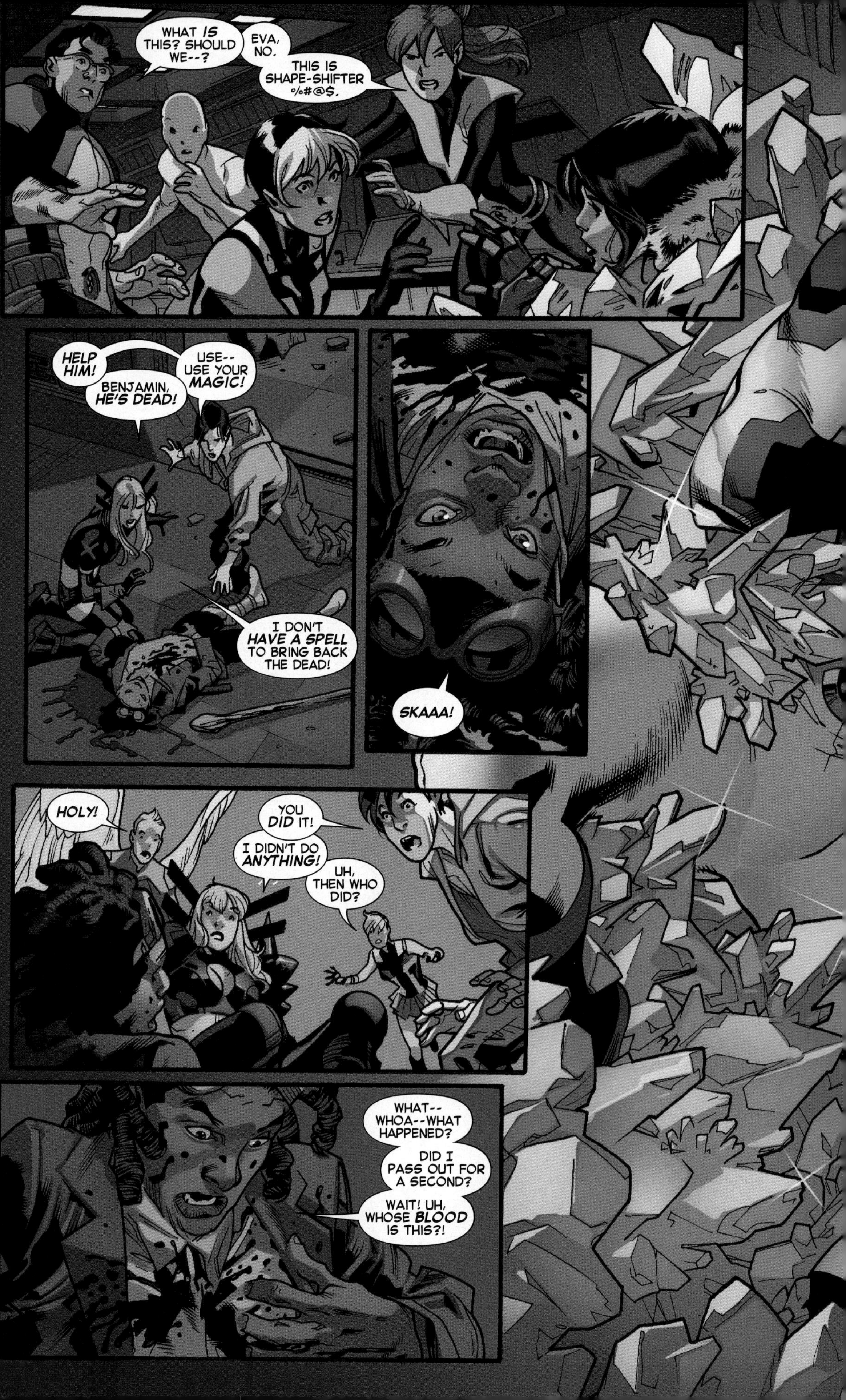
WHAT IS THIS? SHOULD WE--?
EVA, NO.
THIS IS SHAPE-SHIFTER %#@$.
HELP HIM!
USE--USE YOUR MAGIC!
BENJAMIN, HE'S DEAD!
I DON'T HAVE A SPELL TO BRING BACK THE DEAD!
SKAAA!
HOLY!
YOU DID IT!
I DIDN'T DO ANYTHING!
UH, THEN WHO DID?
WHAT--WHOA--WHAT HAPPENED?
DID I PASS OUT FOR A SECOND?
WAIT! UH, WHOSE BLOOD IS THIS?!

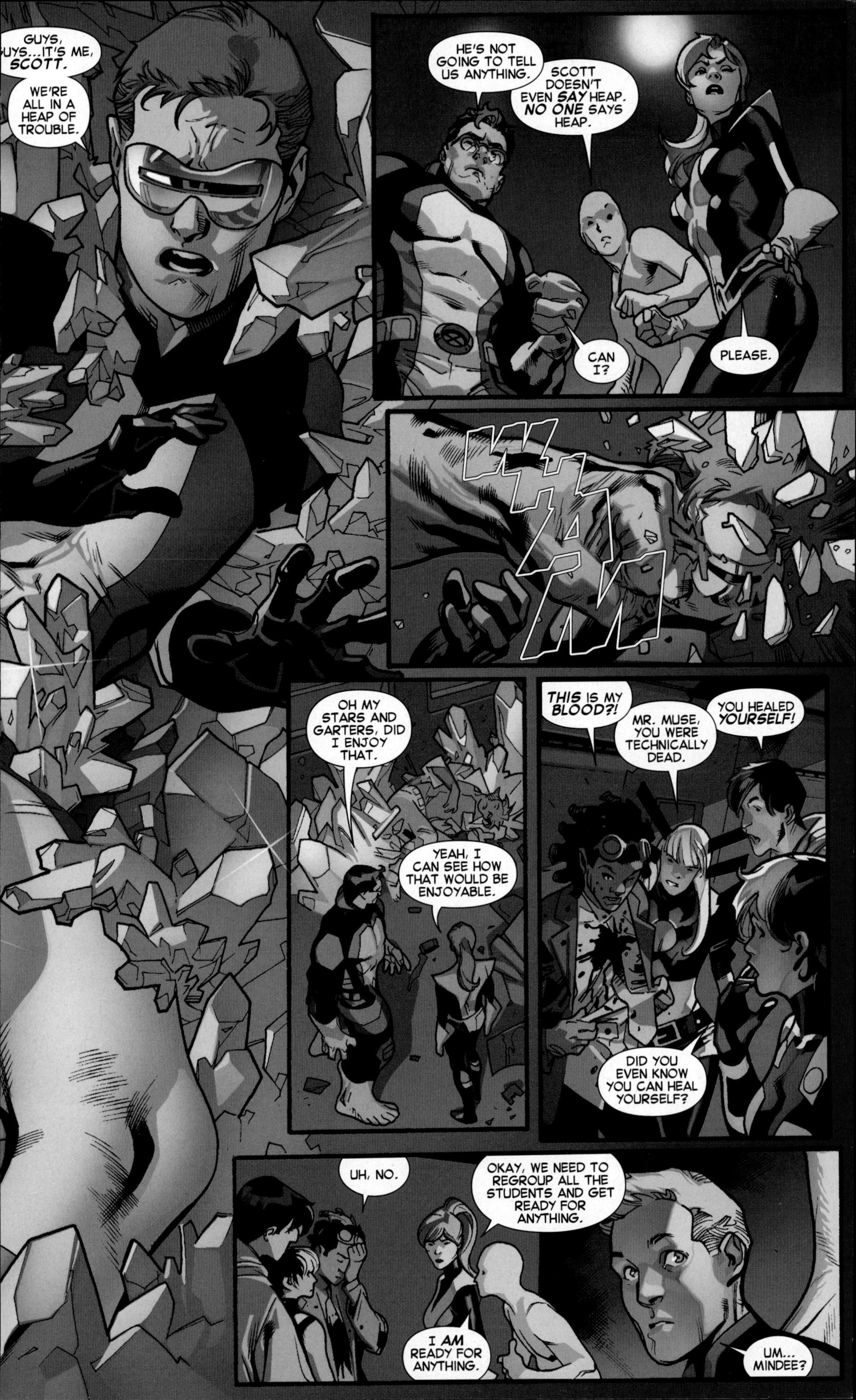
GUYS, GUYS...IT'S ME, SCOTT.
WE'RE ALL IN A HEAP OF TROUBLE.
HE'S NOT GOING TO TELL US ANYTHING.
SCOTT DOESN'T EVEN SAY HEAP. NO ONE SAYS HEAP.
CAN I?
PLEASE.
WHAM
OH MY STARS AND GARTERS, DID I ENJOY THAT.
YEAH, I CAN SEE HOW THAT WOULD BE ENJOYABLE.
THIS is my BLOOD?!
MR. MUSE, YOU WERE TECHNICALLY DEAD.
YOU HEALED YOURSELF!
DID YOU EVEN KNOW YOU CAN HEAL YOURSELF?
UH, NO.
OKAY, WE NEED TO REGROUP ALL THE STUDENTS AND GET READY FOR ANYTHING.
I AM READY FOR ANYTHING.
UM... MINDEE?

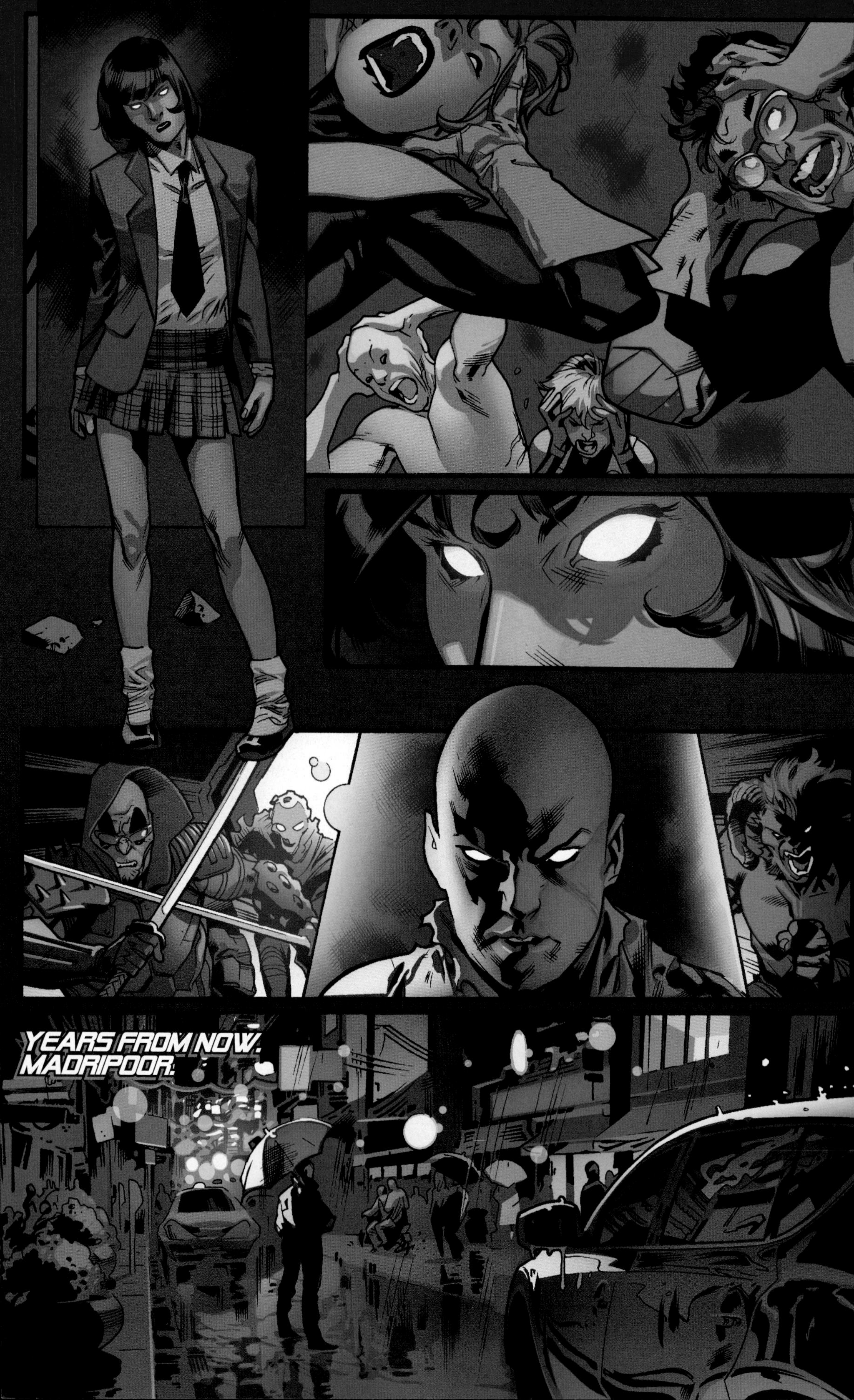
YEARS FROM NOW.
MADRIPOOR.

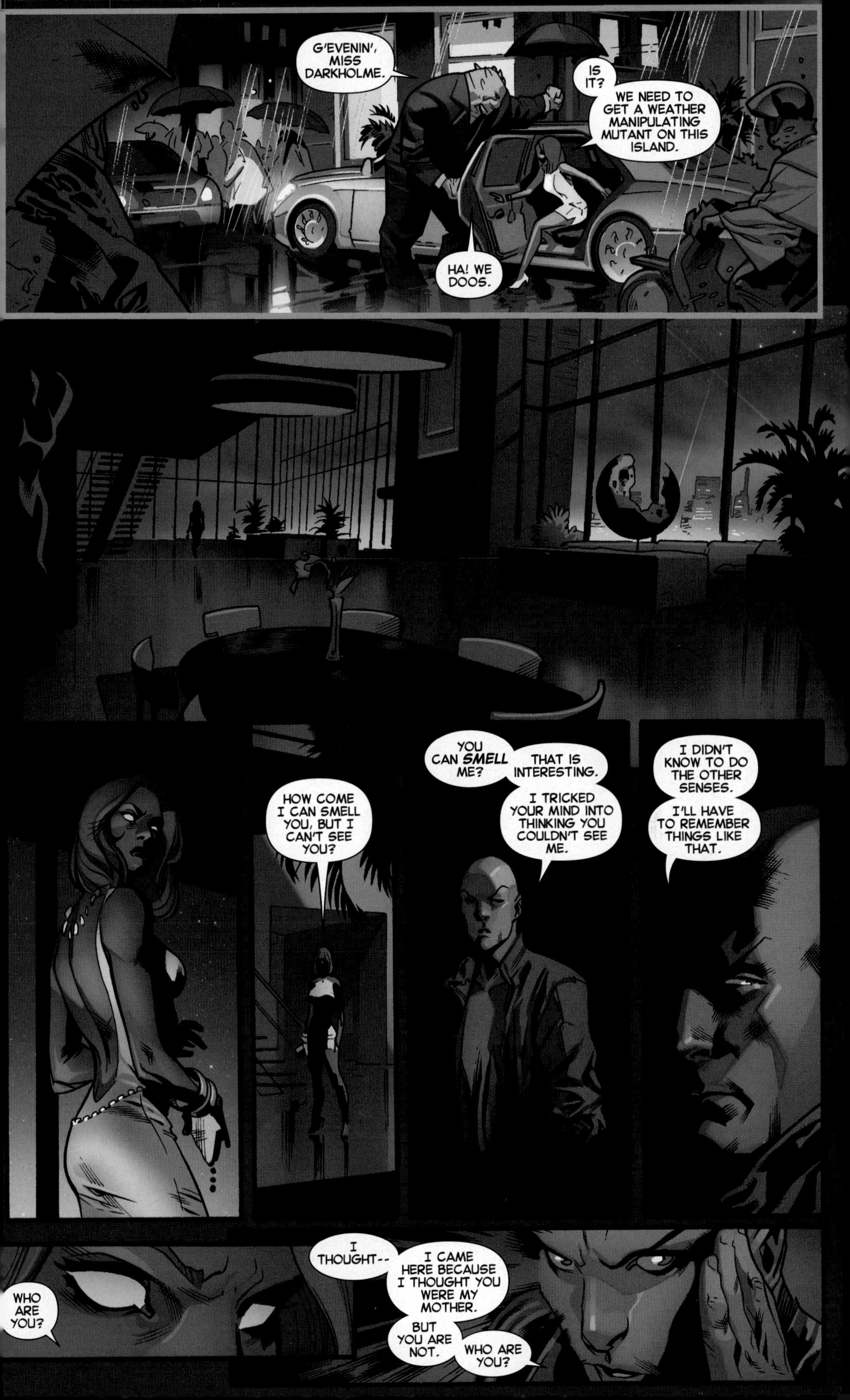
G'EVENIN', MISS DARKHOLME.
IS IT?
WE NEED TO GET A WEATHER MANIPULATING MUTANT ON THIS ISLAND.
HA! WE DOOS.
HOW COME I CAN SMELL YOU, BUT I CAN'T SEE YOU?
YOU CAN *SMELL* ME?
THAT IS INTERESTING.
I TRICKED YOUR MIND INTO THINKING YOU COULDN'T SEE ME.
I DIDN'T KNOW TO DO THE OTHER SENSES.
I'LL HAVE TO REMEMBER THINGS LIKE THAT.
WHO ARE YOU?
I THOUGHT--
I CAME HERE BECAUSE I THOUGHT YOU WERE MY MOTHER.
BUT YOU ARE NOT.
WHO ARE YOU?

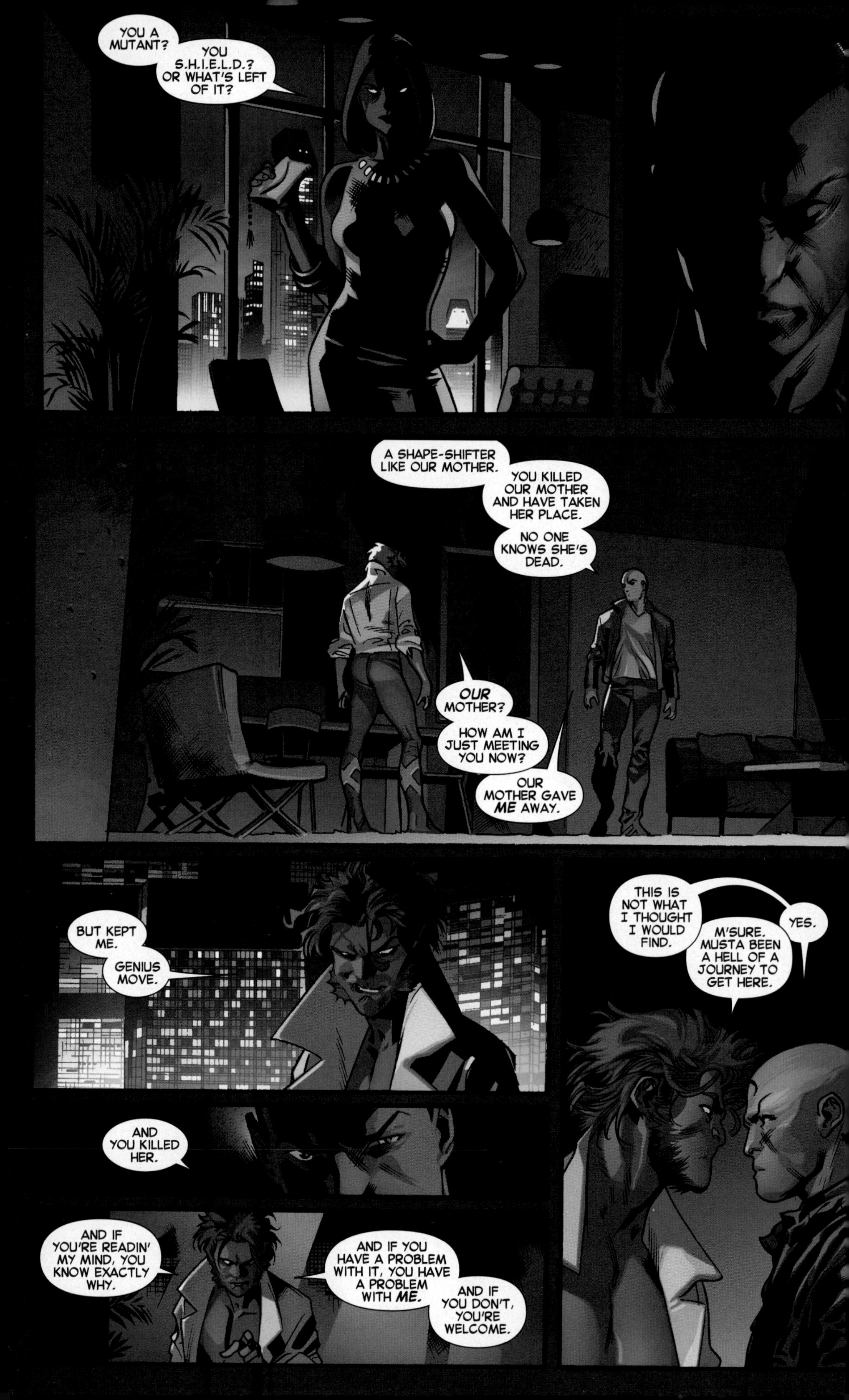

YOU A MUTANT?
YOU S.H.I.E.L.D.? OR WHAT'S LEFT OF IT?
A SHAPE-SHIFTER LIKE OUR MOTHER.
YOU KILLED OUR MOTHER AND HAVE TAKEN HER PLACE.
NO ONE KNOWS SHE'S DEAD.
OUR MOTHER?
HOW AM I JUST MEETING YOU NOW?
OUR MOTHER GAVE ME AWAY.
BUT KEPT ME.
GENIUS MOVE.
AND YOU KILLED HER.
AND IF YOU'RE READIN' MY MIND, YOU KNOW EXACTLY WHY.
AND IF YOU HAVE A PROBLEM WITH IT, YOU HAVE A PROBLEM WITH ME.
AND IF YOU DON'T, YOU'RE WELCOME.
THIS IS NOT WHAT I THOUGHT I WOULD FIND.
YES.
M'SURE. MUSTA BEEN A HELL OF A JOURNEY TO GET HERE.

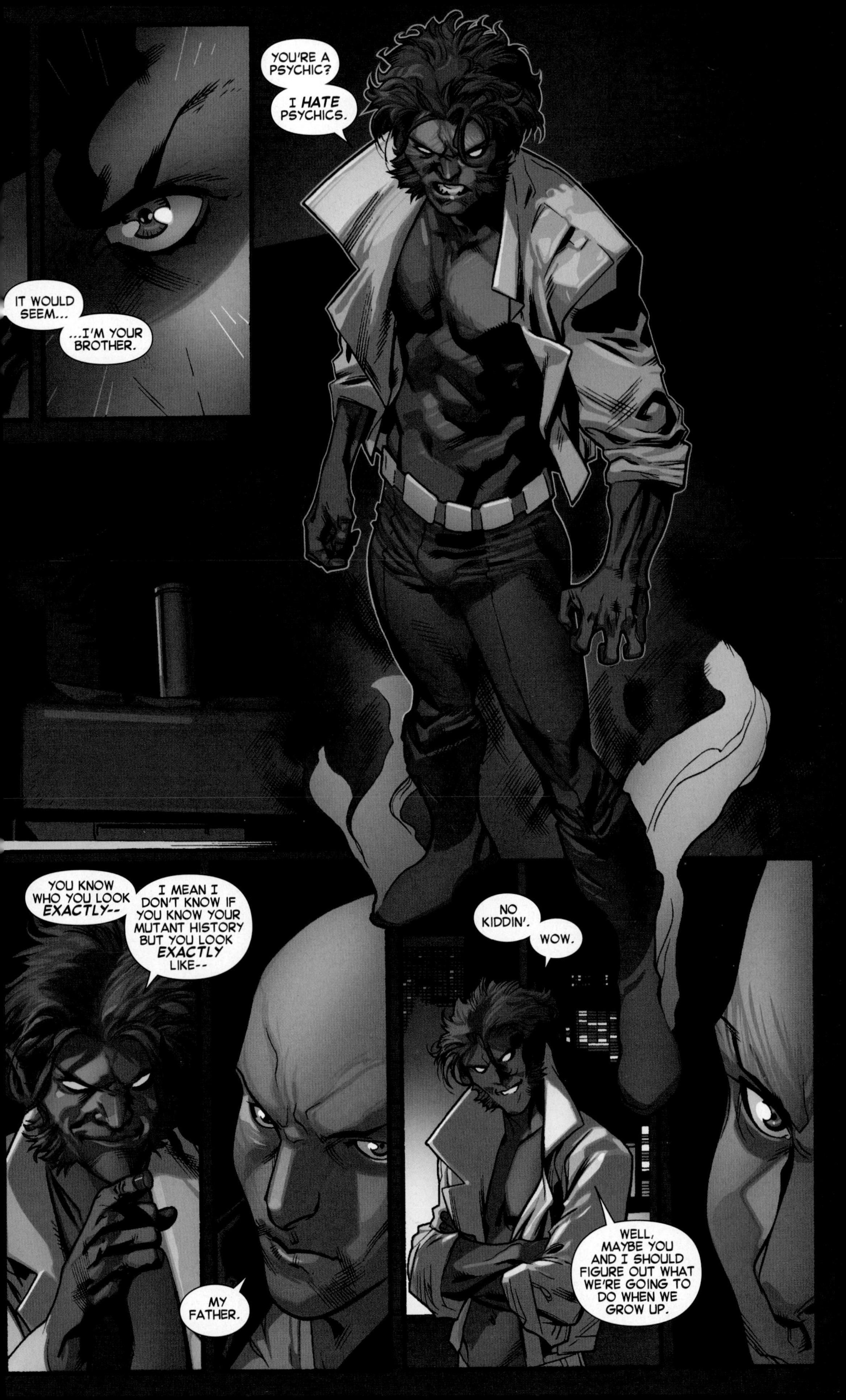

YOU'RE A PSYCHIC?
I HATE PSYCHICS.
IT WOULD SEEM...
...I'M YOUR BROTHER.
YOU KNOW WHO YOU LOOK EXACTLY--
I MEAN I DON'T KNOW IF YOU KNOW YOUR MUTANT HISTORY BUT YOU LOOK EXACTLY LIKE--
MY FATHER.
NO KIDDIN'.
WOW.
WELL, MAYBE YOU AND I SHOULD FIGURE OUT WHAT WE'RE GOING TO DO WHEN WE GROW UP.

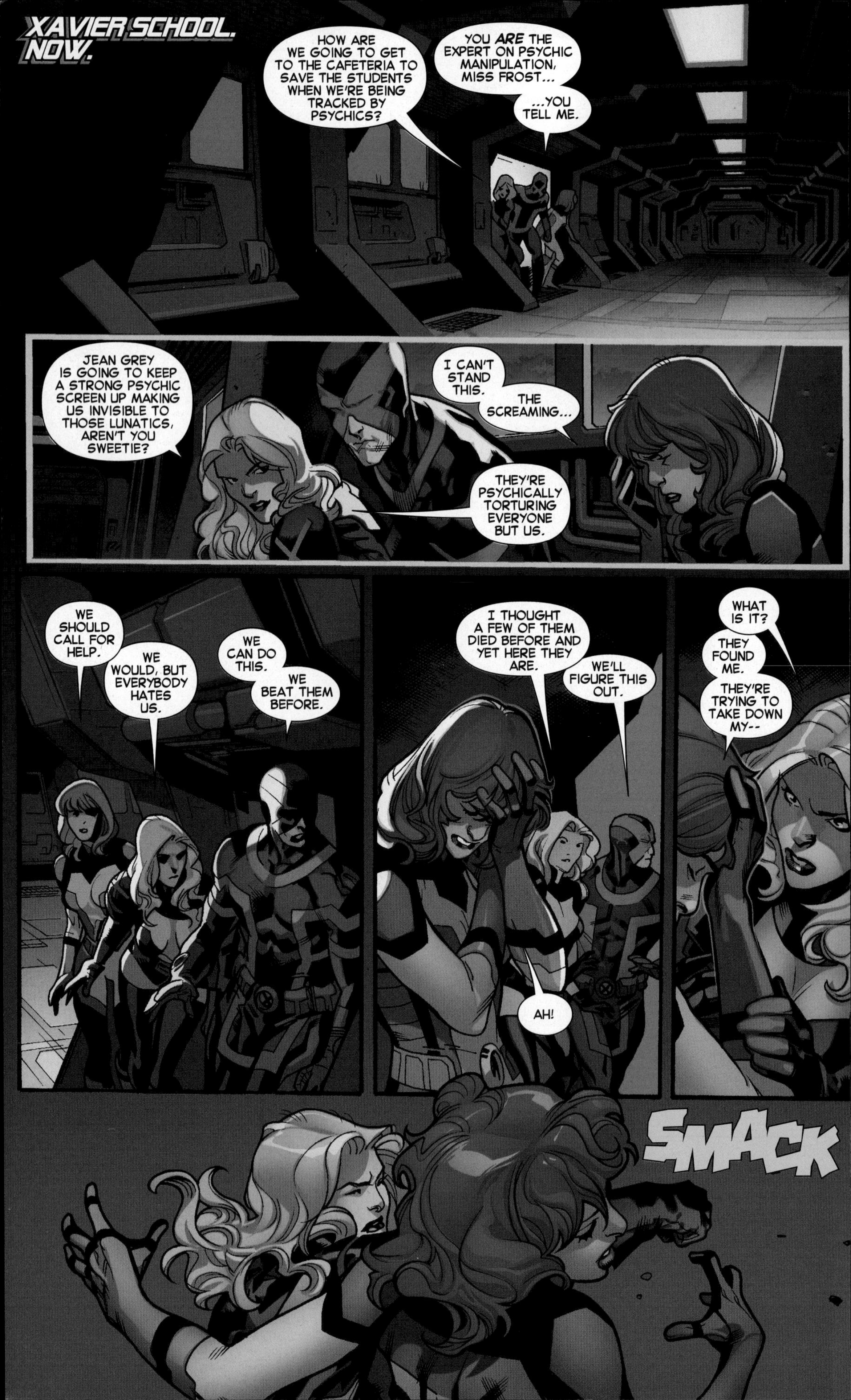
XAVIER SCHOOL. NOW.
HOW ARE WE GOING TO GET TO THE CAFETERIA TO SAVE THE STUDENTS WHEN WE'RE BEING TRACKED BY PSYCHICS?
YOU ARE THE EXPERT ON PSYCHIC MANIPULATION, MISS FROST...
...YOU TELL ME.
JEAN GREY IS GOING TO KEEP A STRONG PSYCHIC SCREEN UP MAKING US INVISIBLE TO THOSE LUNATICS, AREN'T YOU SWEETIE?
I CAN'T STAND THIS.
THE SCREAMING...
THEY'RE PSYCHICALLY TORTURING EVERYONE BUT US.
WE SHOULD CALL FOR HELP.
WE WOULD, BUT EVERYBODY HATES US.
WE CAN DO THIS.
WE BEAT THEM BEFORE.
I THOUGHT A FEW OF THEM DIED BEFORE AND YET HERE THEY ARE.
WE'LL FIGURE THIS OUT.
AH!
WHAT IS IT?
THEY FOUND ME.
THEY'RE TRYING TO TAKE DOWN MY--
SMACK

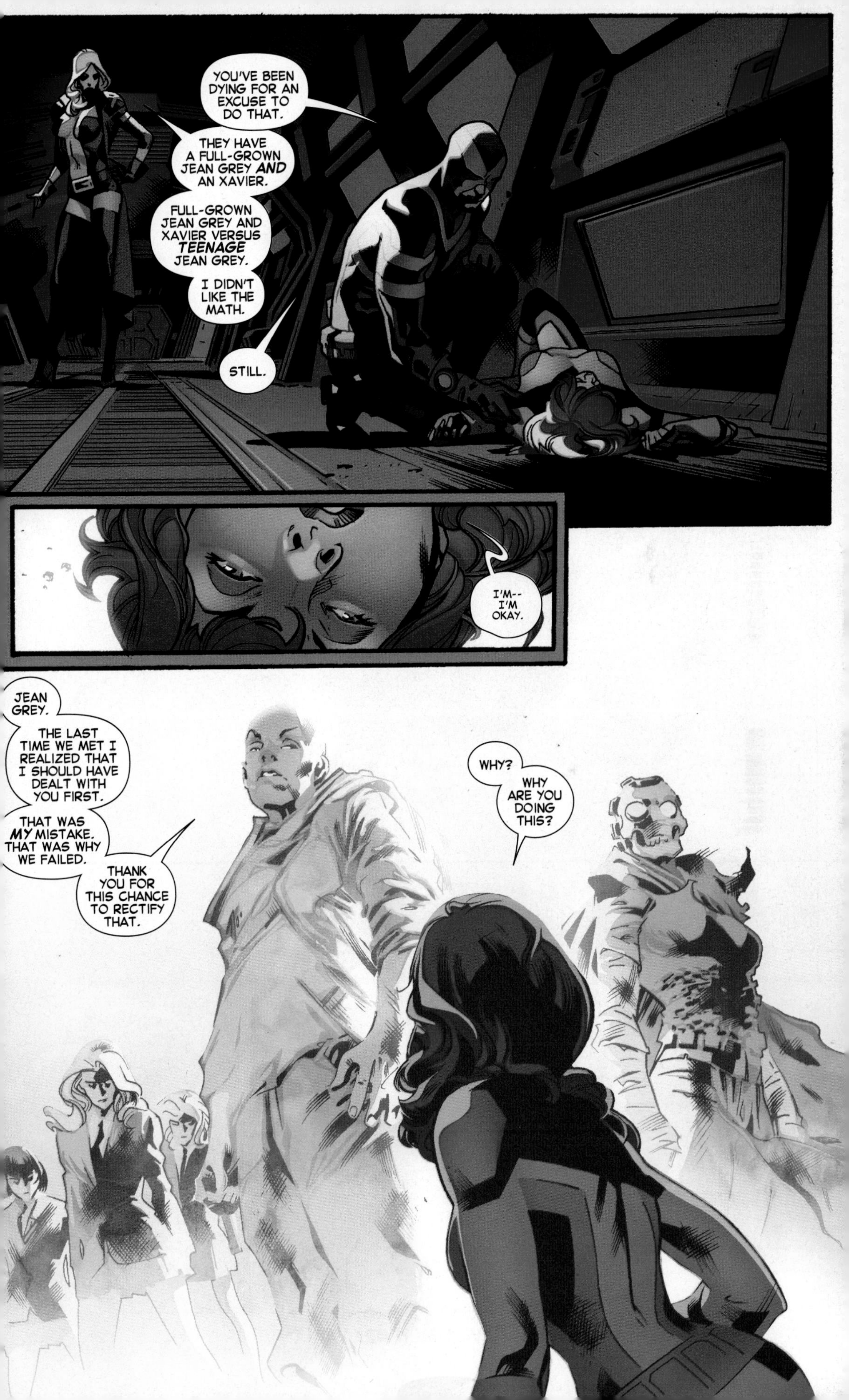
YOU'VE BEEN DYING FOR AN EXCUSE TO DO THAT.
THEY HAVE A FULL-GROWN JEAN GREY AND AN XAVIER.
FULL-GROWN JEAN GREY AND XAVIER VERSUS TEENAGE JEAN GREY.
I DIDN'T LIKE THE MATH.
STILL.
I'M-- I'M OKAY.
JEAN GREY.
THE LAST TIME WE MET I REALIZED THAT I SHOULD HAVE DEALT WITH YOU FIRST.
THAT WAS MY MISTAKE. THAT WAS WHY WE FAILED.
THANK YOU FOR THIS CHANCE TO RECTIFY THAT.
WHY?
WHY ARE YOU DOING THIS?

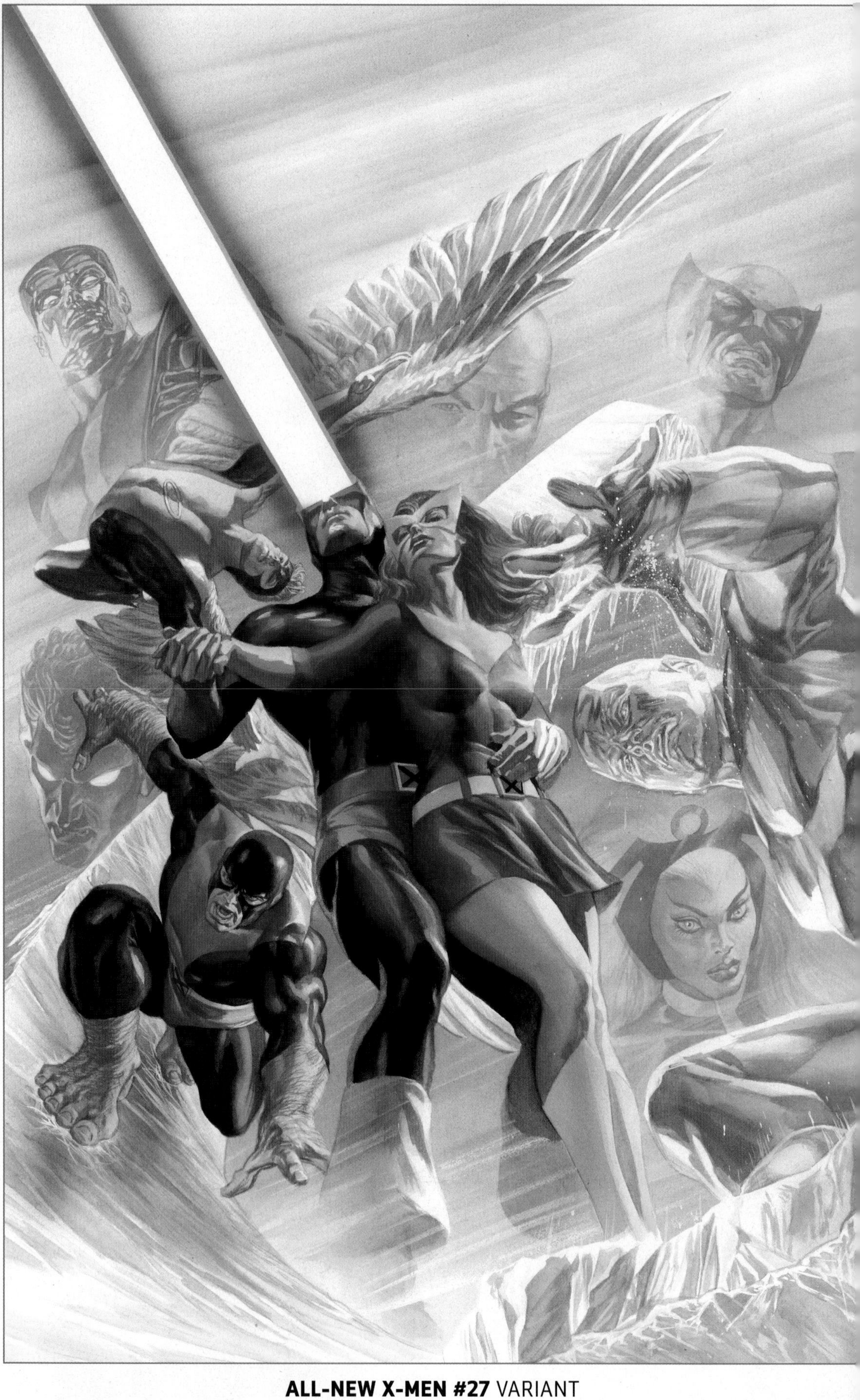

ALL-NEW X-MEN #27 VARIANT
BY ALEX ROSS

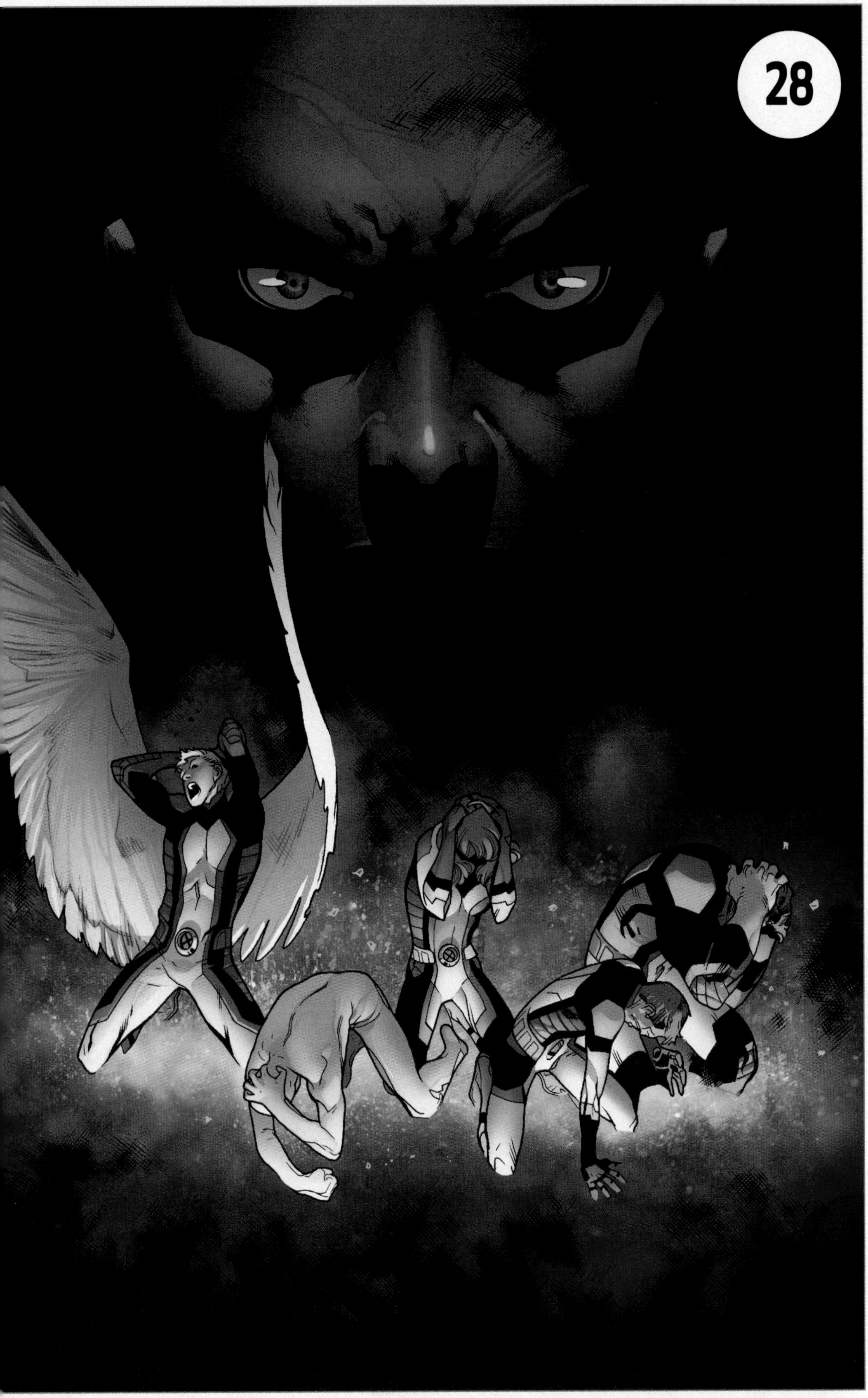
28

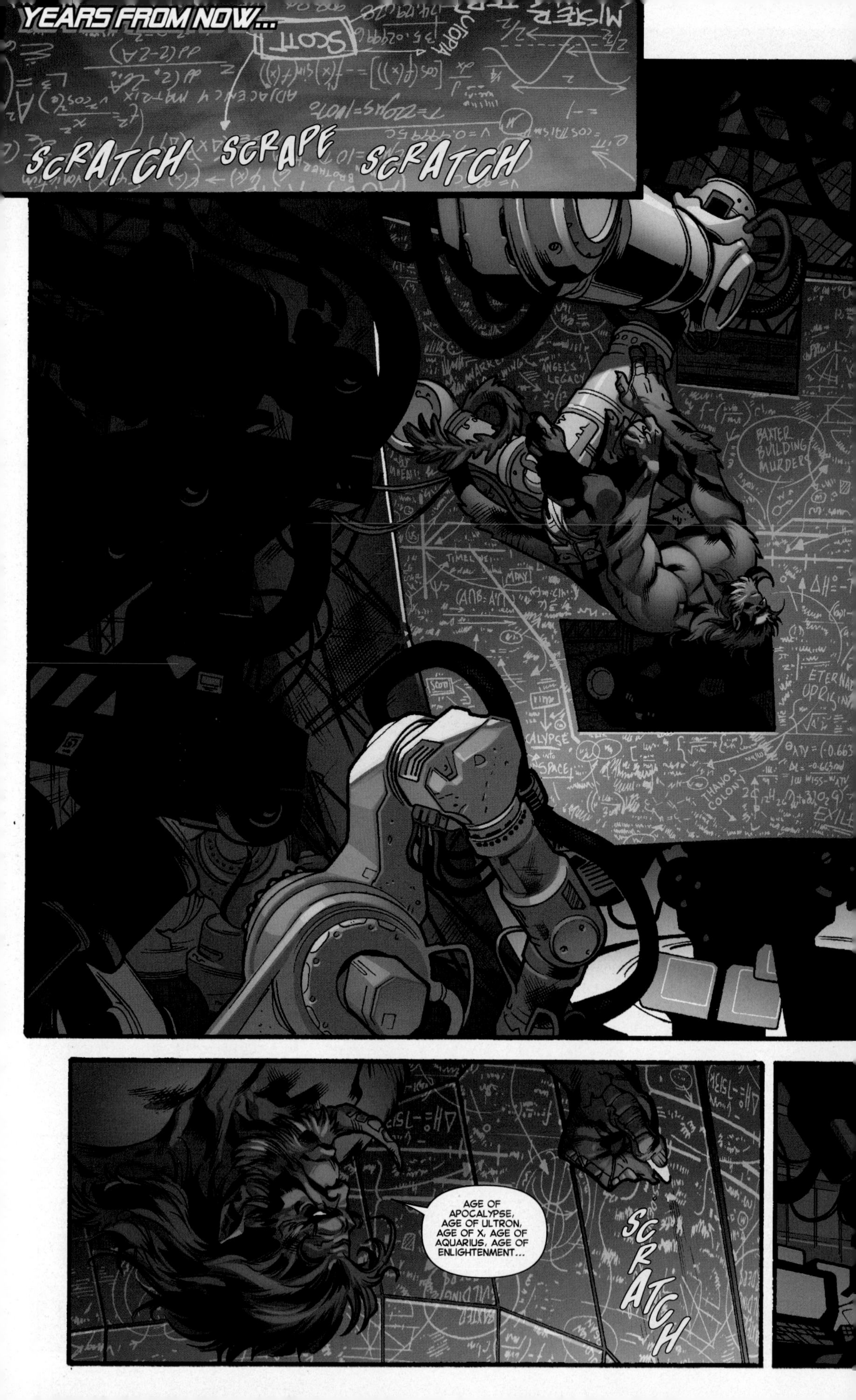
YEARS FROM NOW...
SCRATCH SCRAPE SCRATCH
AGE OF APOCALYPSE, AGE OF ULTRON, AGE OF X, AGE OF AQUARIUS, AGE OF ENLIGHTENMENT...
SCRATCH

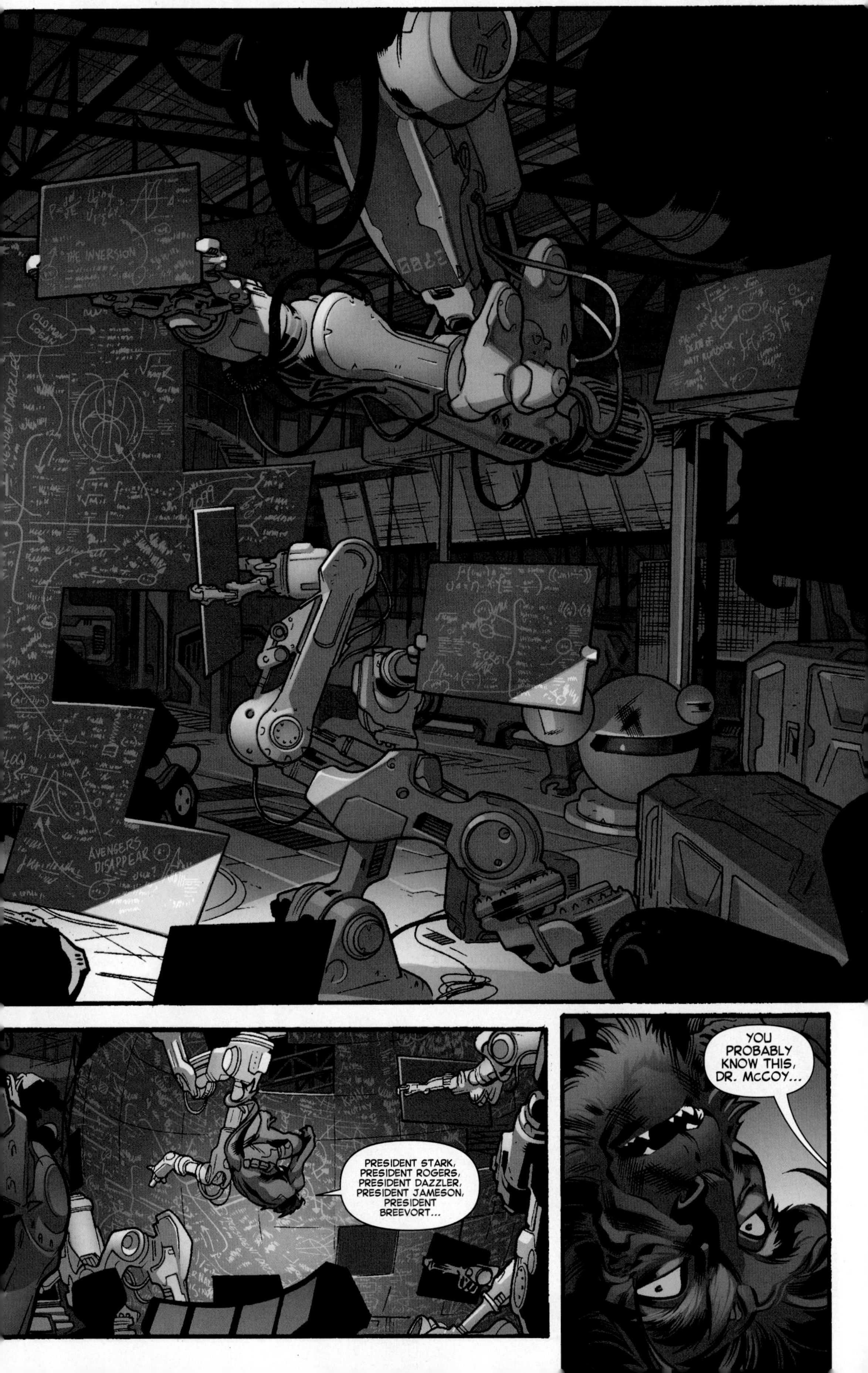
THE INVERSION
OLD MAN LOGAN
SECRET WAR
AVENGERS DISAPPEAR
PRESIDENT STARK, PRESIDENT ROGERS, PRESIDENT DAZZLER, PRESIDENT JAMESON, PRESIDENT BREEVORT...
YOU PROBABLY KNOW THIS, DR. McCOY...

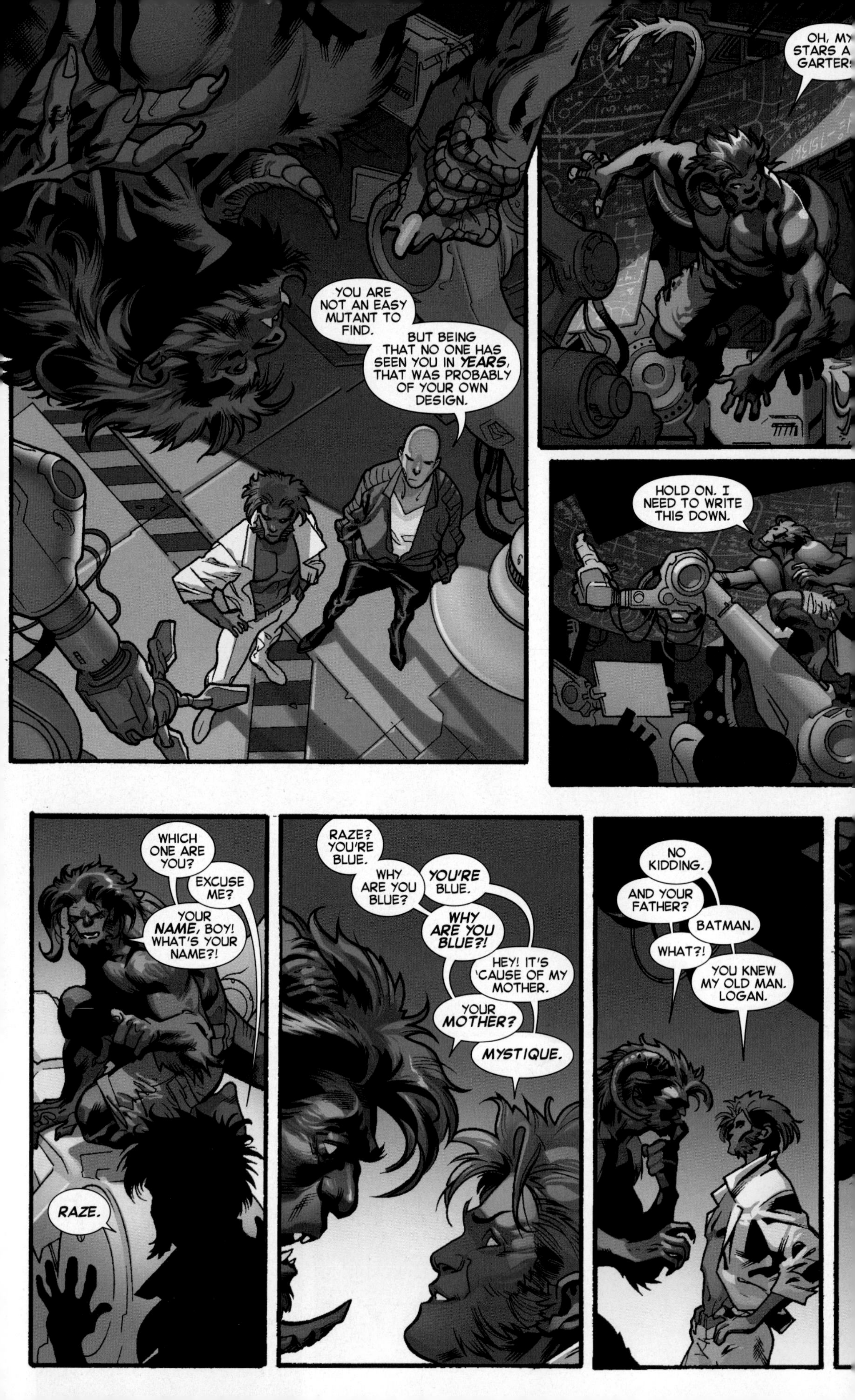
YOU ARE NOT AN EASY MUTANT TO FIND.
BUT BEING THAT NO ONE HAS SEEN YOU IN YEARS, THAT WAS PROBABLY OF YOUR OWN DESIGN.
OH, MY STARS A GARTER
HOLD ON. I NEED TO WRITE THIS DOWN.
WHICH ONE ARE YOU?
EXCUSE ME?
YOUR NAME, BOY! WHAT'S YOUR NAME?!
RAZE.
RAZE? YOU'RE BLUE.
WHY ARE YOU BLUE?
YOU'RE BLUE.
WHY ARE YOU BLUE?!
HEY! IT'S 'CAUSE OF MY MOTHER.
YOUR MOTHER?
MYSTIQUE.
NO KIDDING.
AND YOUR FATHER?
BATMAN.
WHAT?!
YOU KNEW MY OLD MAN. LOGAN.

HEY, HE REALLY DOES SAY THAT.

XAVIER.

JUST LIKE THAT OLD DRAKE GUY SAID.

YOU-- YOU ARE ALIVE.

YOU MIGHT BE THINKING OF MY FATHER.

OR MY FATHER'S FATHER...

YOU'RE-- YOU'RE HIS SON.

HOW OLD ARE YOU, BOY?!

EIGHTEEN. EIGHTEEN YEARS OLD.

WHAT IS ALL THIS?

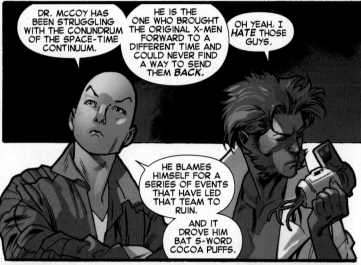

DR. MCCOY HAS BEEN STRUGGLING WITH THE CONUNDRUM OF THE SPACE-TIME CONTINUUM.

HE IS THE ONE WHO BROUGHT THE ORIGINAL X-MEN FORWARD TO A DIFFERENT TIME AND COULD NEVER FIND A WAY TO SEND THEM BACK.

OH YEAH, I HATE THOSE GUYS.

HE BLAMES HIMSELF FOR A SERIES OF EVENTS THAT HAVE LED THAT TEAM TO RUIN.

AND IT DROVE HIM BAT S-WORD COCOA PUFFS.

THE WOLVERINE.

YEAH.

I NEED TO WRITE THAT DOWN.

HIS MIND IS A MESS.

NO KIDDING.

NO.

SO HE'S USELESS.

QUITE THE CONTRARY...

...HE JUST NEEDS A LITTLE HELP PUTTING EVERYTHING BACK WHERE IT BELONGS.

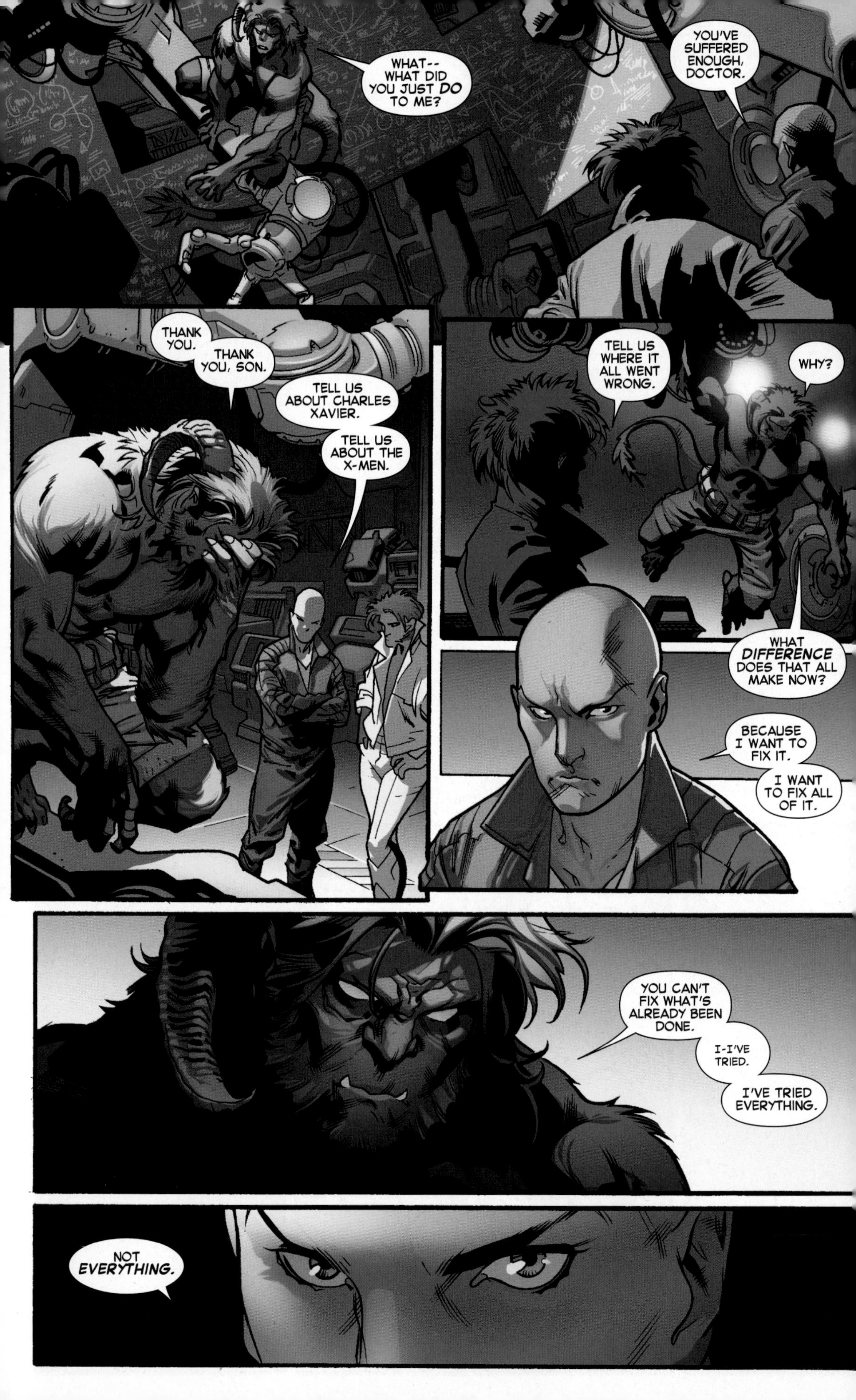
WHAT-- WHAT DID YOU JUST DO TO ME?
YOU'VE SUFFERED ENOUGH, DOCTOR.
THANK YOU.
THANK YOU, SON.
TELL US ABOUT CHARLES XAVIER.
TELL US ABOUT THE X-MEN.
TELL US WHERE IT ALL WENT WRONG.
WHY?
WHAT DIFFERENCE DOES THAT ALL MAKE NOW?
BECAUSE I WANT TO FIX IT.
I WANT TO FIX ALL OF IT.
YOU CAN'T FIX WHAT'S ALREADY BEEN DONE.
I-I'VE TRIED.
I'VE TRIED EVERYTHING.
NOT EVERYTHING.

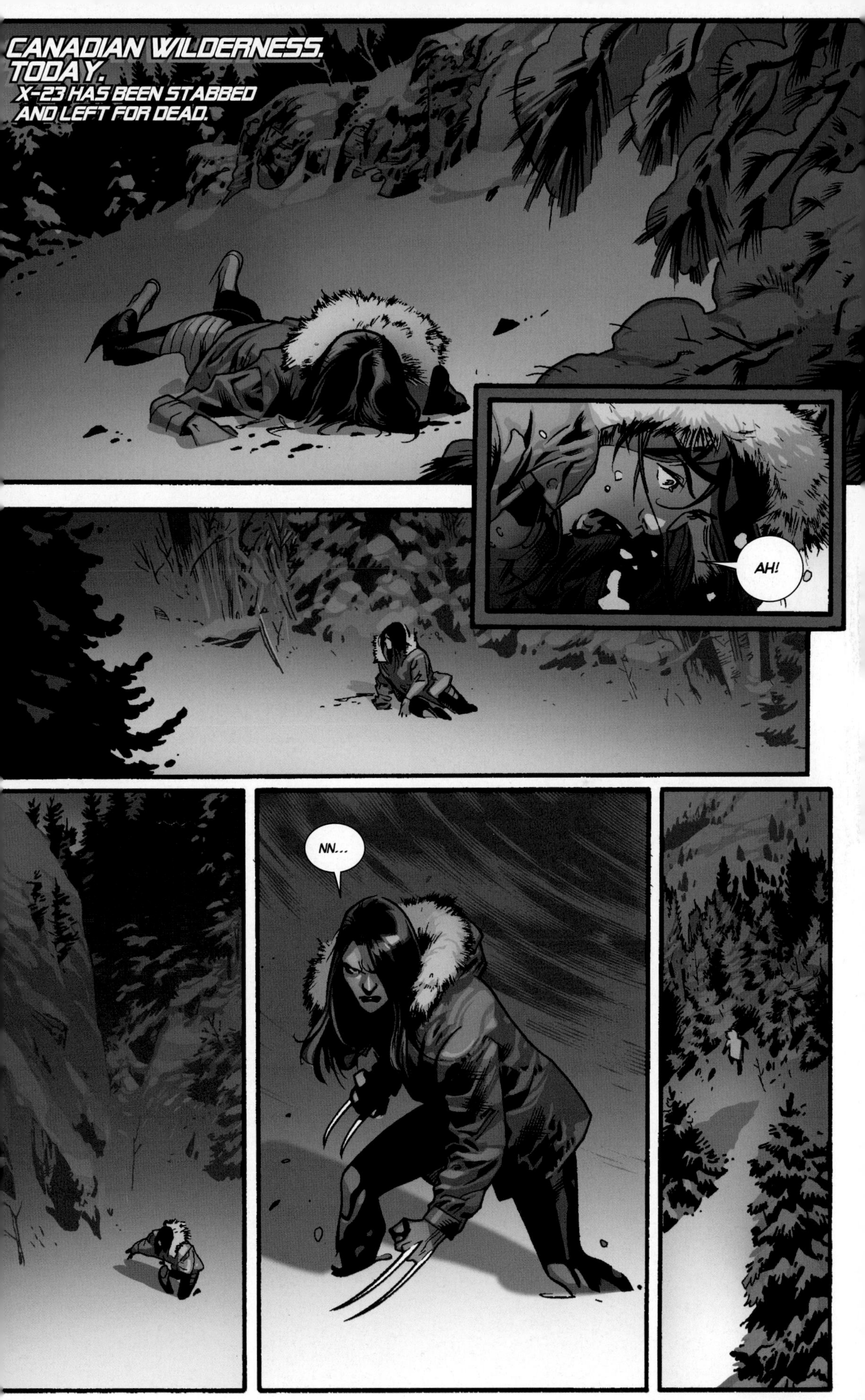
CANADIAN WILDERNESS. TODAY.
X-23 HAS BEEN STABBED AND LEFT FOR DEAD.
AH!
NN...

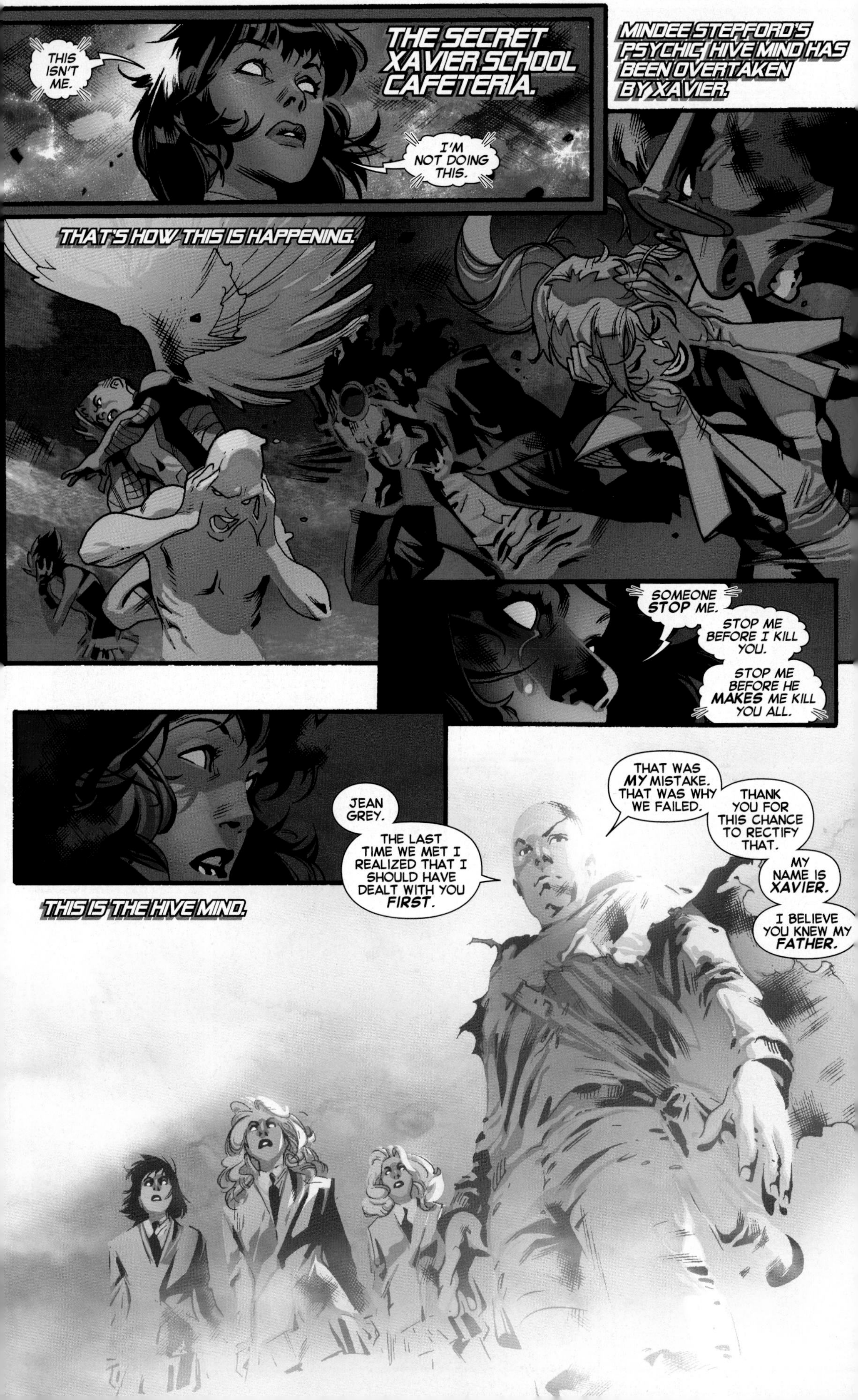
THE SECRET XAVIER SCHOOL CAFETERIA.
THIS ISN'T ME.
I'M NOT DOING THIS.
MINDEE STEPFORD'S PSYCHIC HIVE MIND HAS BEEN OVERTAKEN BY XAVIER.
THAT'S HOW THIS IS HAPPENING.
SOMEONE STOP ME.
STOP ME BEFORE I KILL YOU.
STOP ME BEFORE HE MAKES ME KILL YOU ALL.
THIS IS THE HIVE MIND.
JEAN GREY.
THE LAST TIME WE MET I REALIZED THAT I SHOULD HAVE DEALT WITH YOU FIRST.
THAT WAS MY MISTAKE. THAT WAS WHY WE FAILED.
THANK YOU FOR THIS CHANCE TO RECTIFY THAT.
MY NAME IS XAVIER.
I BELIEVE YOU KNEW MY FATHER.

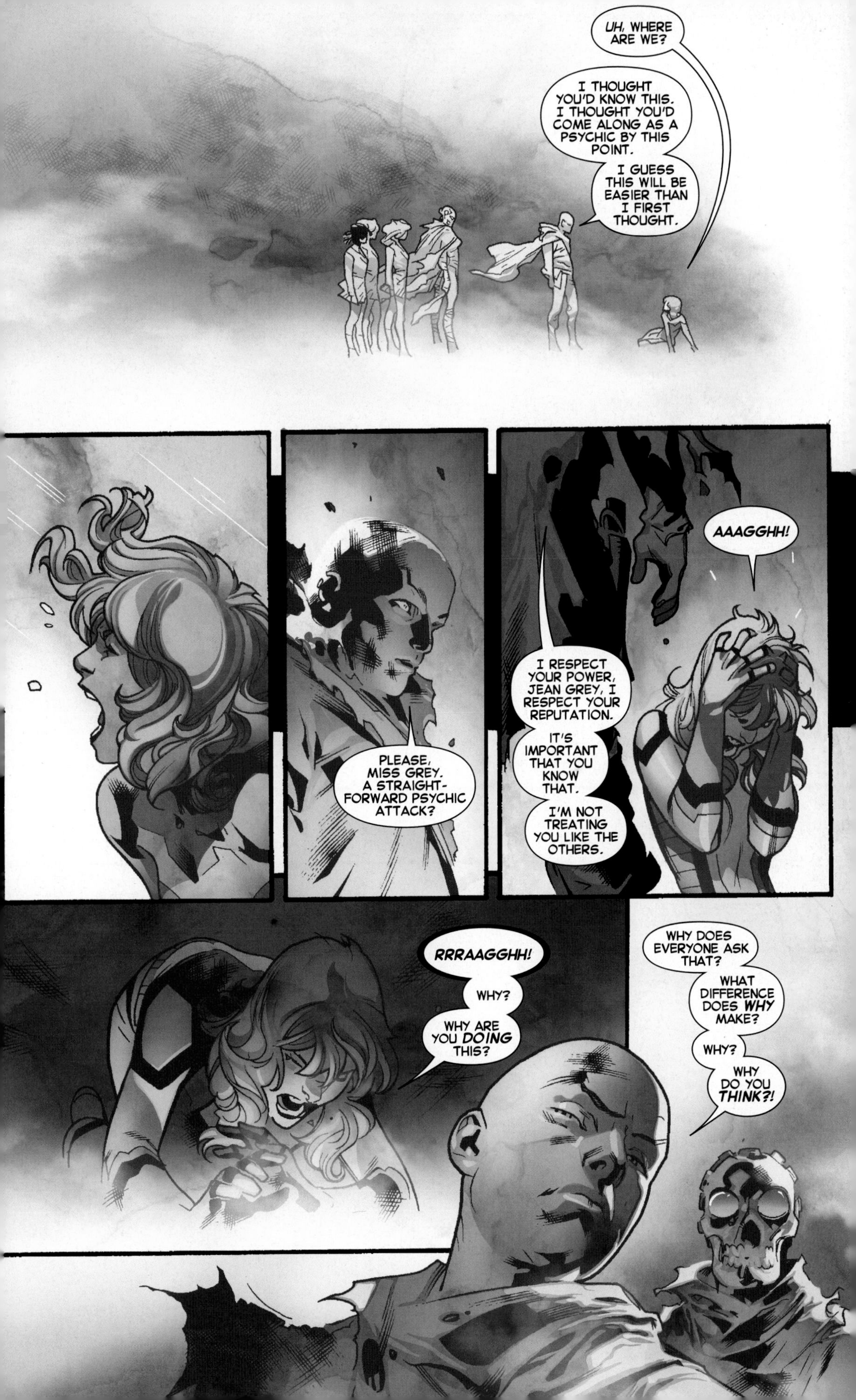
UH, WHERE ARE WE?
I THOUGHT YOU'D KNOW THIS. I THOUGHT YOU'D COME ALONG AS A PSYCHIC BY THIS POINT.
I GUESS THIS WILL BE EASIER THAN I FIRST THOUGHT.
PLEASE, MISS GREY. A STRAIGHT-FORWARD PSYCHIC ATTACK?
AAAGGHH!
I RESPECT YOUR POWER, JEAN GREY, I RESPECT YOUR REPUTATION.
IT'S IMPORTANT THAT YOU KNOW THAT.
I'M NOT TREATING YOU LIKE THE OTHERS.
RRRAAGGHH!
WHY?
WHY ARE YOU DOING THIS?
WHY DOES EVERYONE ASK THAT?
WHAT DIFFERENCE DOES WHY MAKE?
WHY?
WHY DO YOU THINK?!

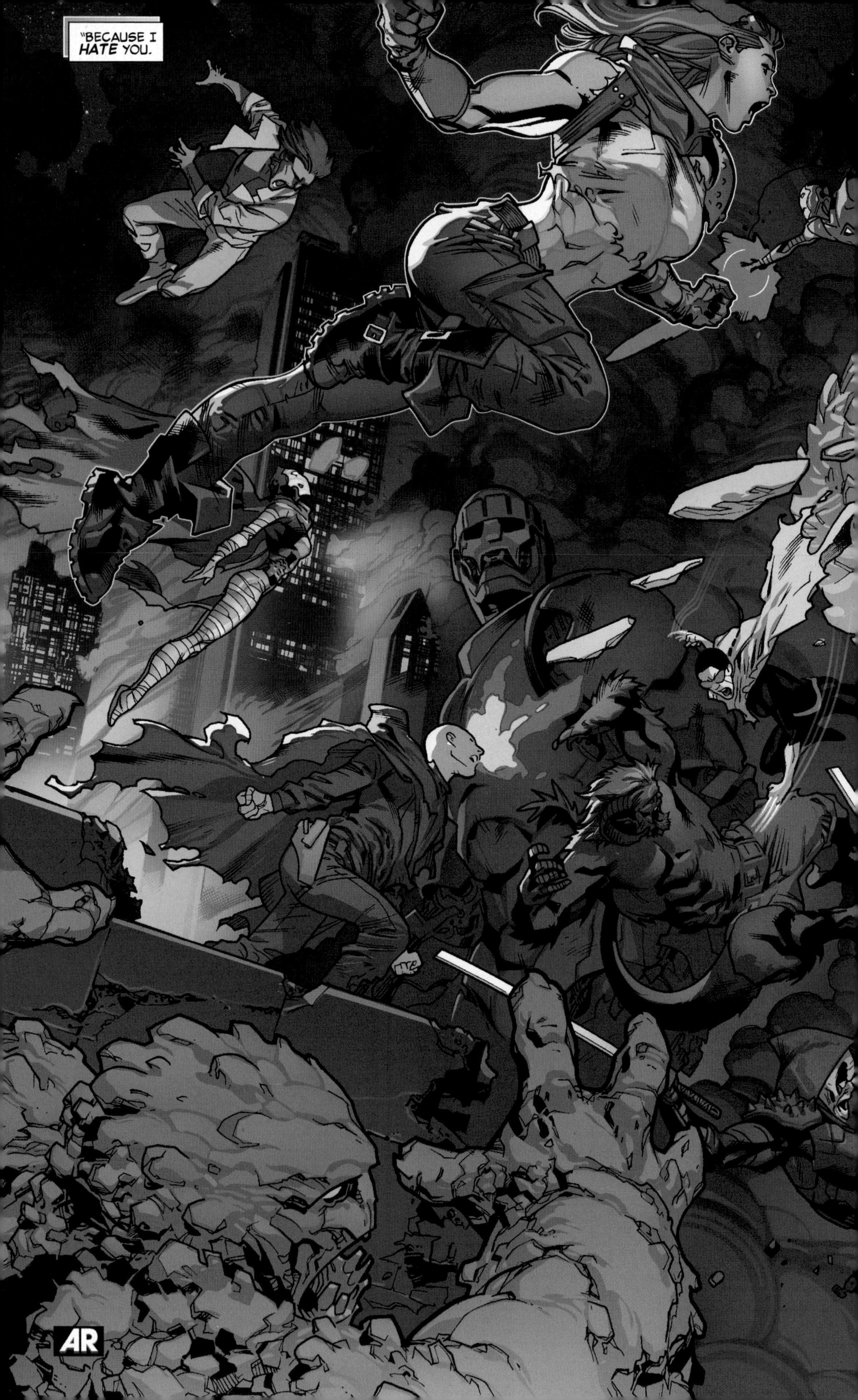
"BECAUSE I HATE YOU.
AR

"I HATE WHO YOU X-MEN ARE, AND I HATE WHO YOU X-MEN WILL BECOME.
"YOU--THEY STAND ON MY FATHER'S GRAVE AND THEY SPEAK OF HIS LEGACY AND THEY HAVE DONE NOTHING BUT MAKE A MOCKERY OF IT.
"IF HE WAS ALIVE TODAY HE WOULD BE DISGUSTED.
"BUT HE'S NOT ALIVE BECAUSE THE X-MEN MURDERED HIM.
"THE X-MEN MURDERED HIM AND THEN WENT ON LIKE NOTHING HAPPENED.
"THEY MOVED INTO HIS HOUSE AND THEY TOOK HIS MONEY AND THEY DIDN'T EVEN HAVE THE COURTESY TO KEEP HIS NAME ON THE SCHOOL HE BUILT.
"YOU WANT TO KNOW WHY THIS IS HAPPENING? BECAUSE YOU DESERVE IT.
"BECAUSE YOU DON'T CARE ABOUT ANYTHING BUT YOURSELVES.
"YOU DON'T LOOK FIVE FEET IN FRONT OF YOU.
"YOU DON'T THINK ABOUT HOW YOUR ACTIONS AFFECT THE FUTURE.
"WELL NOW YOU DO."

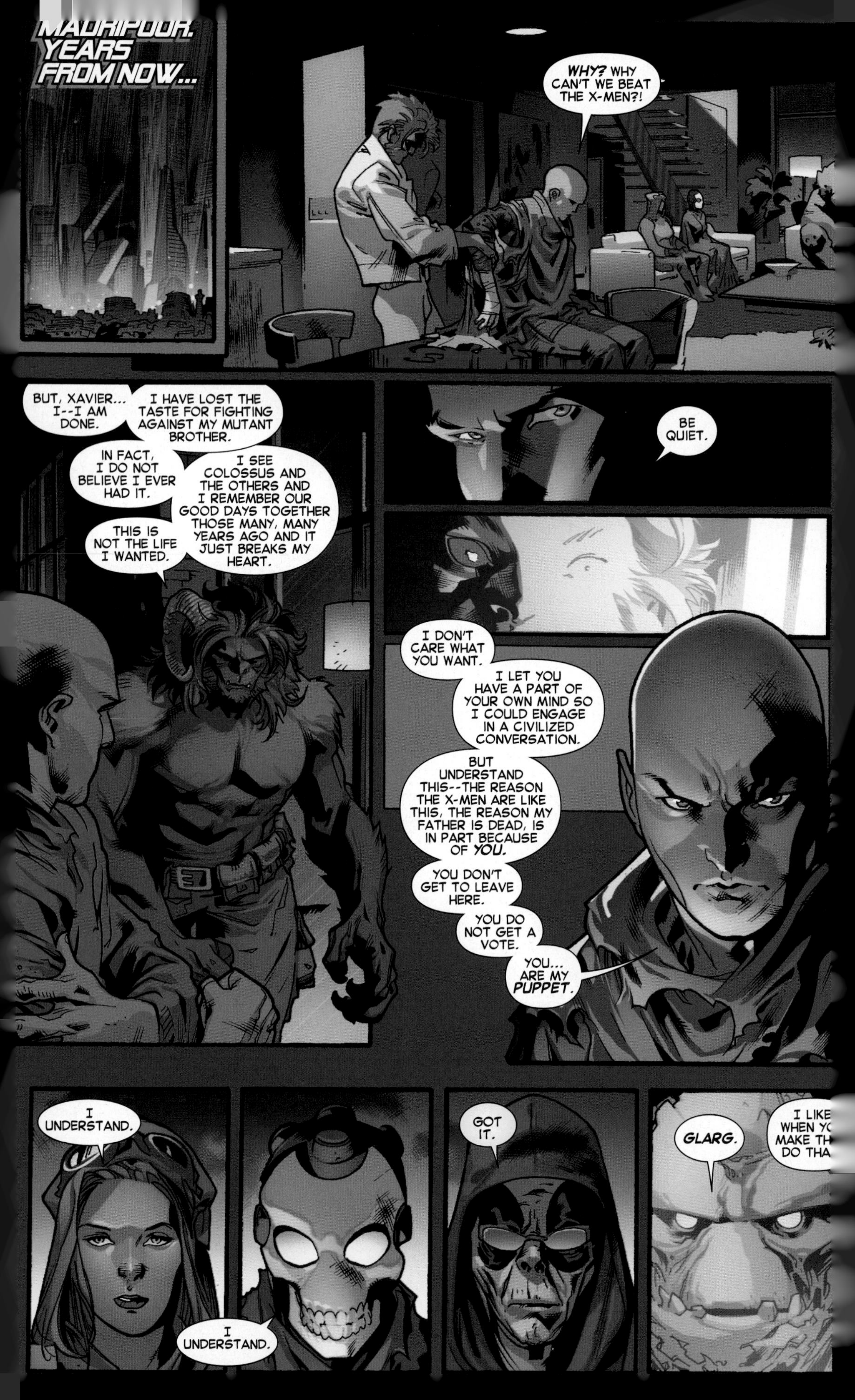
MADRIPOOR. YEARS FROM NOW...
WHY? WHY CAN'T WE BEAT THE X-MEN?!
BUT, XAVIER... I--I AM DONE.
I HAVE LOST THE TASTE FOR FIGHTING AGAINST MY MUTANT BROTHER.
IN FACT, I DO NOT BELIEVE I EVER HAD IT.
I SEE COLOSSUS AND THE OTHERS AND I REMEMBER OUR GOOD DAYS TOGETHER THOSE MANY, MANY YEARS AGO AND IT JUST BREAKS MY HEART.
THIS IS NOT THE LIFE I WANTED.
BE QUIET.
I DON'T CARE WHAT YOU WANT.
I LET YOU HAVE A PART OF YOUR OWN MIND SO I COULD ENGAGE IN A CIVILIZED CONVERSATION.
BUT UNDERSTAND THIS--THE REASON THE X-MEN ARE LIKE THIS, THE REASON MY FATHER IS DEAD, IS IN PART BECAUSE OF YOU.
YOU DON'T GET TO LEAVE HERE.
YOU DO NOT GET A VOTE.
YOU... ARE MY PUPPET.
I UNDERSTAND.
I UNDERSTAND.
GOT IT.
GLARG.
I LIKE WHEN YO MAKE TH DO THA

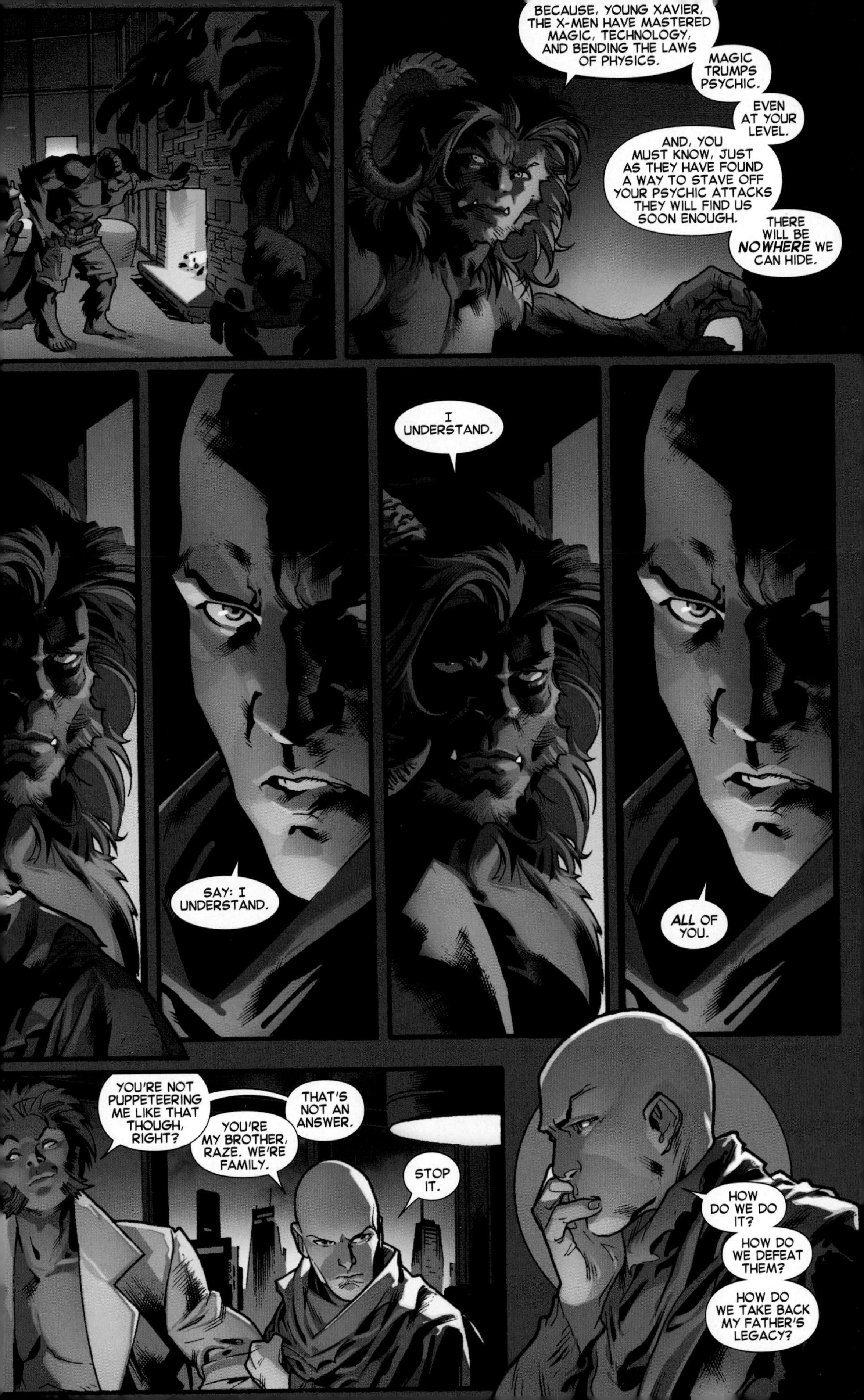
BECAUSE, YOUNG XAVIER, THE X-MEN HAVE MASTERED MAGIC, TECHNOLOGY, AND BENDING THE LAWS OF PHYSICS.
MAGIC TRUMPS PSYCHIC.
EVEN AT YOUR LEVEL.
AND, YOU MUST KNOW, JUST AS THEY HAVE FOUND A WAY TO STAVE OFF YOUR PSYCHIC ATTACKS THEY WILL FIND US SOON ENOUGH.
THERE WILL BE **NOWHERE** WE CAN HIDE.
SAY: I UNDERSTAND.
I UNDERSTAND.
ALL OF YOU.
YOU'RE NOT PUPPETEERING ME LIKE THAT THOUGH, RIGHT?
THAT'S NOT AN ANSWER.
YOU'RE MY BROTHER, RAZE. WE'RE FAMILY.
STOP IT.
HOW DO WE DO IT?
HOW DO WE DEFEAT THEM?
HOW DO WE TAKE BACK MY FATHER'S LEGACY?

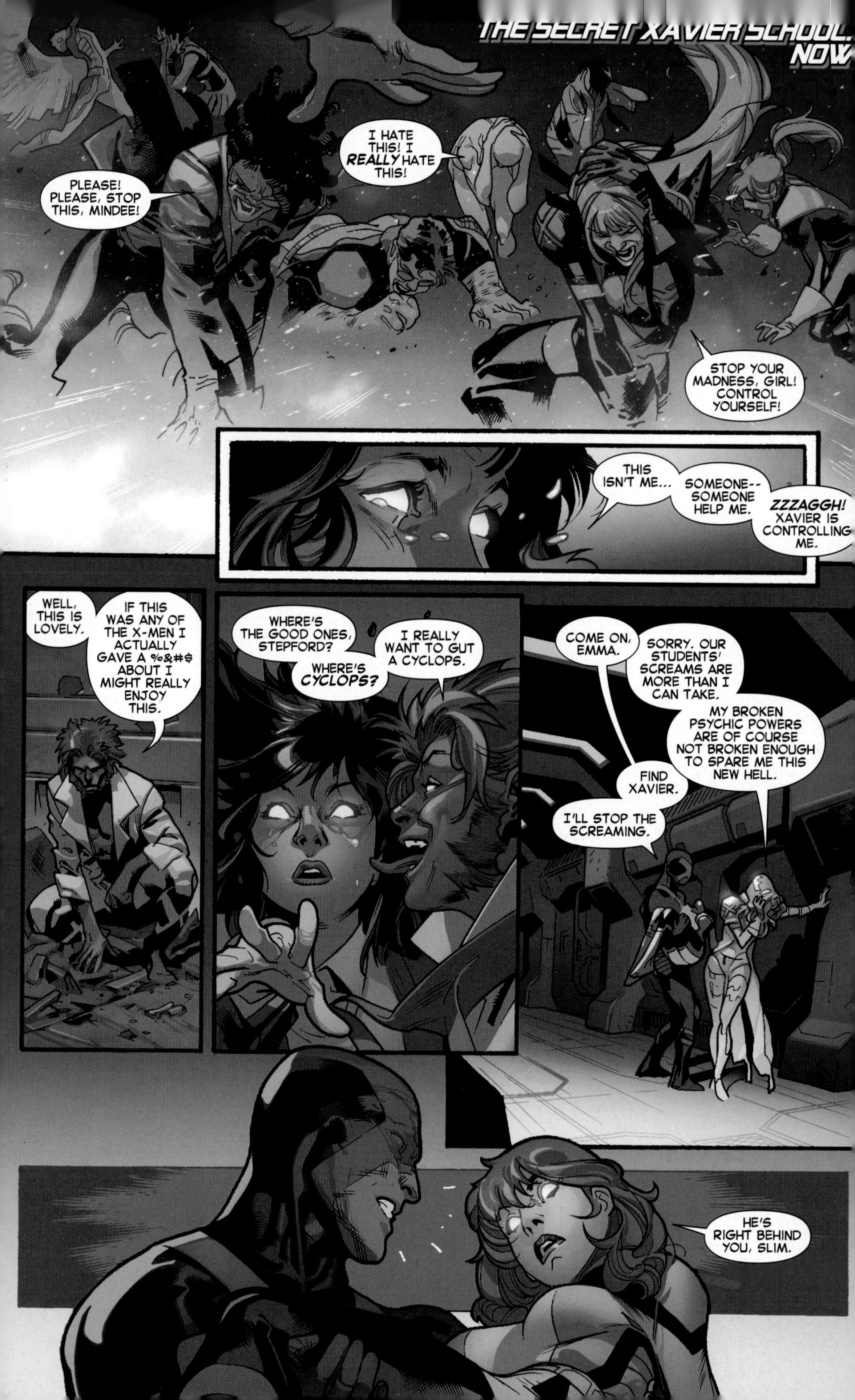
THE SECRET XAVIER SCHOOL. NOW
PLEASE! PLEASE, STOP THIS, MINDEE!
I HATE THIS! I REALLY HATE THIS!
STOP YOUR MADNESS, GIRL! CONTROL YOURSELF!
THIS ISN'T ME...
SOMEONE-- SOMEONE HELP ME.
ZZZAGGH! XAVIER IS CONTROLLING ME.
WELL, THIS IS LOVELY.
IF THIS WAS ANY OF THE X-MEN I ACTUALLY GAVE A %&#$ ABOUT I MIGHT REALLY ENJOY THIS.
WHERE'S THE GOOD ONES, STEPFORD?
WHERE'S CYCLOPS?
I REALLY WANT TO GUT A CYCLOPS.
COME ON, EMMA.
SORRY. OUR STUDENTS' SCREAMS ARE MORE THAN I CAN TAKE.
MY BROKEN PSYCHIC POWERS ARE OF COURSE NOT BROKEN ENOUGH TO SPARE ME THIS NEW HELL.
FIND XAVIER.
I'LL STOP THE SCREAMING.
HE'S RIGHT BEHIND YOU, SLIM.

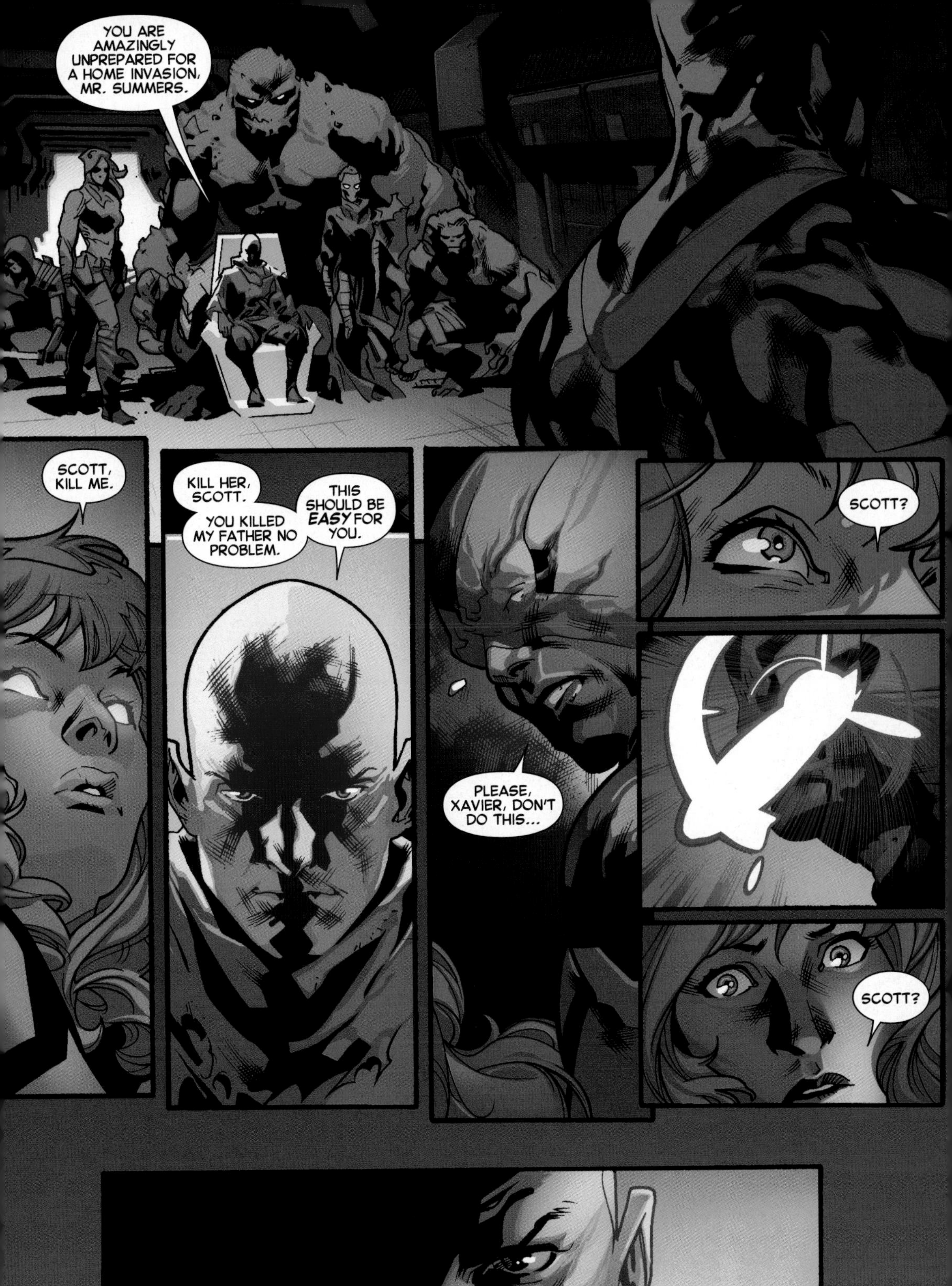

YOU ARE AMAZINGLY UNPREPARED FOR A HOME INVASION, MR. SUMMERS.
SCOTT, KILL ME.
KILL HER, SCOTT.
YOU KILLED MY FATHER NO PROBLEM.
THIS SHOULD BE EASY FOR YOU.
PLEASE, XAVIER, DON'T DO THIS...
SCOTT?
SCOTT?

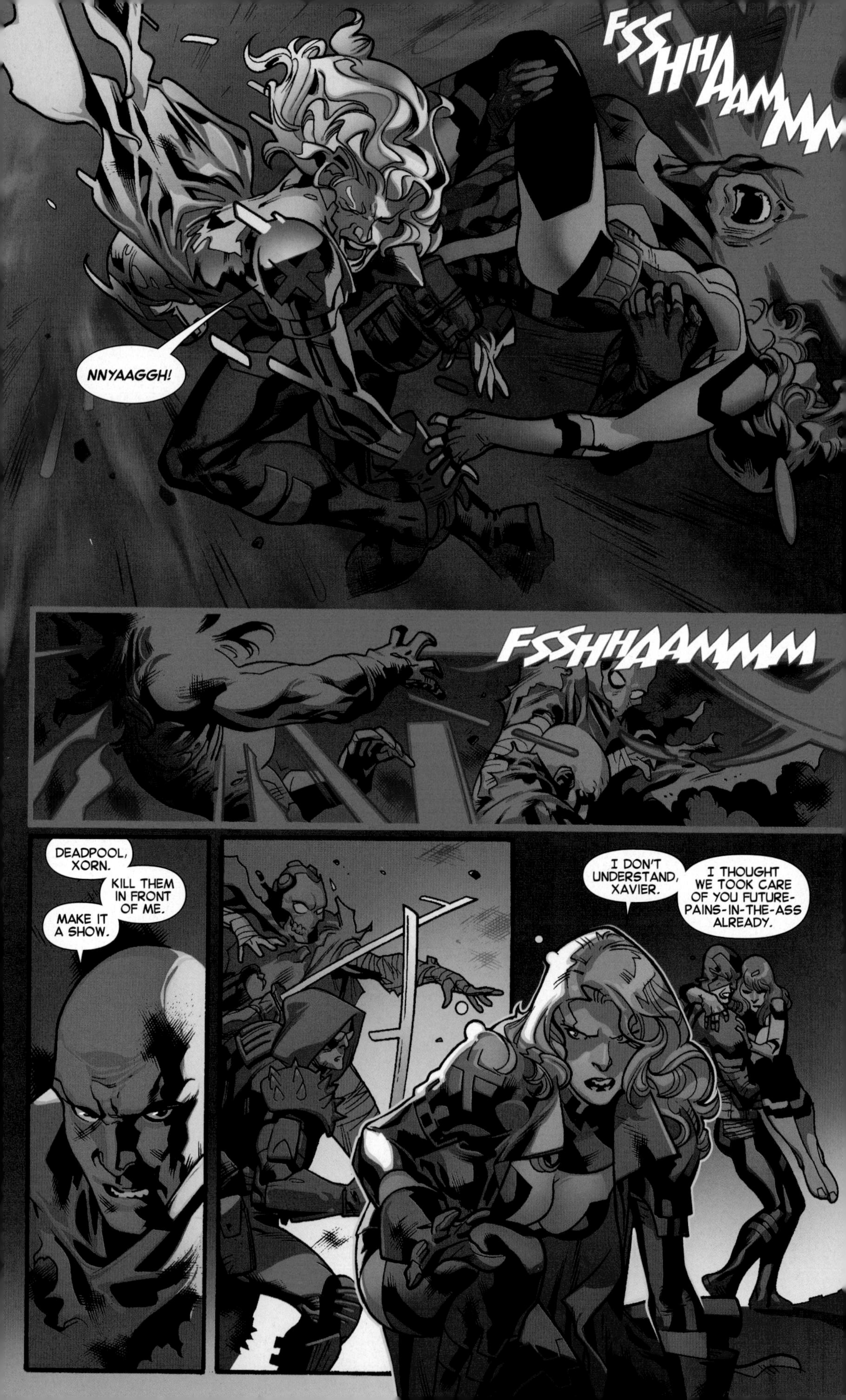
FSSHHAAMMM
NNYAAGGH!
FSSHHAAMMM
DEADPOOL, XORN.
KILL THEM IN FRONT OF ME.
MAKE IT A SHOW.
I DON'T UNDERSTAND, XAVIER.
I THOUGHT WE TOOK CARE OF YOU FUTURE-PAINS-IN-THE-ASS ALREADY.

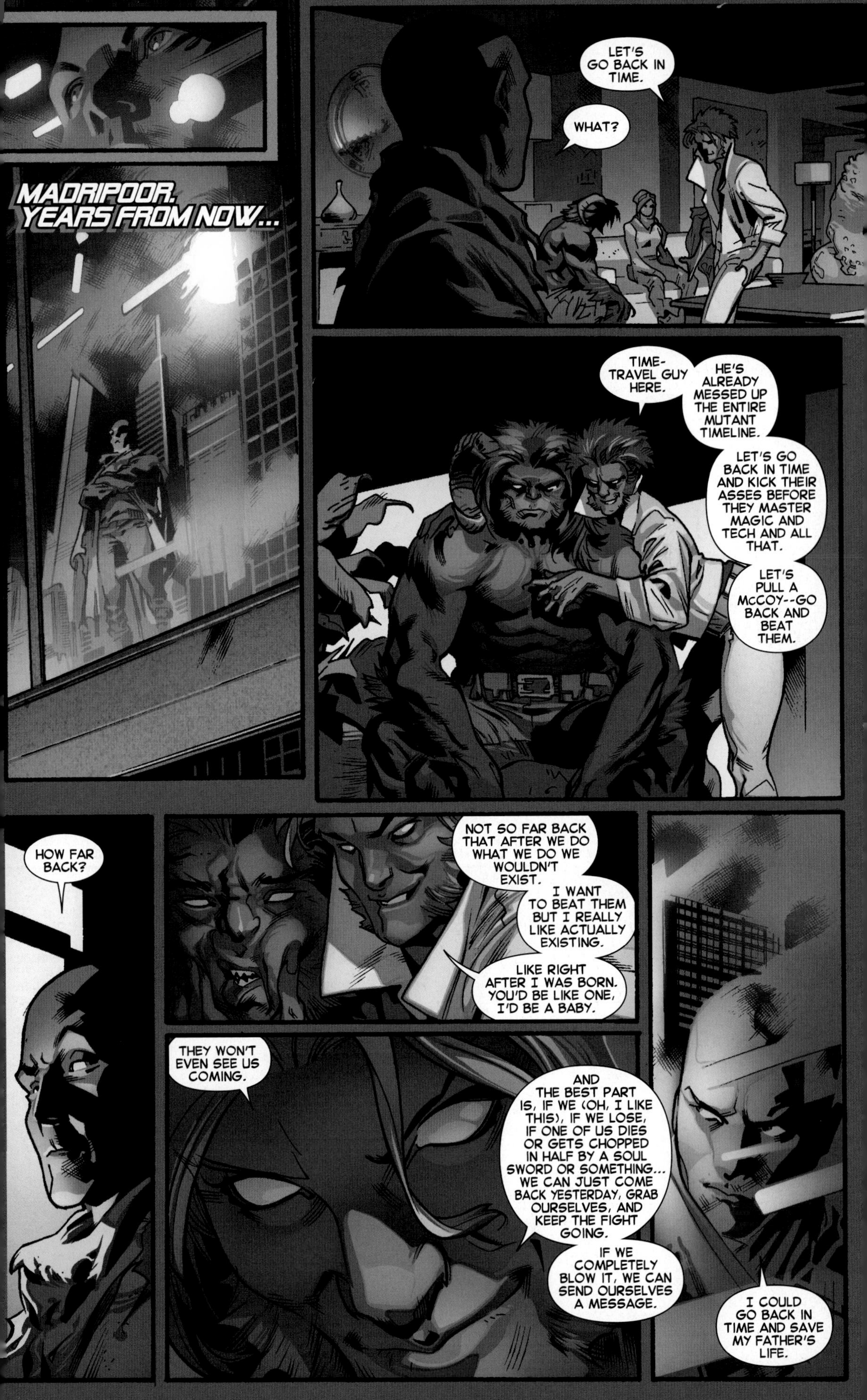
MADRIPOOR. YEARS FROM NOW...
LET'S GO BACK IN TIME.
WHAT?
TIME-TRAVEL GUY HERE.
HE'S ALREADY MESSED UP THE ENTIRE MUTANT TIMELINE.
LET'S GO BACK IN TIME AND KICK THEIR ASSES BEFORE THEY MASTER MAGIC AND TECH AND ALL THAT.
LET'S PULL A McCOY--GO BACK AND BEAT THEM.
HOW FAR BACK?
NOT SO FAR BACK THAT AFTER WE DO WHAT WE DO WE WOULDN'T EXIST.
I WANT TO BEAT THEM BUT I REALLY LIKE ACTUALLY EXISTING.
LIKE RIGHT AFTER I WAS BORN. YOU'D BE LIKE ONE, I'D BE A BABY.
THEY WON'T EVEN SEE US COMING.
AND THE BEST PART IS, IF WE (OH, I LIKE THIS), IF WE LOSE, IF ONE OF US DIES OR GETS CHOPPED IN HALF BY A SOUL SWORD OR SOMETHING... WE CAN JUST COME BACK YESTERDAY, GRAB OURSELVES, AND KEEP THE FIGHT GOING.
IF WE COMPLETELY BLOW IT, WE CAN SEND OURSELVES A MESSAGE.
I COULD GO BACK IN TIME AND SAVE MY FATHER'S LIFE.

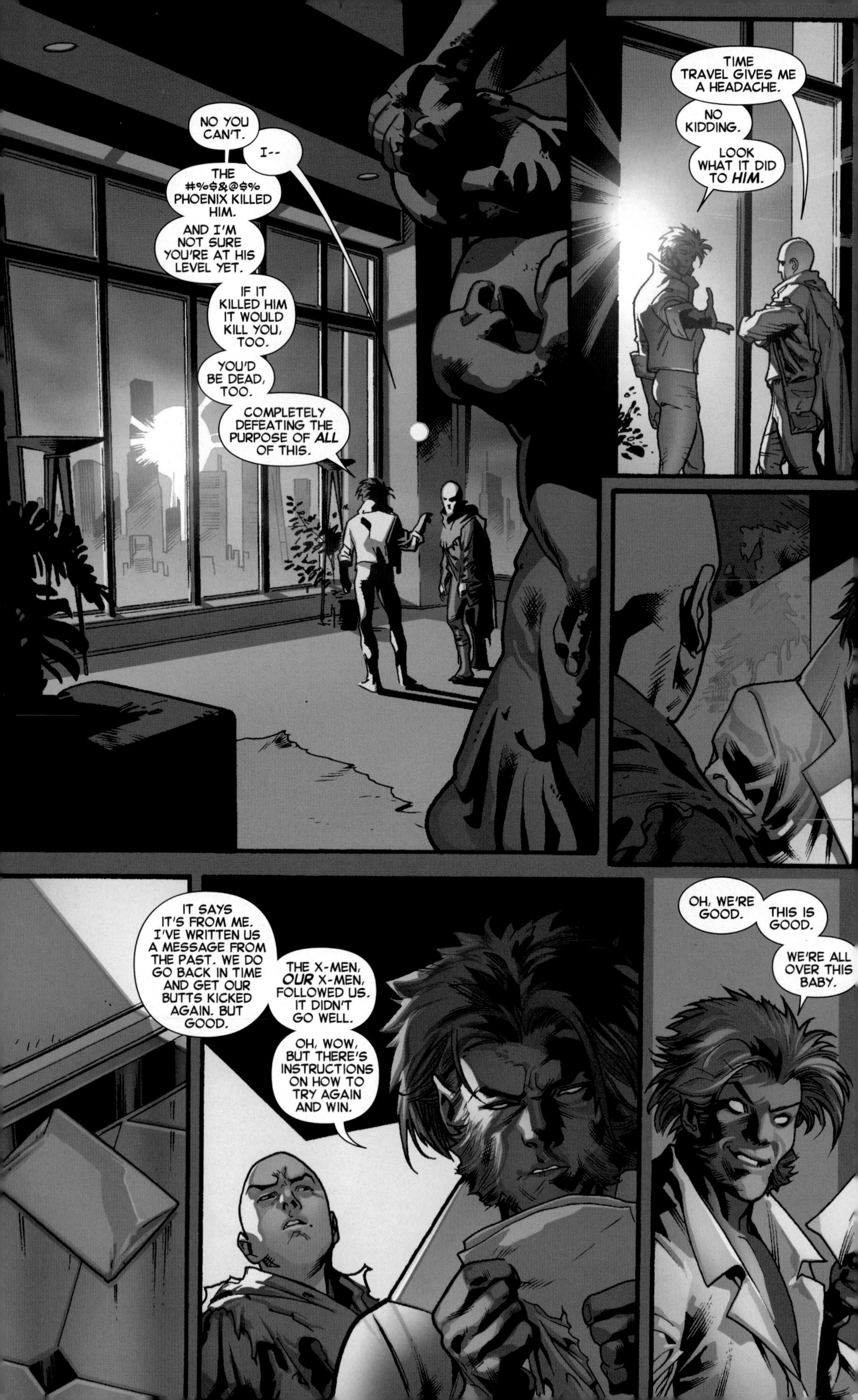
NO YOU CAN'T.
I--
THE #%$&@$% PHOENIX KILLED HIM.
AND I'M NOT SURE YOU'RE AT HIS LEVEL YET.
IF IT KILLED HIM IT WOULD KILL YOU, TOO.
YOU'D BE DEAD, TOO.
COMPLETELY DEFEATING THE PURPOSE OF ALL OF THIS.
TIME TRAVEL GIVES ME A HEADACHE.
NO KIDDING.
LOOK WHAT IT DID TO HIM.
IT SAYS IT'S FROM ME. I'VE WRITTEN US A MESSAGE FROM THE PAST. WE DO GO BACK IN TIME AND GET OUR BUTTS KICKED AGAIN. BUT GOOD.
THE X-MEN, OUR X-MEN, FOLLOWED US. IT DIDN'T GO WELL.
OH, WOW, BUT THERE'S INSTRUCTIONS ON HOW TO TRY AGAIN AND WIN.
OH, WE'RE GOOD.
THIS IS GOOD.
WE'RE ALL OVER THIS BABY.

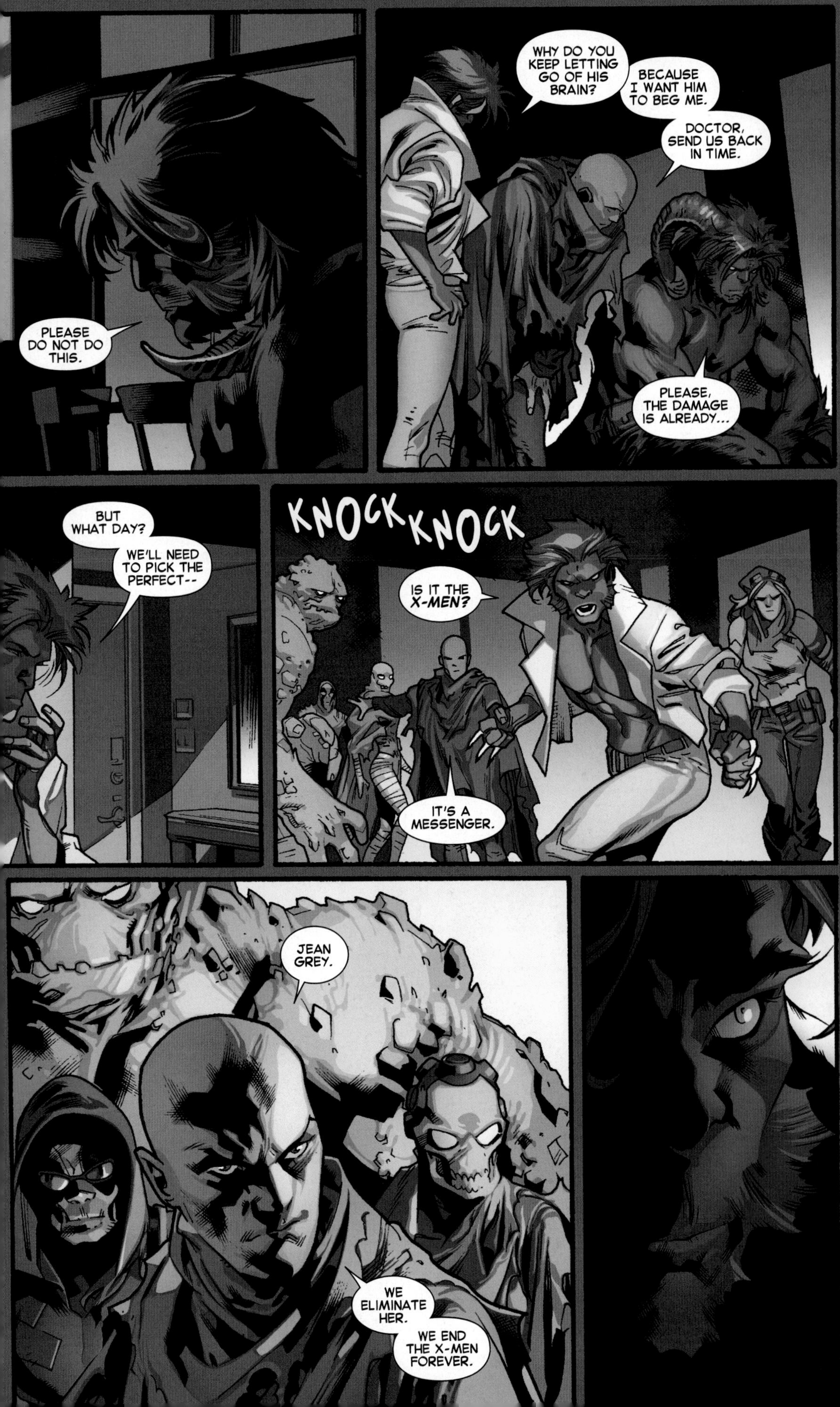
PLEASE DO NOT DO THIS.
WHY DO YOU KEEP LETTING GO OF HIS BRAIN?
BECAUSE I WANT HIM TO BEG ME.
DOCTOR, SEND US BACK IN TIME.
PLEASE, THE DAMAGE IS ALREADY...
BUT WHAT DAY?
WE'LL NEED TO PICK THE PERFECT--
KNOCK KNOCK
IS IT THE X-MEN?
IT'S A MESSENGER.
JEAN GREY.
WE ELIMINATE HER.
WE END THE X-MEN FOREVER.

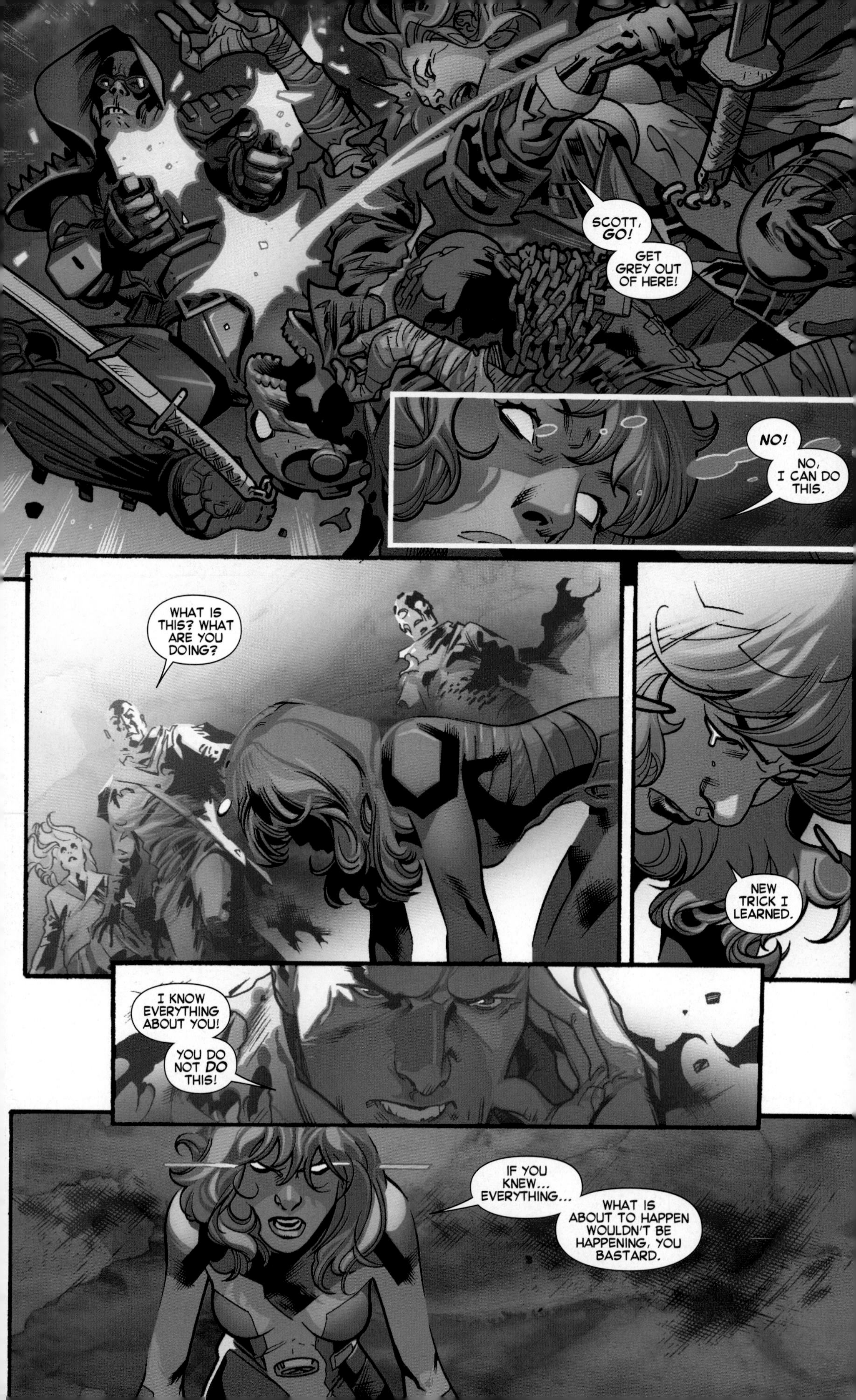
SCOTT, GO!
GET GREY OUT OF HERE!
NO!
NO, I CAN DO THIS.
WHAT IS THIS? WHAT ARE YOU DOING?
NEW TRICK I LEARNED.
I KNOW EVERYTHING ABOUT YOU!
YOU DO NOT DO THIS!
IF YOU KNEW... EVERYTHING...
WHAT IS ABOUT TO HAPPEN WOULDN'T BE HAPPENING, YOU BASTARD.

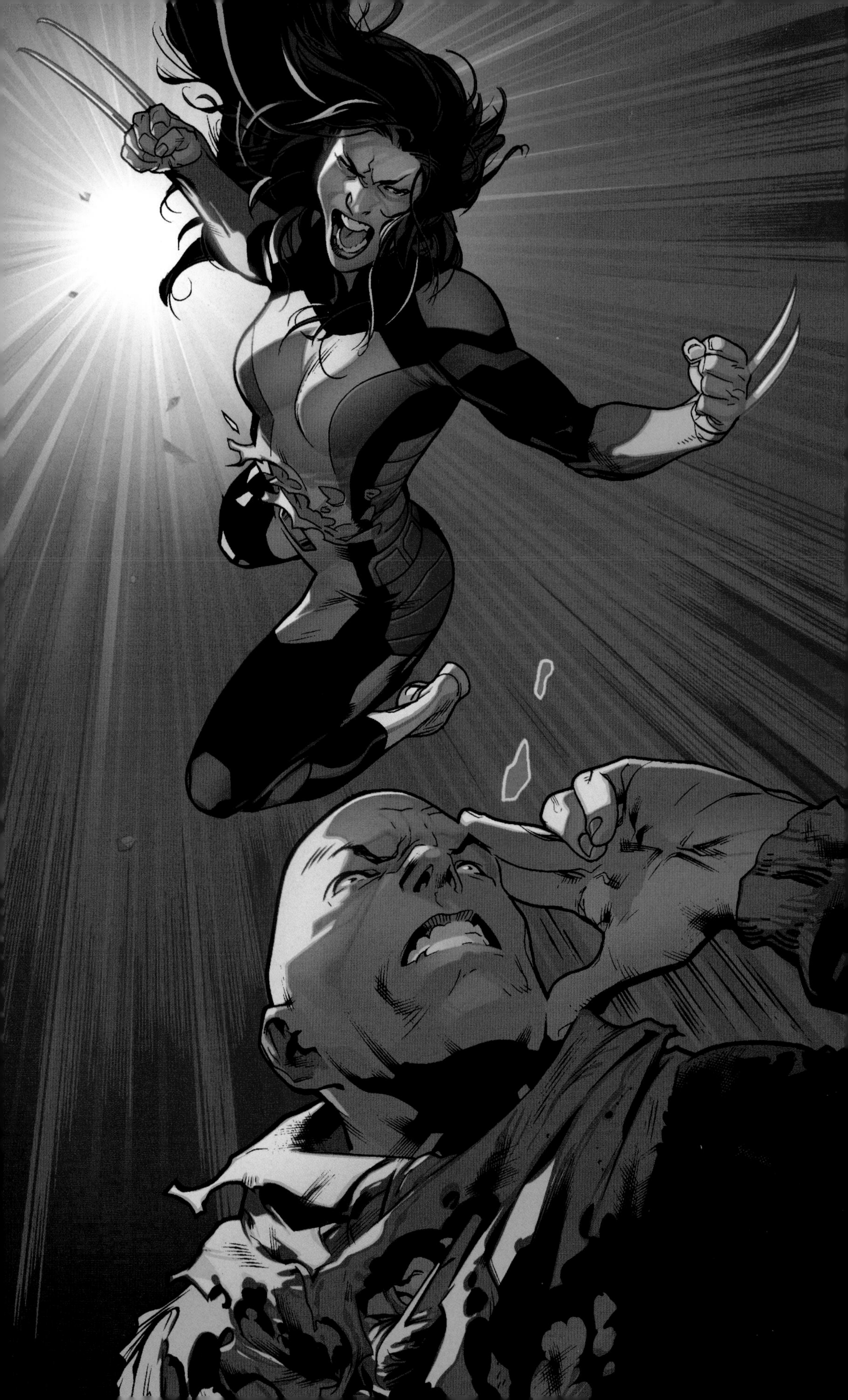

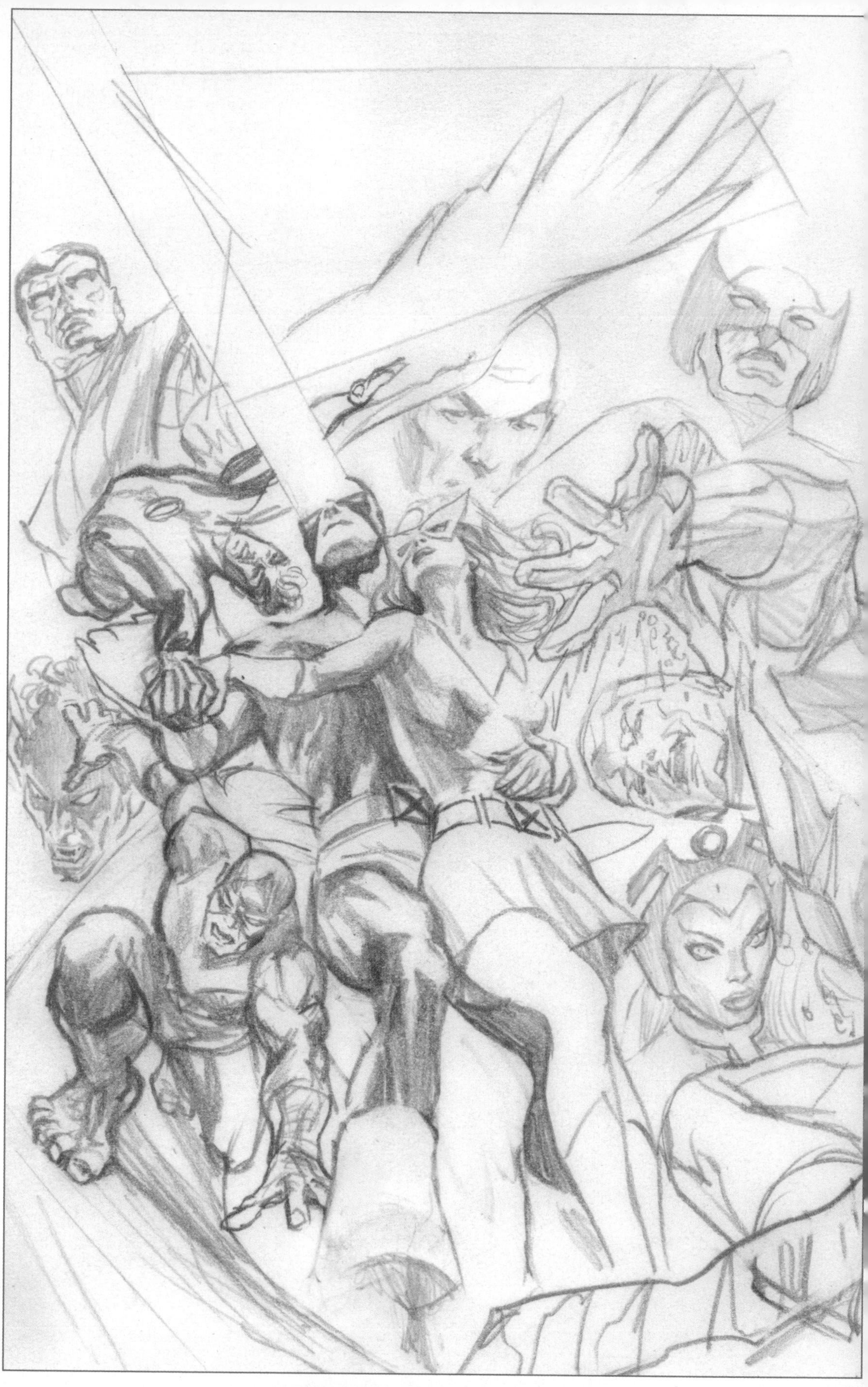

ALL-NEW X-MEN #27 SKETCH VARIANT
BY ALEX ROSS

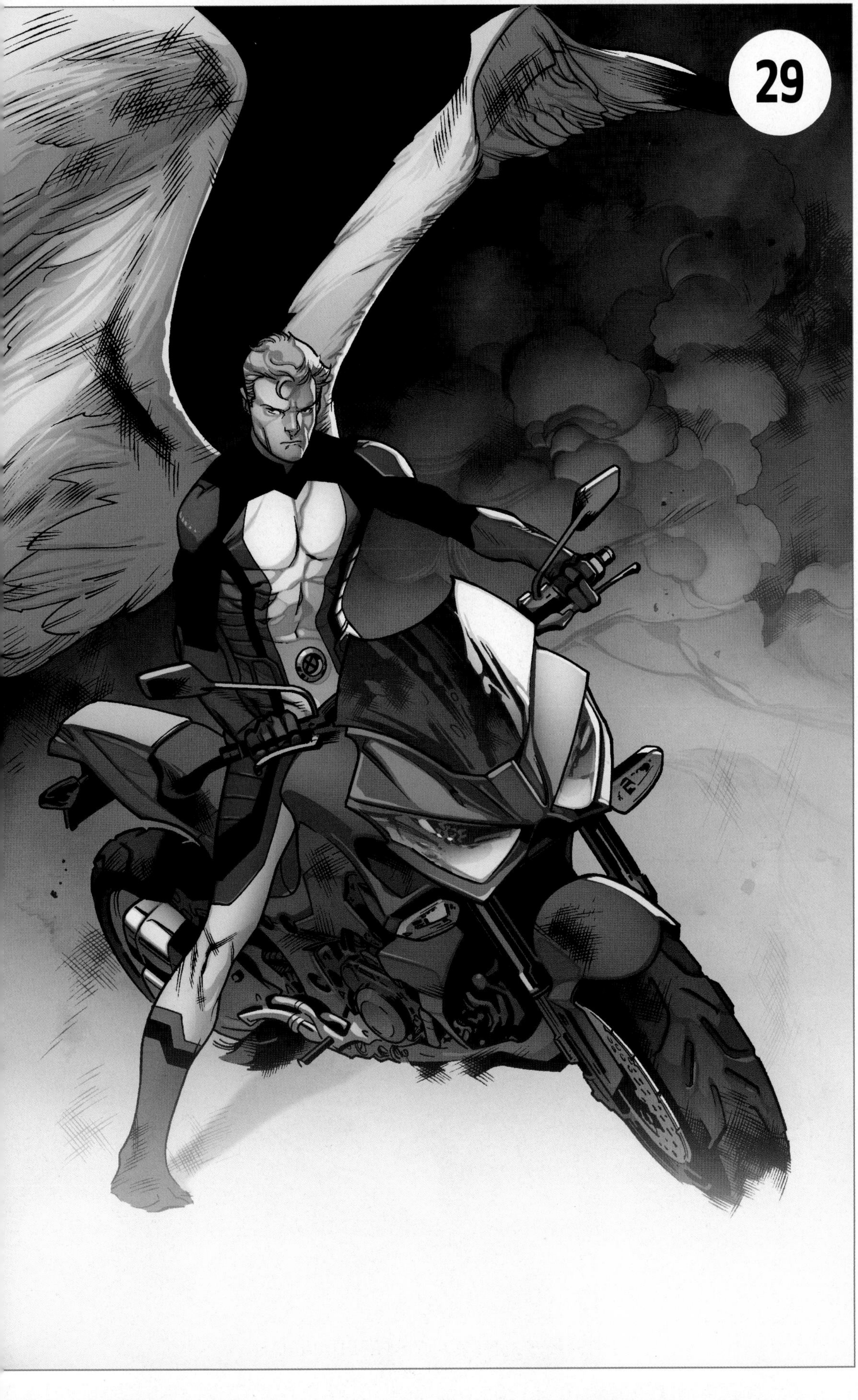

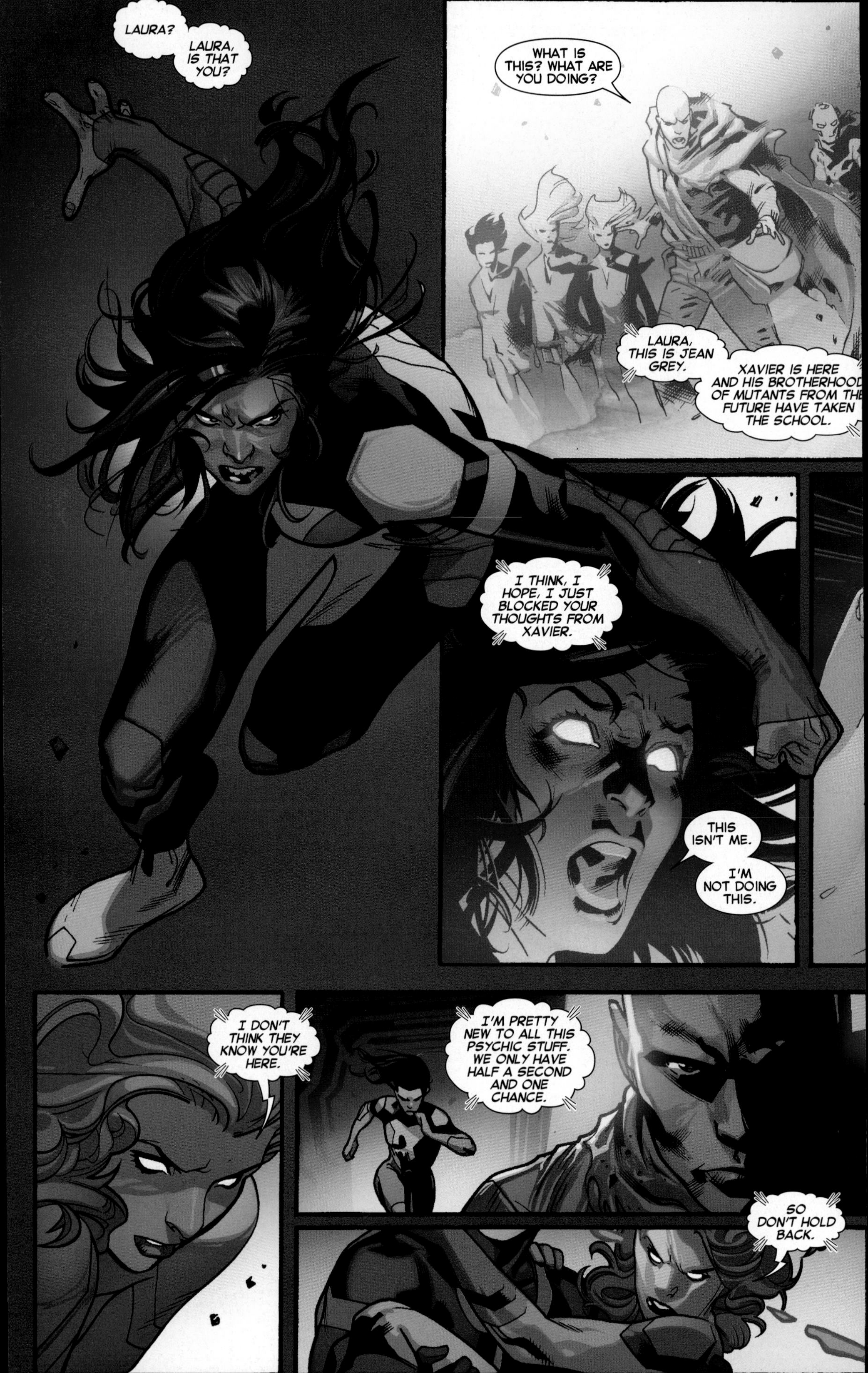
LAURA?
LAURA, IS THAT YOU?
WHAT IS THIS? WHAT ARE YOU DOING?
LAURA, THIS IS JEAN GREY.
XAVIER IS HERE AND HIS BROTHERHOOD OF MUTANTS FROM THE FUTURE HAVE TAKEN THE SCHOOL.
I THINK, I HOPE, I JUST BLOCKED YOUR THOUGHTS FROM XAVIER.
THIS ISN'T ME.
I'M NOT DOING THIS.
I DON'T THINK THEY KNOW YOU'RE HERE.
I'M PRETTY NEW TO ALL THIS PSYCHIC STUFF. WE ONLY HAVE HALF A SECOND AND ONE CHANCE.
SO DON'T HOLD BACK.

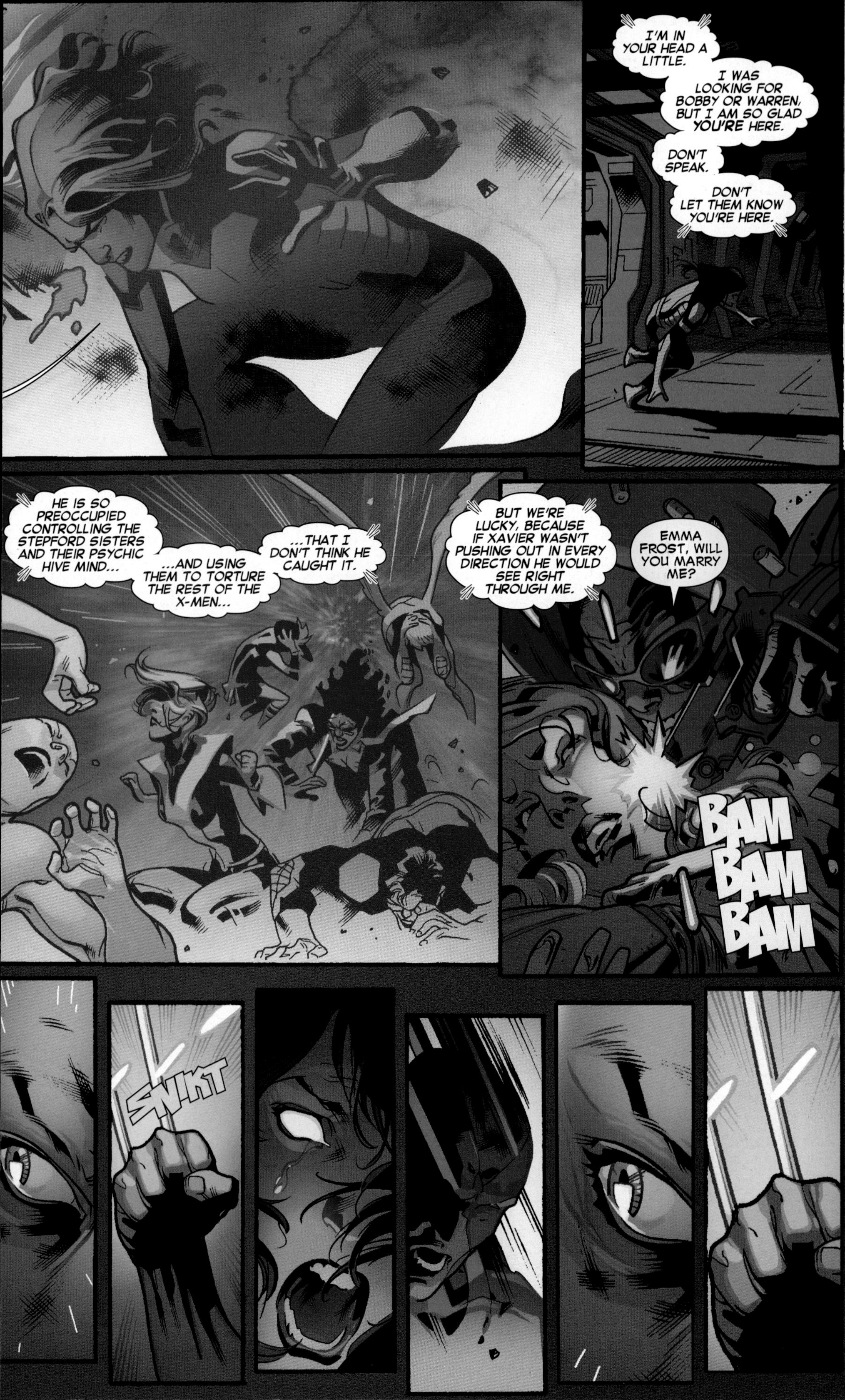
I'M IN YOUR HEAD A LITTLE.
I WAS LOOKING FOR BOBBY OR WARREN, BUT I AM SO GLAD YOU'RE HERE.
DON'T SPEAK.
DON'T LET THEM KNOW YOU'RE HERE.
HE IS SO PREOCCUPIED CONTROLLING THE STEPFORD SISTERS AND THEIR PSYCHIC HIVE MIND...
...AND USING THEM TO TORTURE THE REST OF THE X-MEN...
...THAT I DON'T THINK HE CAUGHT IT.
BUT WE'RE LUCKY, BECAUSE IF XAVIER WASN'T PUSHING OUT IN EVERY DIRECTION HE WOULD SEE RIGHT THROUGH ME.
EMMA FROST, WILL YOU MARRY ME?
BAM BAM BAM
SNIKT

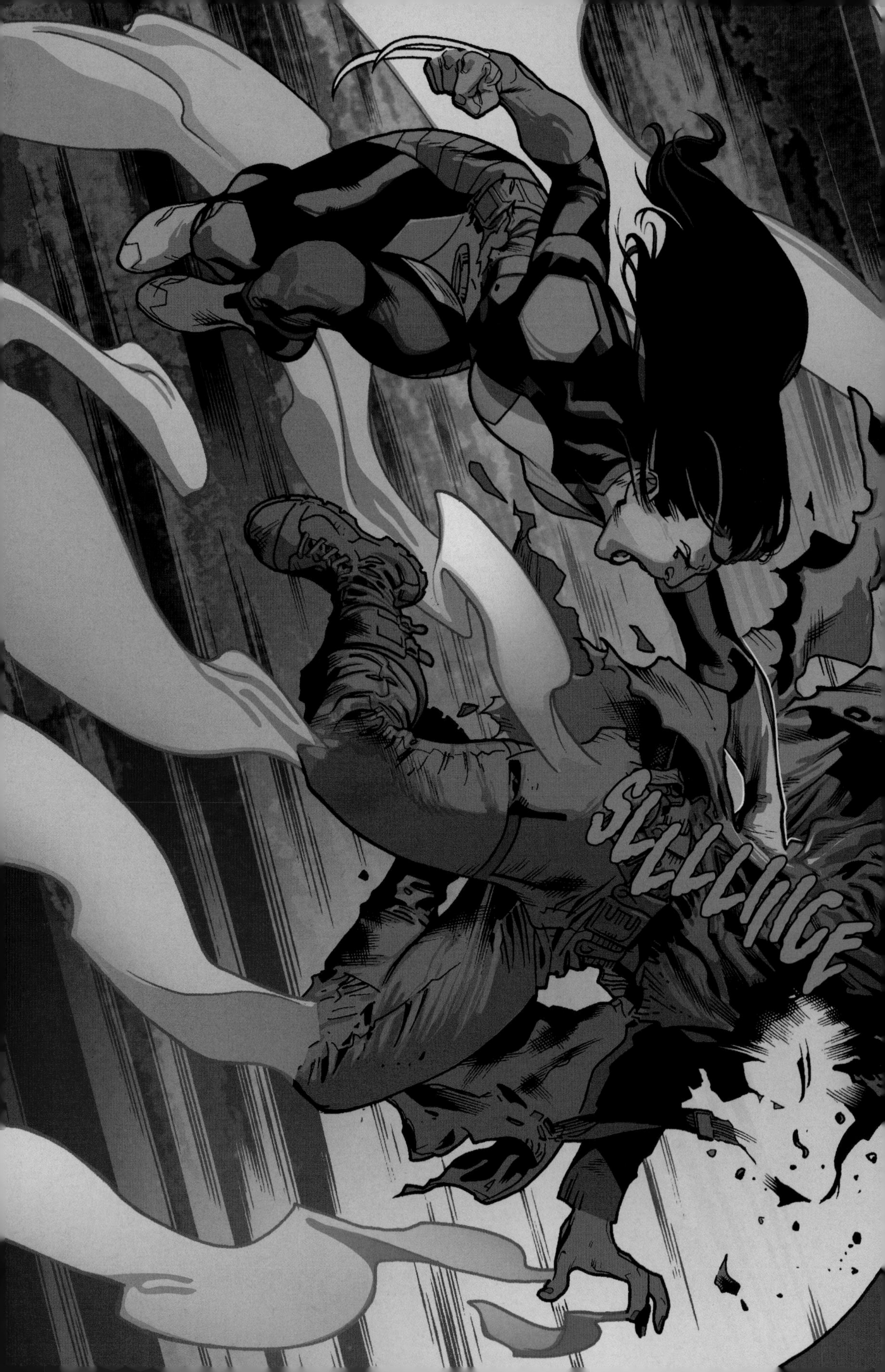
SLLLIIICE

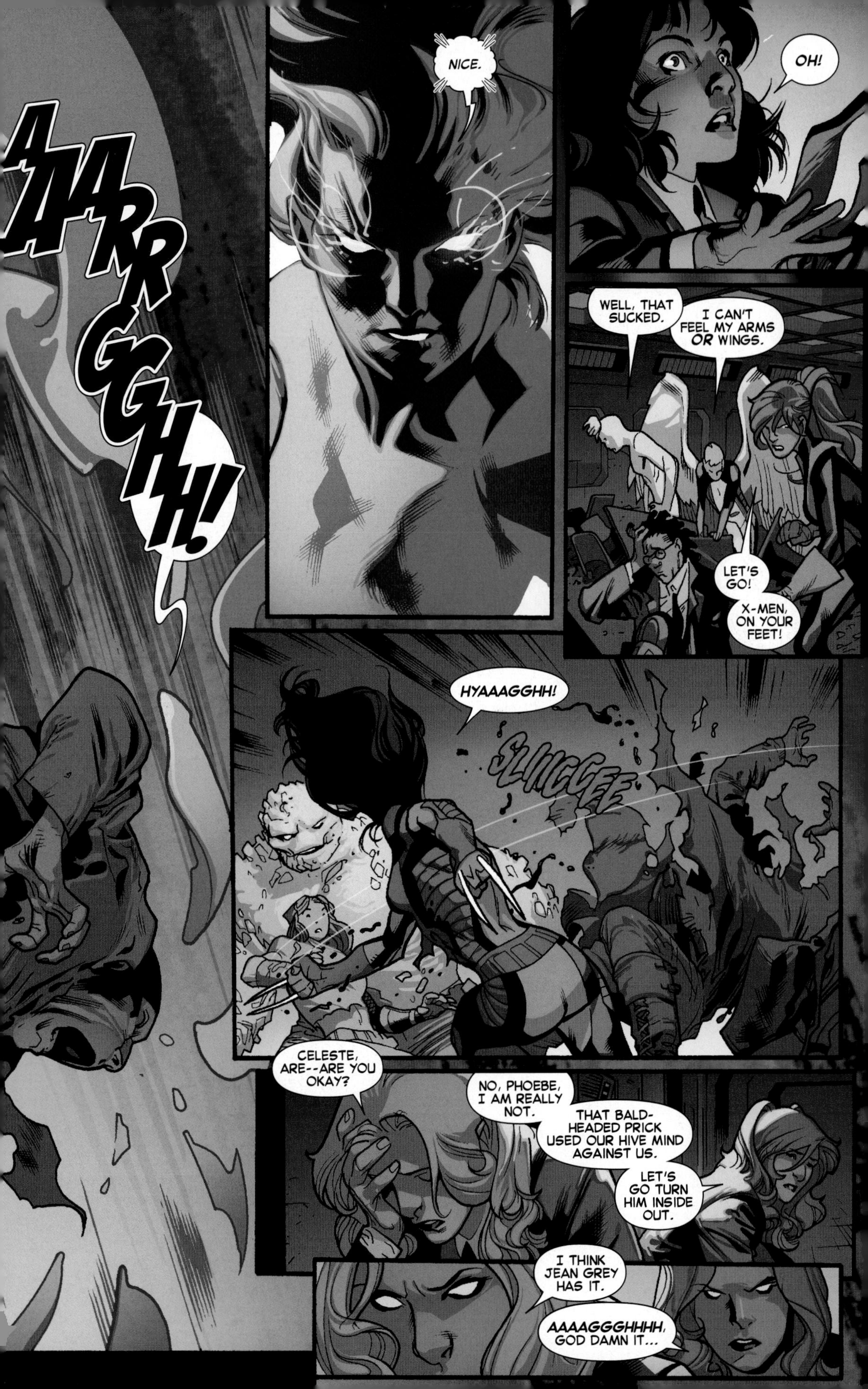
AAARRGGHH!
NICE.
OH!
WELL, THAT SUCKED.
I CAN'T FEEL MY ARMS OR WINGS.
LET'S GO!
X-MEN, ON YOUR FEET!
HYAAAGGHH!
SLIICCEE
CELESTE, ARE--ARE YOU OKAY?
NO, PHOEBE, I AM REALLY NOT.
THAT BALD-HEADED PRICK USED OUR HIVE MIND AGAINST US.
LET'S GO TURN HIM INSIDE OUT.
I THINK JEAN GREY HAS IT.
AAAAGGGHHHH, GOD DAMN IT...

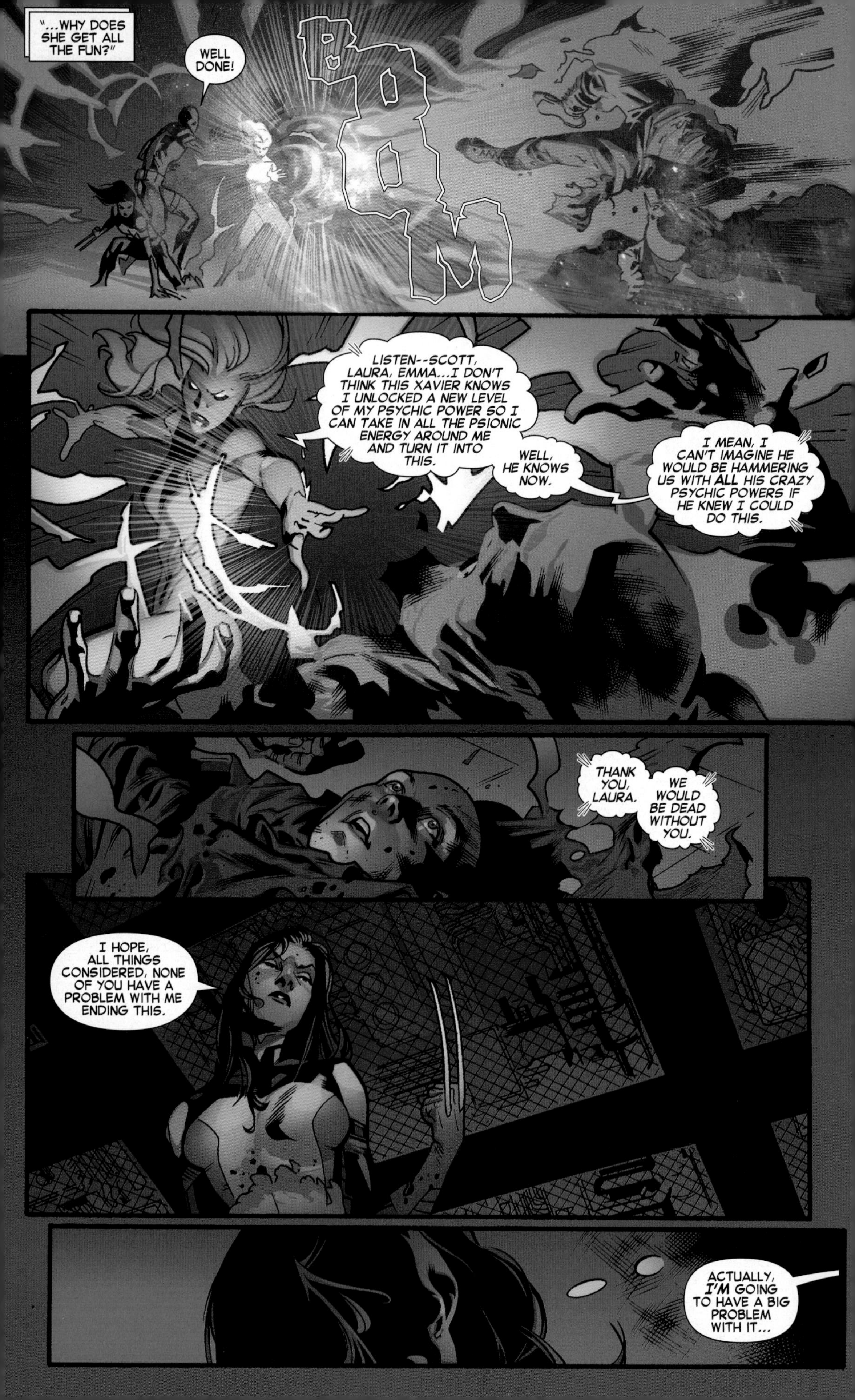
"...WHY DOES SHE GET ALL THE FUN?"
WELL DONE!
BOOM
LISTEN--SCOTT, LAURA, EMMA...I DON'T THINK THIS XAVIER KNOWS I UNLOCKED A NEW LEVEL OF MY PSYCHIC POWER SO I CAN TAKE IN ALL THE PSIONIC ENERGY AROUND ME AND TURN IT INTO THIS.
WELL, HE KNOWS NOW.
I MEAN, I CAN'T IMAGINE HE WOULD BE HAMMERING US WITH ALL HIS CRAZY PSYCHIC POWERS IF HE KNEW I COULD DO THIS.
THANK YOU, LAURA.
WE WOULD BE DEAD WITHOUT YOU.
I HOPE, ALL THINGS CONSIDERED, NONE OF YOU HAVE A PROBLEM WITH ME ENDING THIS.
ACTUALLY, I'M GOING TO HAVE A BIG PROBLEM WITH IT...

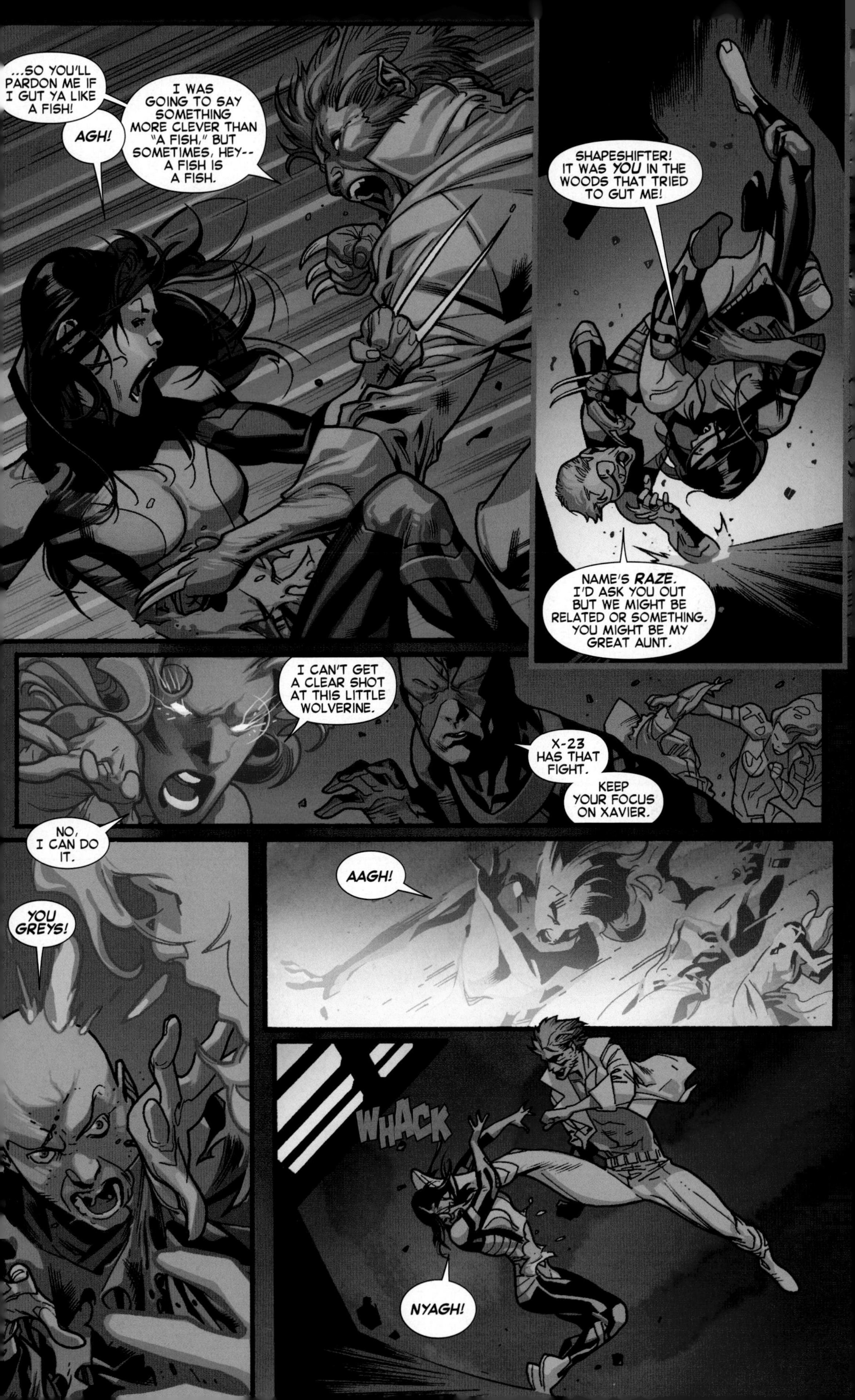
...SO YOU'LL PARDON ME IF I GUT YA LIKE A FISH!
AGH!
I WAS GOING TO SAY SOMETHING MORE CLEVER THAN "A FISH," BUT SOMETIMES, HEY-- A FISH IS A FISH.
SHAPESHIFTER! IT WAS YOU IN THE WOODS THAT TRIED TO GUT ME!
NAME'S RAZE. I'D ASK YOU OUT BUT WE MIGHT BE RELATED OR SOMETHING. YOU MIGHT BE MY GREAT AUNT.
I CAN'T GET A CLEAR SHOT AT THIS LITTLE WOLVERINE.
X-23 HAS THAT FIGHT.
KEEP YOUR FOCUS ON XAVIER.
NO, I CAN DO IT.
YOU GREYS!
AAGH!
WHACK
NYAGH!

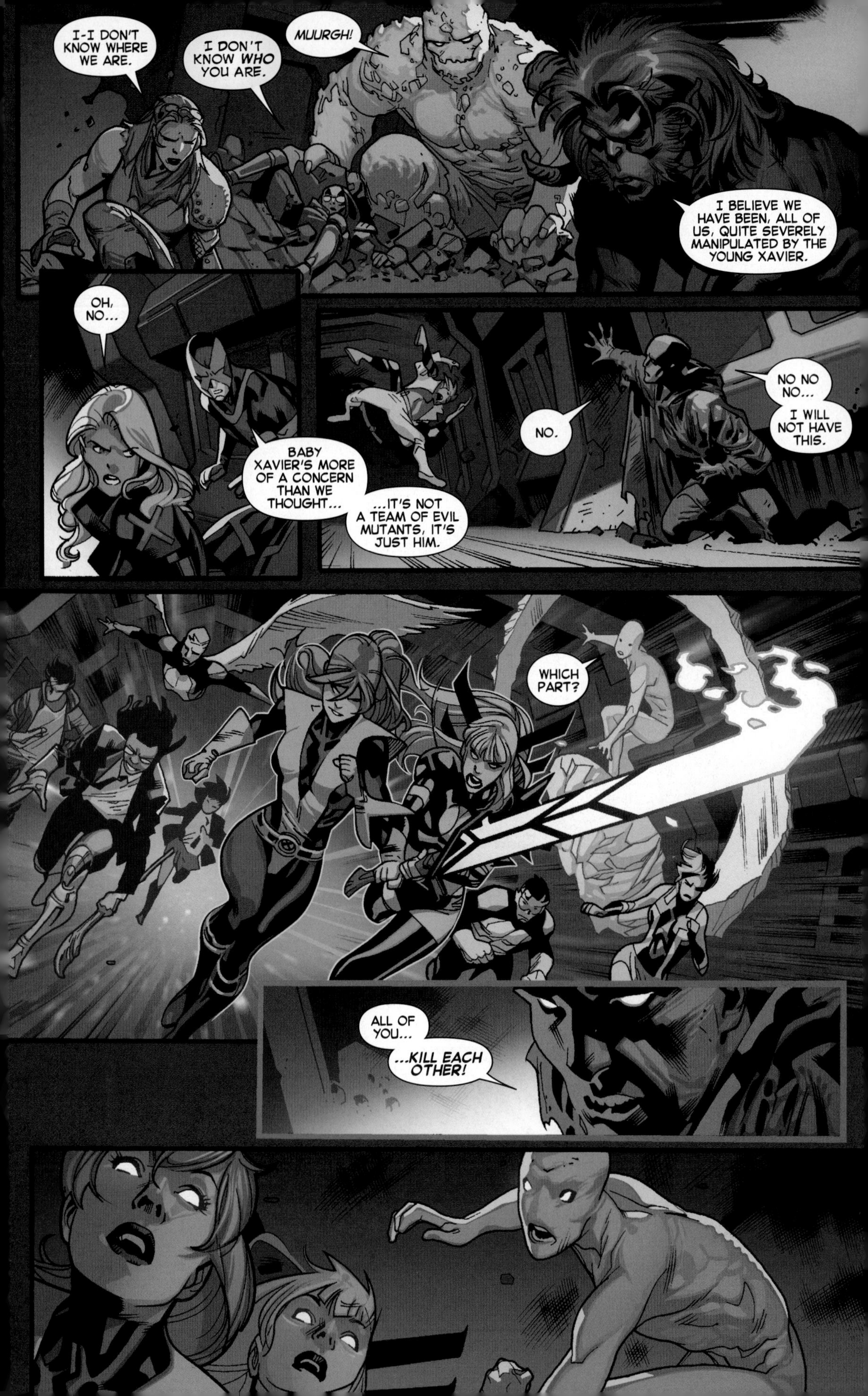
I-I DON'T KNOW WHERE WE ARE.
I DON'T KNOW WHO YOU ARE.
MUURGH!
I BELIEVE WE HAVE BEEN, ALL OF US, QUITE SEVERELY MANIPULATED BY THE YOUNG XAVIER.
OH, NO...
BABY XAVIER'S MORE OF A CONCERN THAN WE THOUGHT...
...IT'S NOT A TEAM OF EVIL MUTANTS, IT'S JUST HIM.
NO.
NO NO NO...
I WILL NOT HAVE THIS.
WHICH PART?
ALL OF YOU...
...KILL EACH OTHER!

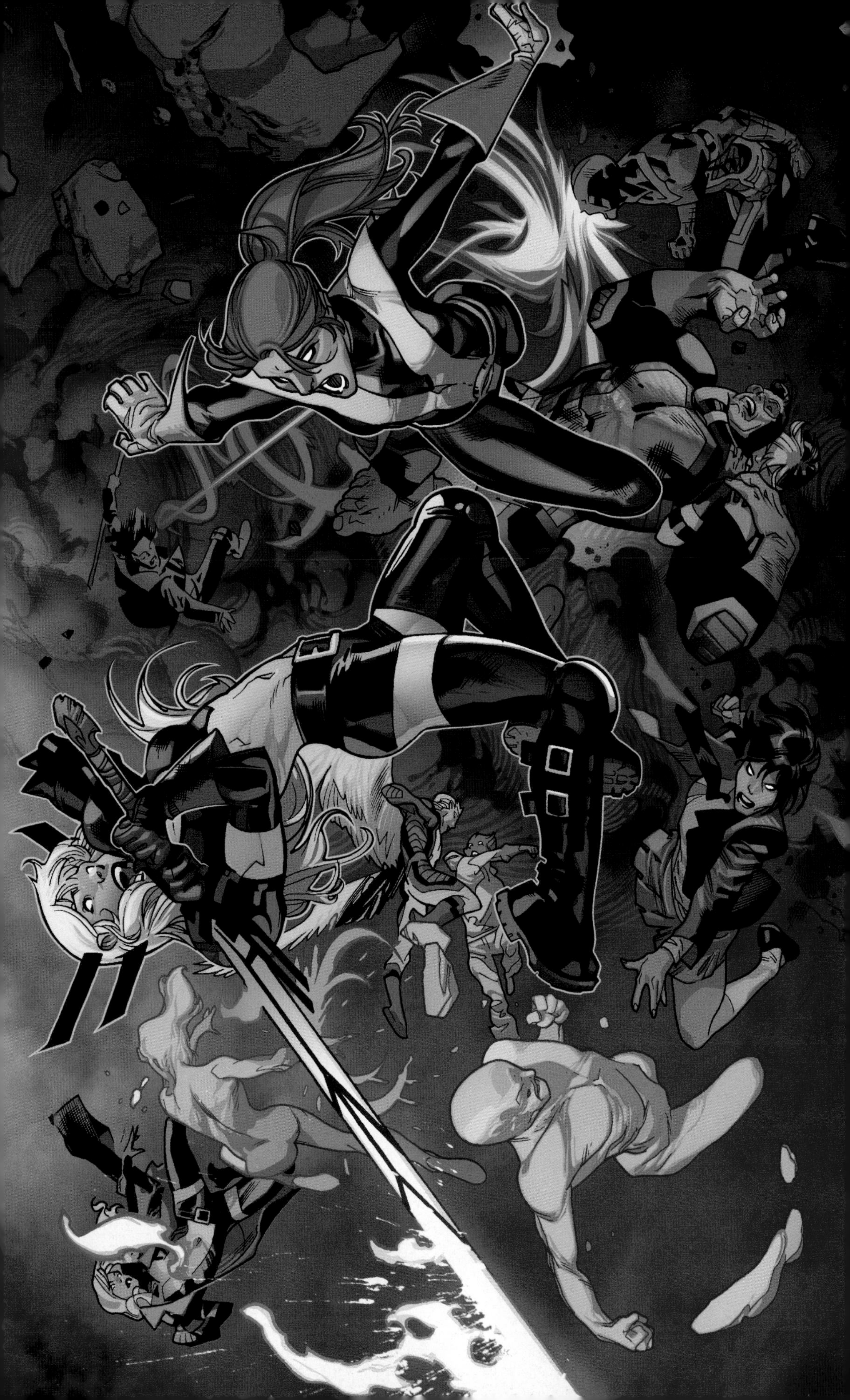

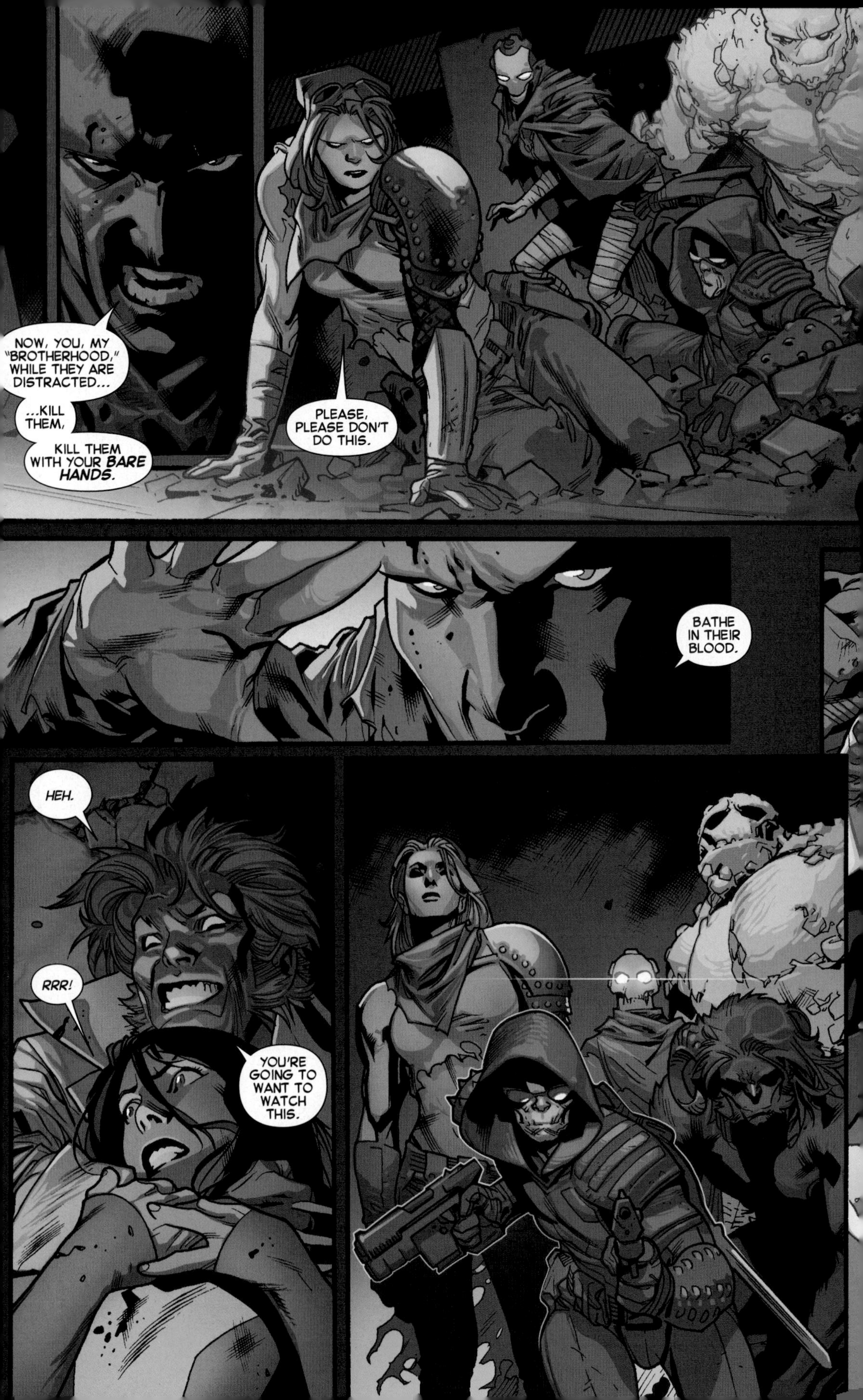

NOW, YOU, MY "BROTHERHOOD," WHILE THEY ARE DISTRACTED...
...KILL THEM,
KILL THEM WITH YOUR **BARE HANDS.**
PLEASE, PLEASE DON'T DO THIS.
BATHE IN THEIR BLOOD.
HEH.
RRR!
YOU'RE GOING TO WANT TO WATCH THIS.

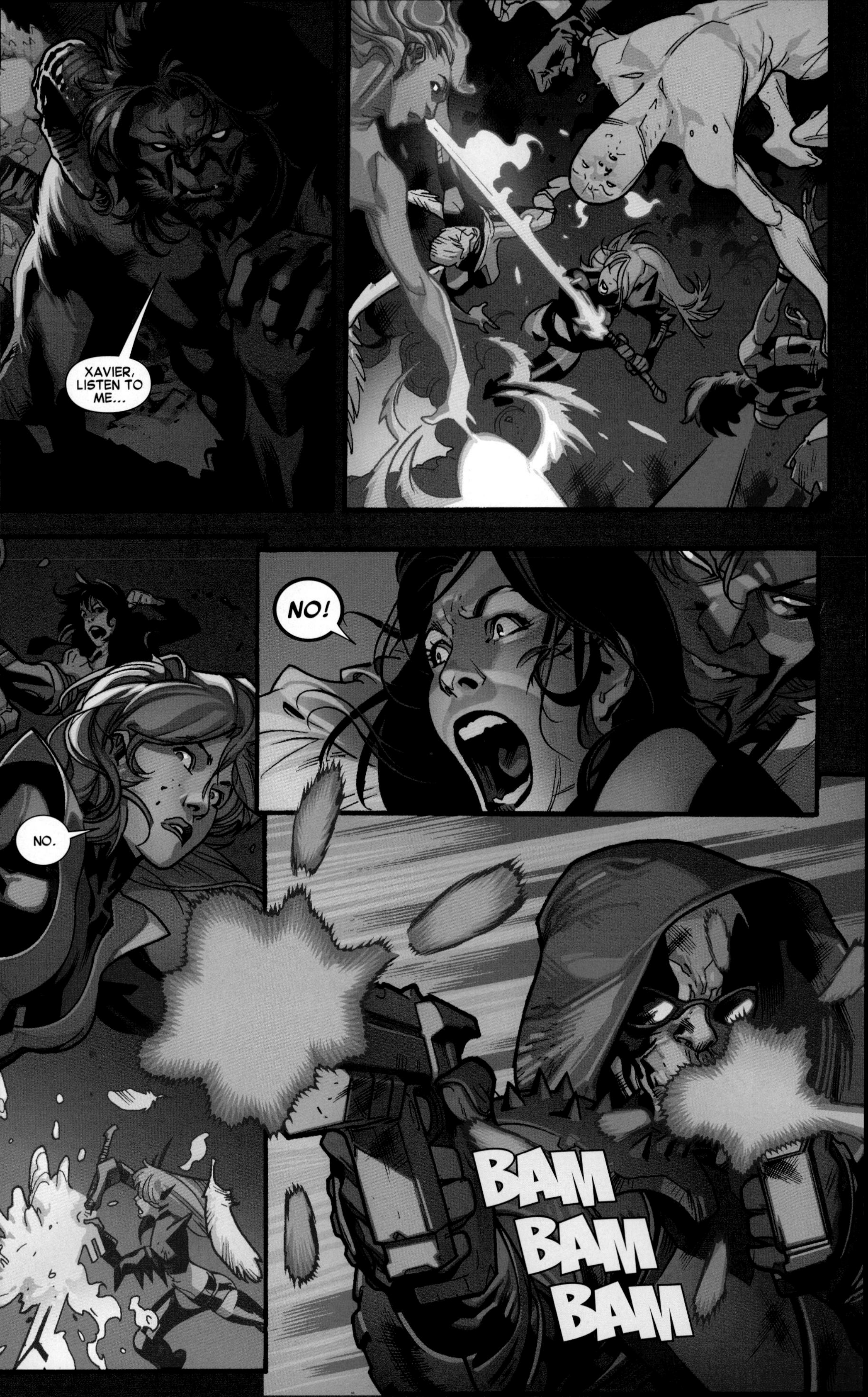
XAVIER, LISTEN TO ME...
NO!
NO.
BAM
BAM
BAM

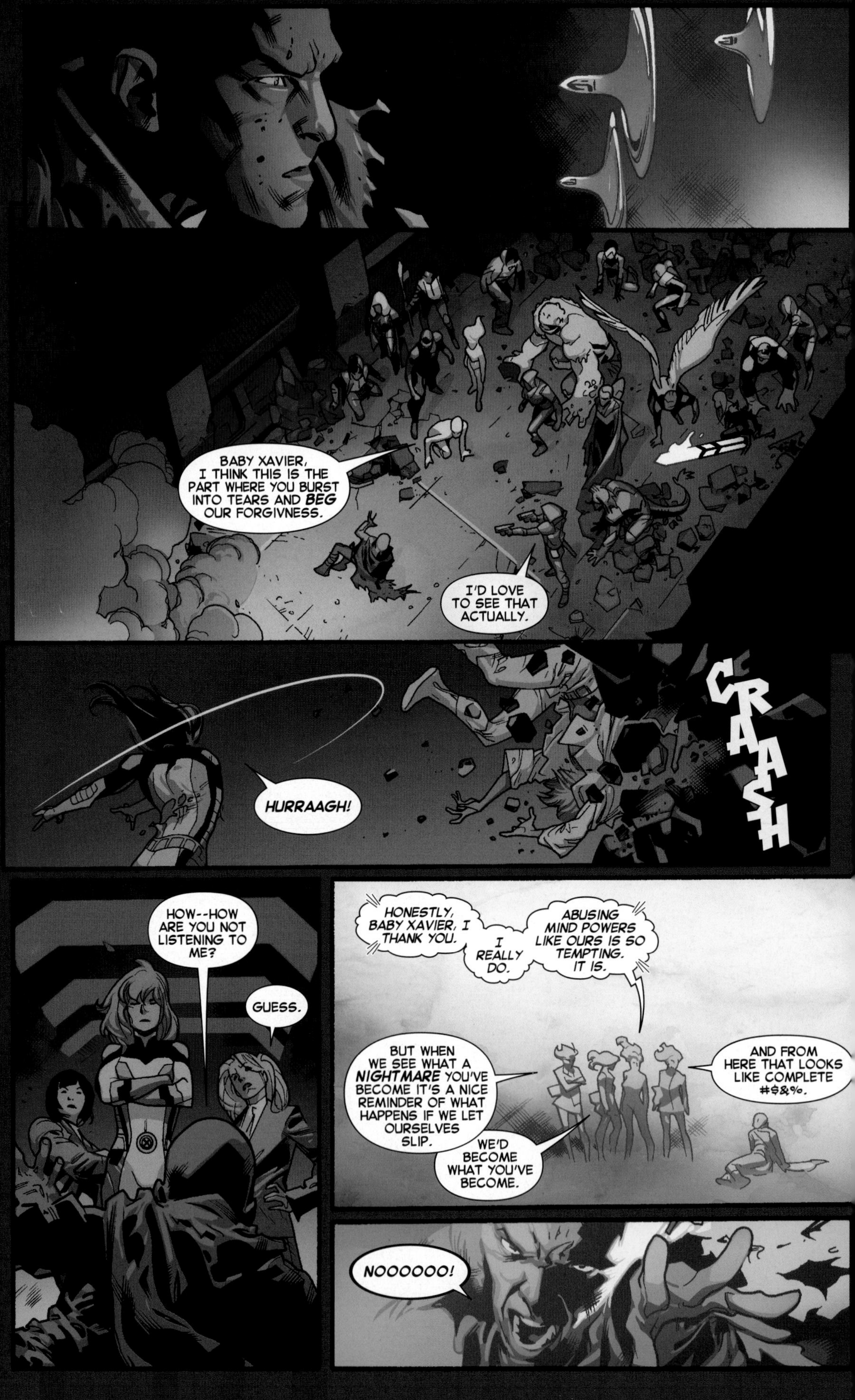
BABY XAVIER, I THINK THIS IS THE PART WHERE YOU BURST INTO TEARS AND BEG OUR FORGIVNESS.
I'D LOVE TO SEE THAT ACTUALLY.
HURRAAGH!
CRASH
HOW--HOW ARE YOU NOT LISTENING TO ME?
GUESS.
HONESTLY, BABY XAVIER, I THANK YOU.
I REALLY DO.
ABUSING MIND POWERS LIKE OURS IS SO TEMPTING. IT IS.
BUT WHEN WE SEE WHAT A NIGHTMARE YOU'VE BECOME IT'S A NICE REMINDER OF WHAT HAPPENS IF WE LET OURSELVES SLIP.
WE'D BECOME WHAT YOU'VE BECOME.
AND FROM HERE THAT LOOKS LIKE COMPLETE #$&%.
NOOOOOO!

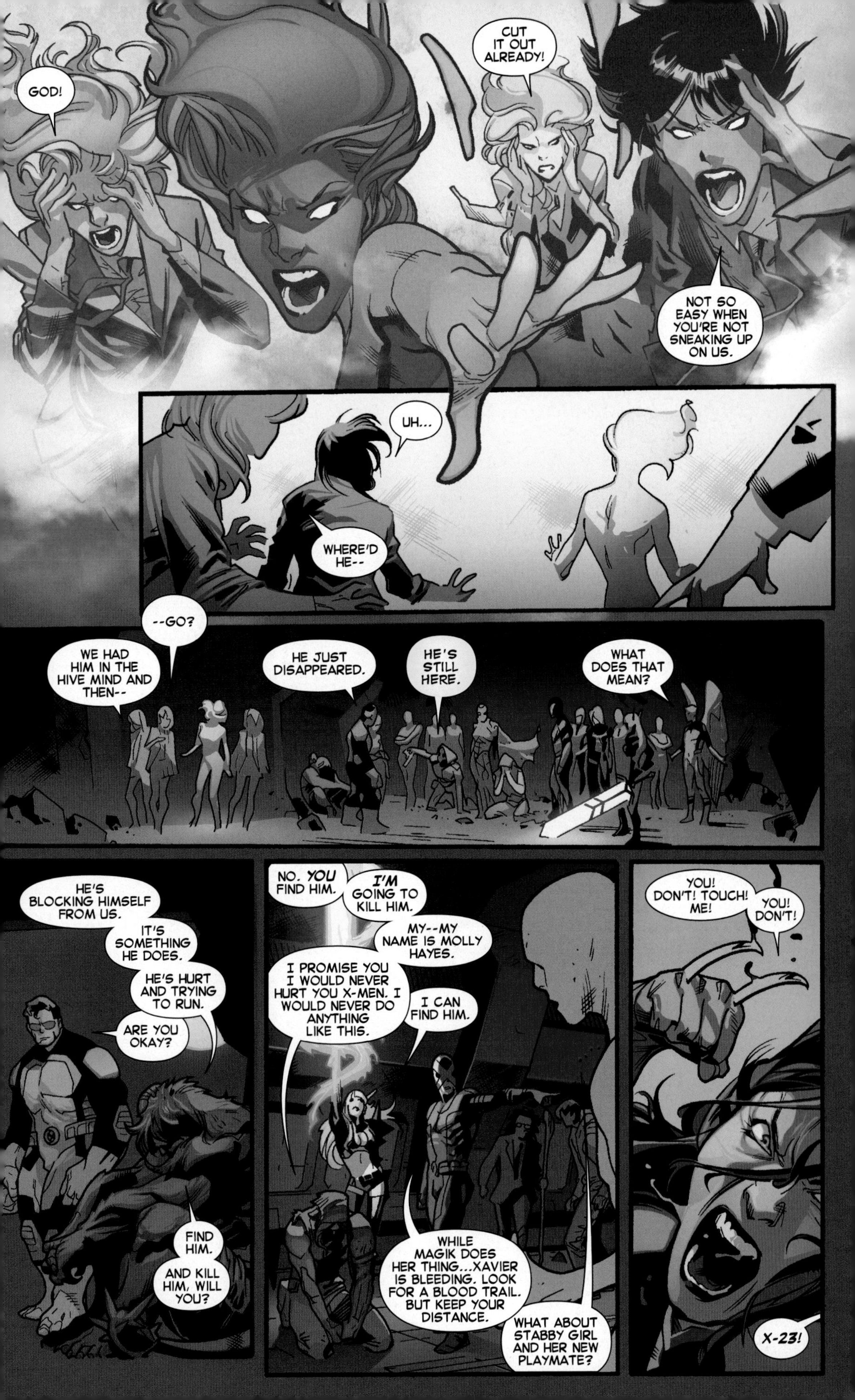
GOD!
CUT IT OUT ALREADY!
NOT SO EASY WHEN YOU'RE NOT SNEAKING UP ON US.
UH...
WHERE'D HE--
--GO?
WE HAD HIM IN THE HIVE MIND AND THEN--
HE JUST DISAPPEARED.
HE'S STILL HERE.
WHAT DOES THAT MEAN?
HE'S BLOCKING HIMSELF FROM US.
IT'S SOMETHING HE DOES.
HE'S HURT AND TRYING TO RUN.
ARE YOU OKAY?
FIND HIM.
AND KILL HIM, WILL YOU?
NO. YOU FIND HIM.
I'M GOING TO KILL HIM.
MY--MY NAME IS MOLLY HAYES.
I PROMISE YOU I WOULD NEVER HURT YOU X-MEN. I WOULD NEVER DO ANYTHING LIKE THIS.
I CAN FIND HIM.
WHILE MAGIK DOES HER THING...XAVIER IS BLEEDING. LOOK FOR A BLOOD TRAIL. BUT KEEP YOUR DISTANCE.
WHAT ABOUT STABBY GIRL AND HER NEW PLAYMATE?
YOU! DON'T! TOUCH! ME!
YOU! DON'T!
X-23!

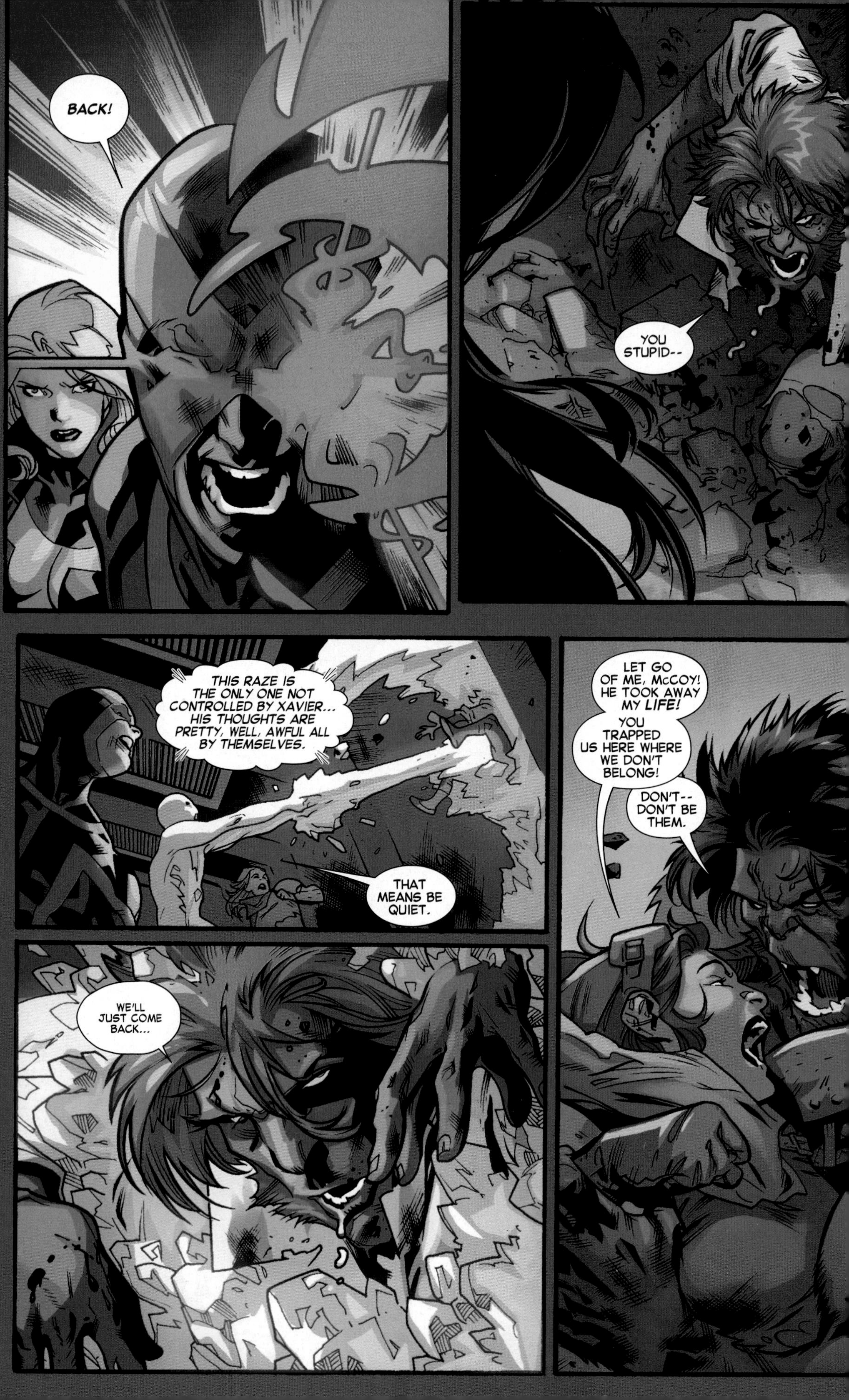
BACK!
YOU STUPID--
THIS RAZE IS THE ONLY ONE NOT CONTROLLED BY XAVIER... HIS THOUGHTS ARE PRETTY, WELL, AWFUL ALL BY THEMSELVES.
THAT MEANS BE QUIET.
LET GO OF ME, McCOY! HE TOOK AWAY MY LIFE!
YOU TRAPPED US HERE WHERE WE DON'T BELONG!
DON'T-- DON'T BE THEM.
WE'LL JUST COME BACK...

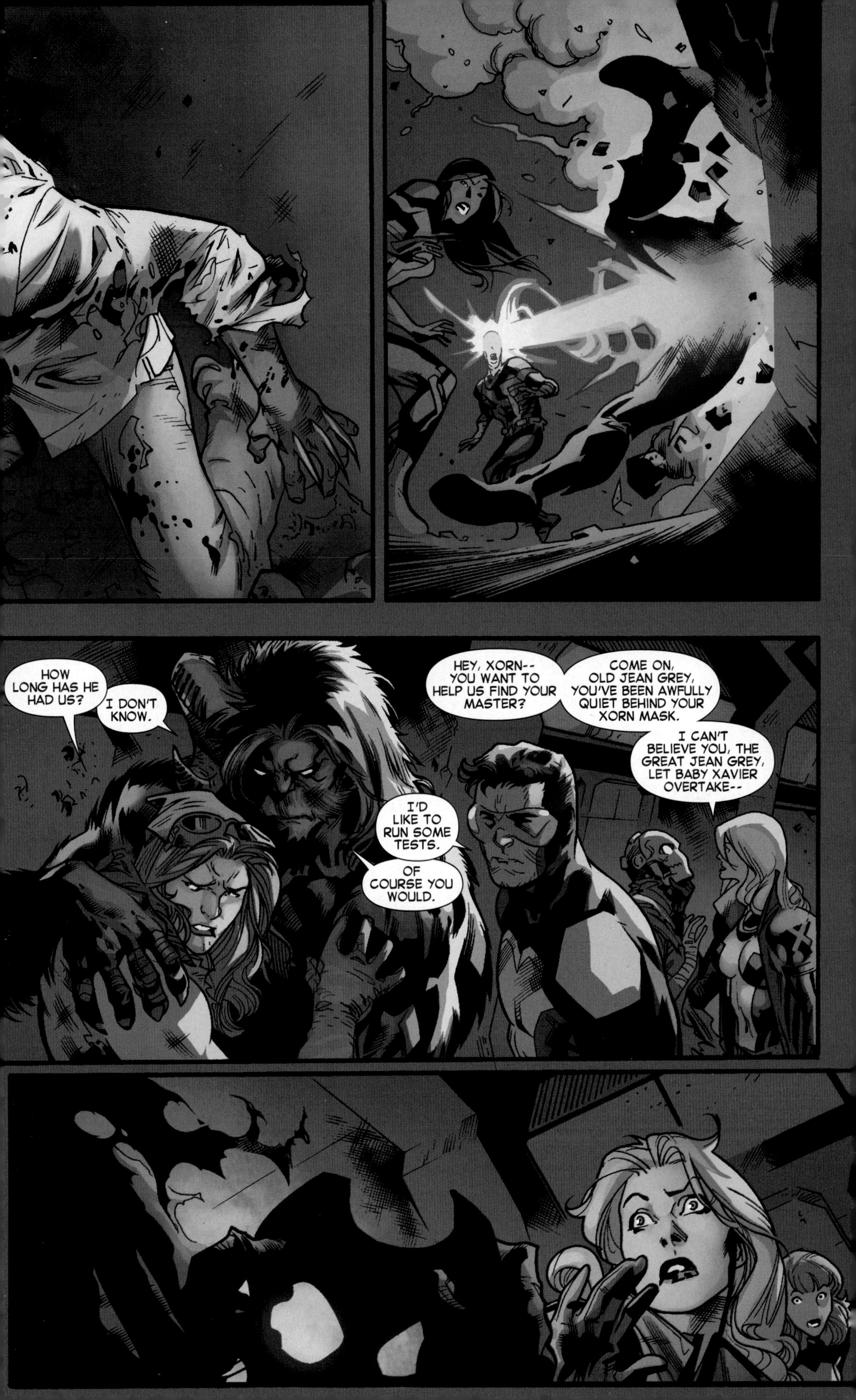
HOW LONG HAS HE HAD US?
I DON'T KNOW.
HEY, XORN-- YOU WANT TO HELP US FIND YOUR MASTER?
COME ON, OLD JEAN GREY, YOU'VE BEEN AWFULLY QUIET BEHIND YOUR XORN MASK.
I CAN'T BELIEVE YOU, THE GREAT JEAN GREY, LET BABY XAVIER OVERTAKE--
I'D LIKE TO RUN SOME TESTS.
OF COURSE YOU WOULD.

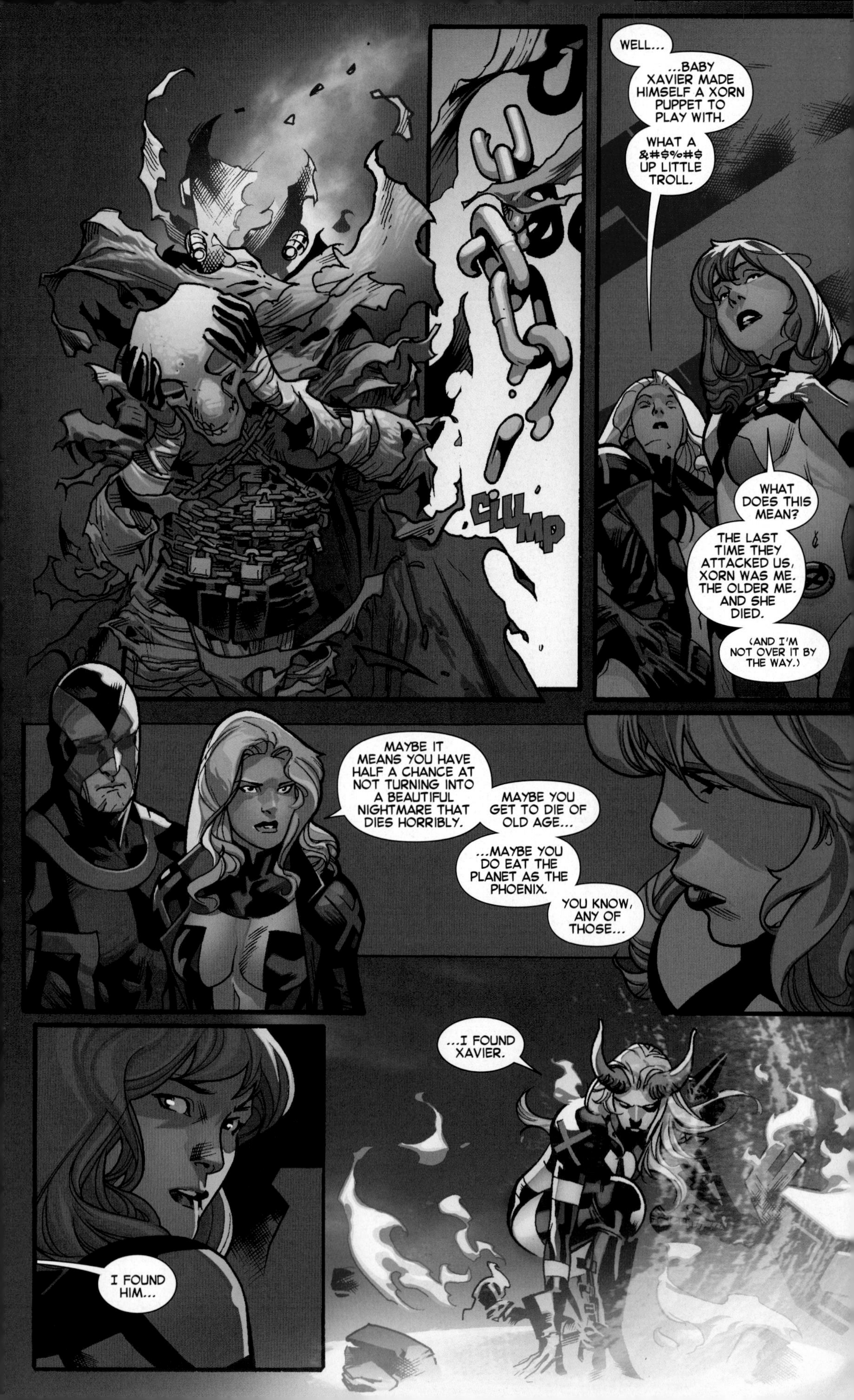
CLLUMP
WELL...
...BABY XAVIER MADE HIMSELF A XORN PUPPET TO PLAY WITH.
WHAT A &#$%#$ UP LITTLE TROLL.
WHAT DOES THIS MEAN?
THE LAST TIME THEY ATTACKED US, XORN WAS ME. THE OLDER ME. AND SHE DIED.
(AND I'M NOT OVER IT BY THE WAY.)
MAYBE IT MEANS YOU HAVE HALF A CHANCE AT NOT TURNING INTO A BEAUTIFUL NIGHTMARE THAT DIES HORRIBLY.
MAYBE YOU GET TO DIE OF OLD AGE...
...MAYBE YOU DO EAT THE PLANET AS THE PHOENIX.
YOU KNOW, ANY OF THOSE...
I FOUND HIM...
...I FOUND XAVIER.

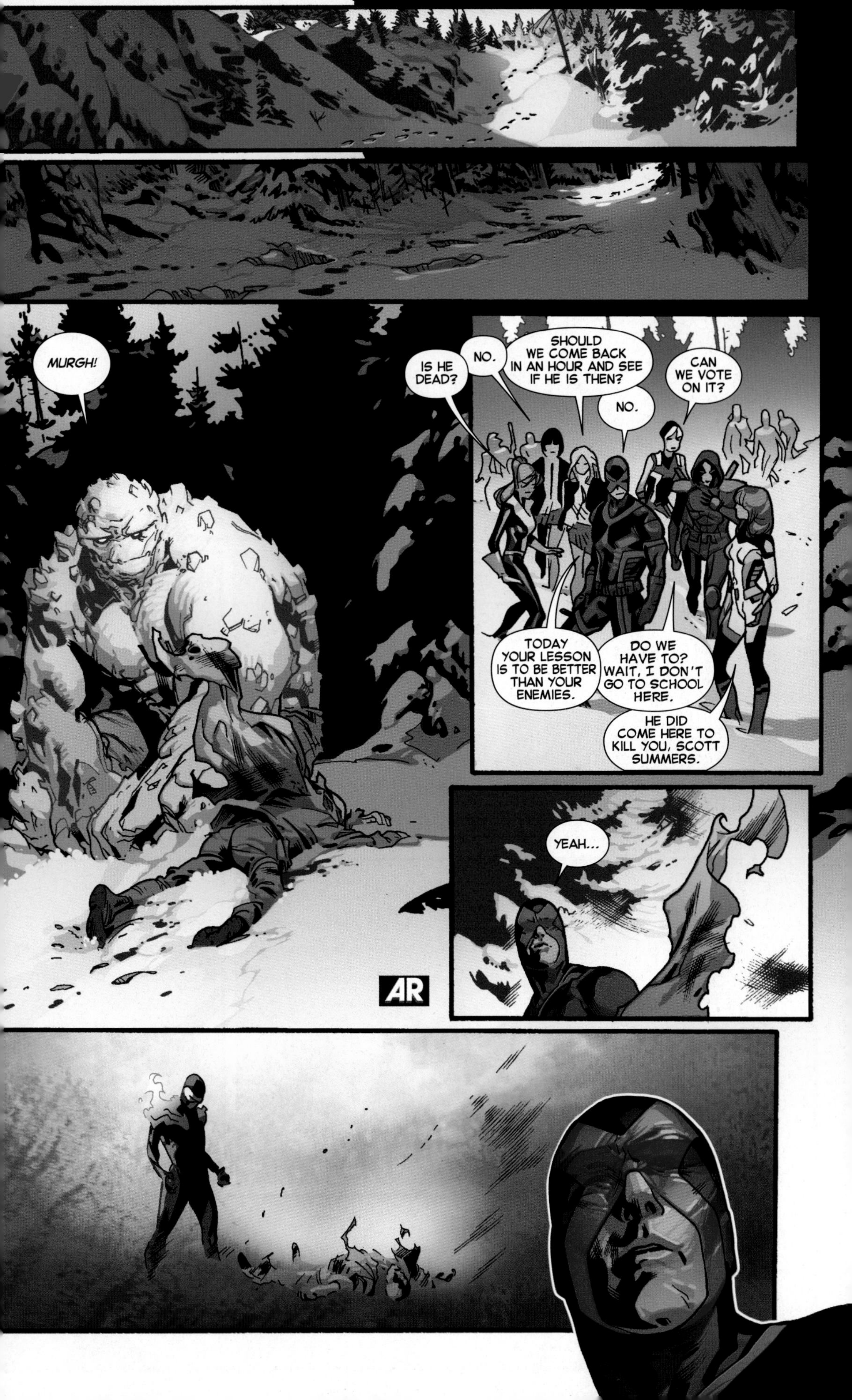
MURGH!
IS HE DEAD?
NO.
SHOULD WE COME BACK IN AN HOUR AND SEE IF HE IS THEN?
NO.
CAN WE VOTE ON IT?
TODAY YOUR LESSON IS TO BE BETTER THAN YOUR ENEMIES.
DO WE HAVE TO? WAIT, I DON'T GO TO SCHOOL HERE.
HE DID COME HERE TO KILL YOU, SCOTT SUMMERS.
YEAH...
AR

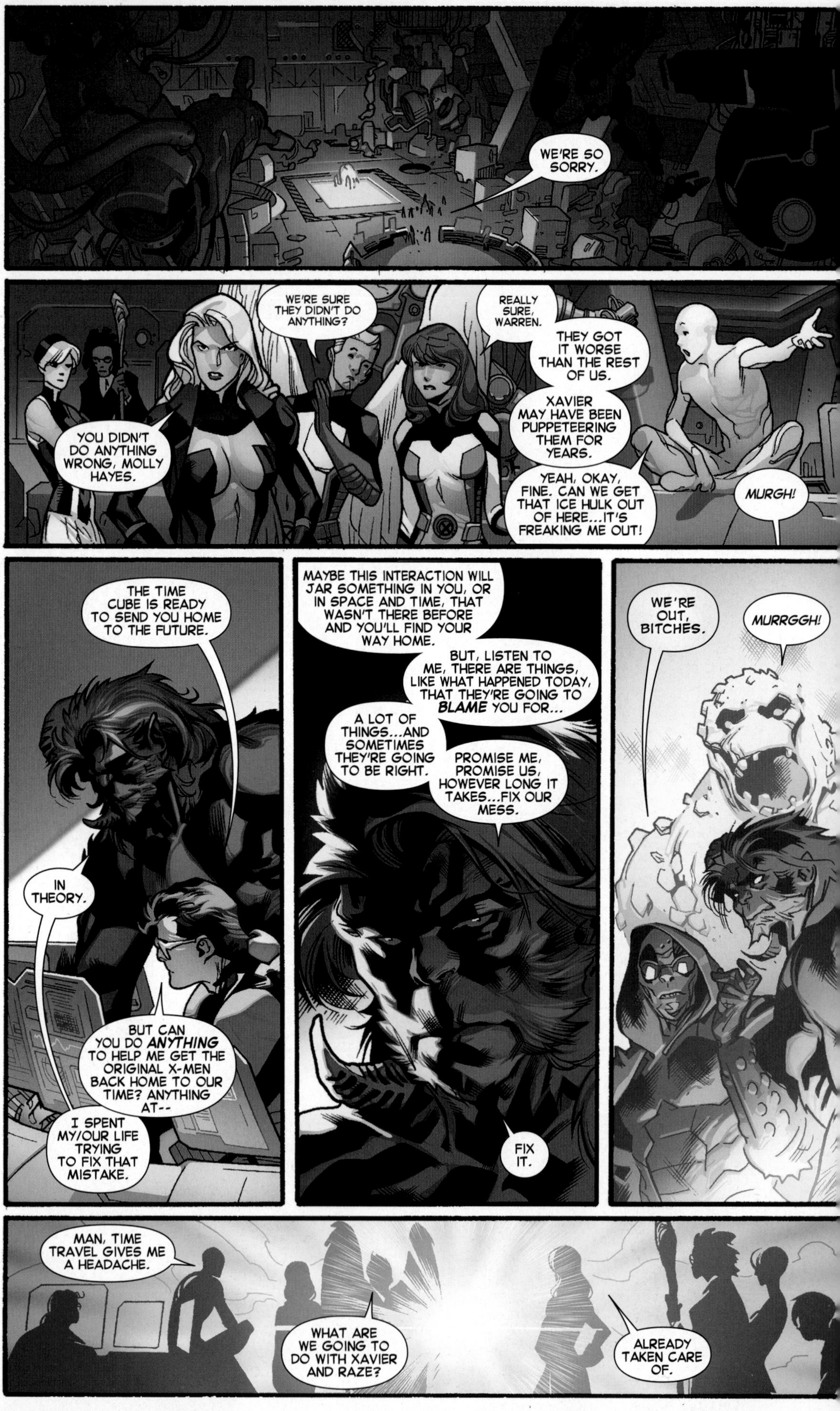
WE'RE SO SORRY.
WE'RE SURE THEY DIDN'T DO ANYTHING?
REALLY SURE, WARREN.
YOU DIDN'T DO ANYTHING WRONG, MOLLY HAYES.
THEY GOT IT WORSE THAN THE REST OF US.
XAVIER MAY HAVE BEEN PUPPETEERING THEM FOR YEARS.
YEAH, OKAY, FINE. CAN WE GET THAT ICE HULK OUT OF HERE...IT'S FREAKING ME OUT!
MURGH!
THE TIME CUBE IS READY TO SEND YOU HOME TO THE FUTURE.
IN THEORY.
BUT CAN YOU DO ANYTHING TO HELP ME GET THE ORIGINAL X-MEN BACK HOME TO OUR TIME? ANYTHING AT--
I SPENT MY/OUR LIFE TRYING TO FIX THAT MISTAKE.
MAYBE THIS INTERACTION WILL JAR SOMETHING IN YOU, OR IN SPACE AND TIME, THAT WASN'T THERE BEFORE AND YOU'LL FIND YOUR WAY HOME.
BUT, LISTEN TO ME, THERE ARE THINGS, LIKE WHAT HAPPENED TODAY, THAT THEY'RE GOING TO BLAME YOU FOR...
A LOT OF THINGS...AND SOMETIMES THEY'RE GOING TO BE RIGHT.
PROMISE ME, PROMISE US, HOWEVER LONG IT TAKES...FIX OUR MESS.
FIX IT.
WE'RE OUT, BITCHES.
MURRGGH!
MAN, TIME TRAVEL GIVES ME A HEADACHE.
WHAT ARE WE GOING TO DO WITH XAVIER AND RAZE?
ALREADY TAKEN CARE OF.

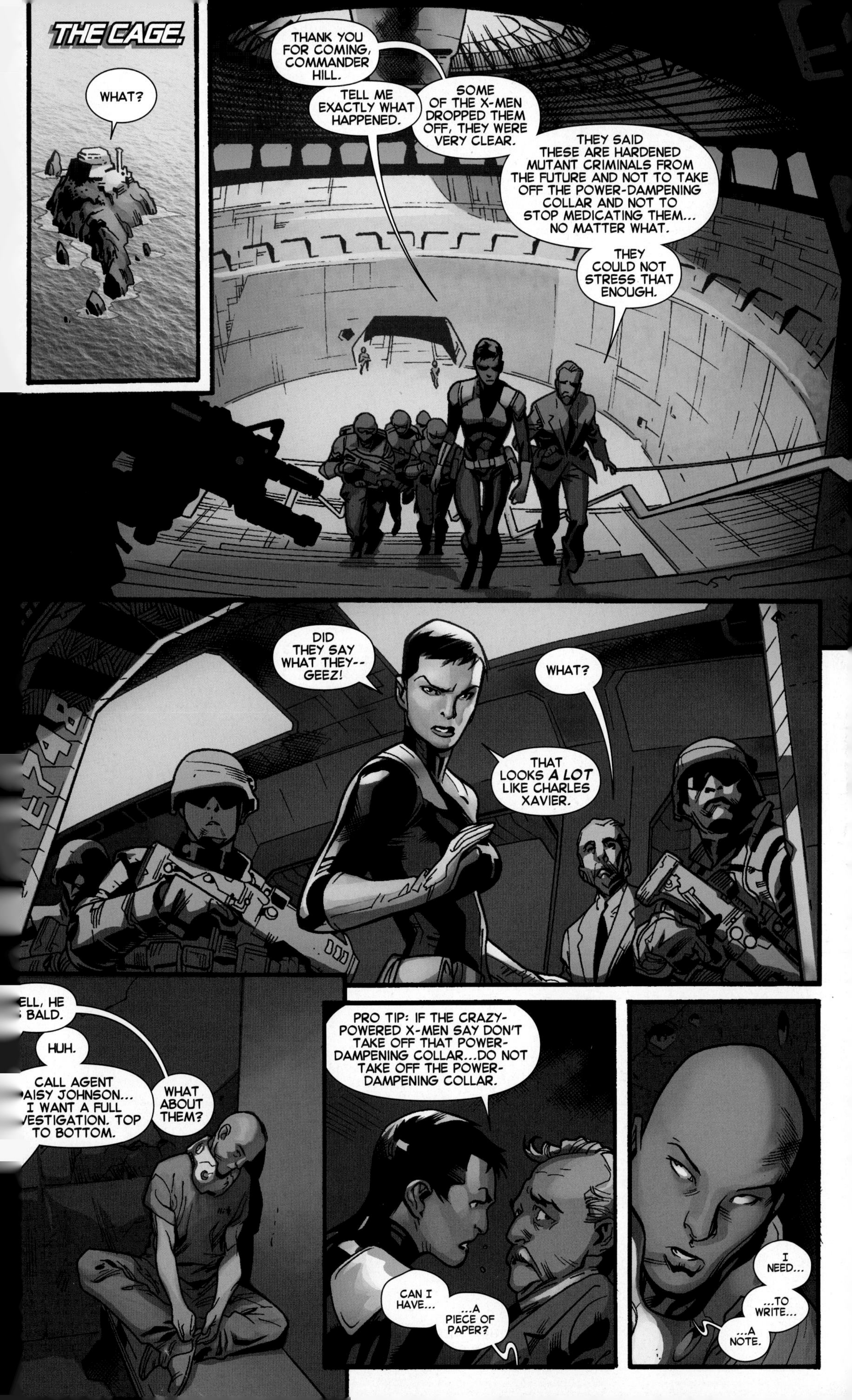
THE CAGE.
WHAT?
THANK YOU FOR COMING, COMMANDER HILL.
TELL ME EXACTLY WHAT HAPPENED.
SOME OF THE X-MEN DROPPED THEM OFF, THEY WERE VERY CLEAR.
THEY SAID THESE ARE HARDENED MUTANT CRIMINALS FROM THE FUTURE AND NOT TO TAKE OFF THE POWER-DAMPENING COLLAR AND NOT TO STOP MEDICATING THEM... NO MATTER WHAT.
THEY COULD NOT STRESS THAT ENOUGH.
DID THEY SAY WHAT THEY-- GEEZ!
WHAT?
THAT LOOKS A LOT LIKE CHARLES XAVIER.
ELL, HE BALD.
HUH.
CALL AGENT AISY JOHNSON... I WANT A FULL VESTIGATION. TOP TO BOTTOM.
WHAT ABOUT THEM?
PRO TIP: IF THE CRAZY-POWERED X-MEN SAY DON'T TAKE OFF THAT POWER-DAMPENING COLLAR...DO NOT TAKE OFF THE POWER-DAMPENING COLLAR.
CAN I HAVE...
...A PIECE OF PAPER?
I NEED...
...TO WRITE...
...A NOTE.

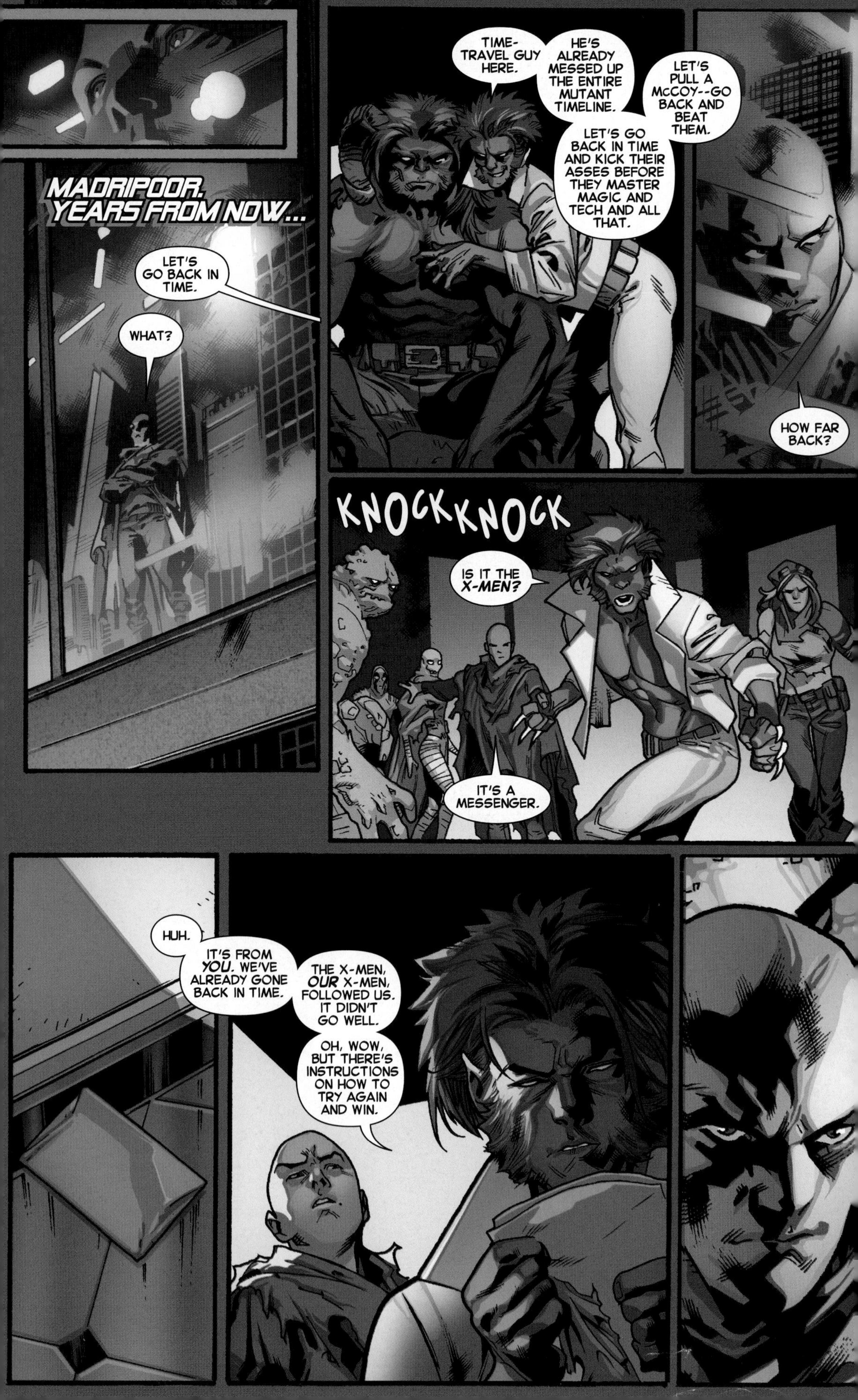
MADRIPOOR. YEARS FROM NOW...
LET'S GO BACK IN TIME.
WHAT?
TIME-TRAVEL GUY HERE.
HE'S ALREADY MESSED UP THE ENTIRE MUTANT TIMELINE.
LET'S GO BACK IN TIME AND KICK THEIR ASSES BEFORE THEY MASTER MAGIC AND TECH AND ALL THAT.
LET'S PULL A McCOY--GO BACK AND BEAT THEM.
HOW FAR BACK?
KNOCK KNOCK
IS IT THE X-MEN?
IT'S A MESSENGER.
HUH.
IT'S FROM YOU. WE'VE ALREADY GONE BACK IN TIME.
THE X-MEN, OUR X-MEN, FOLLOWED US. IT DIDN'T GO WELL.
OH, WOW, BUT THERE'S INSTRUCTIONS ON HOW TO TRY AGAIN AND WIN.

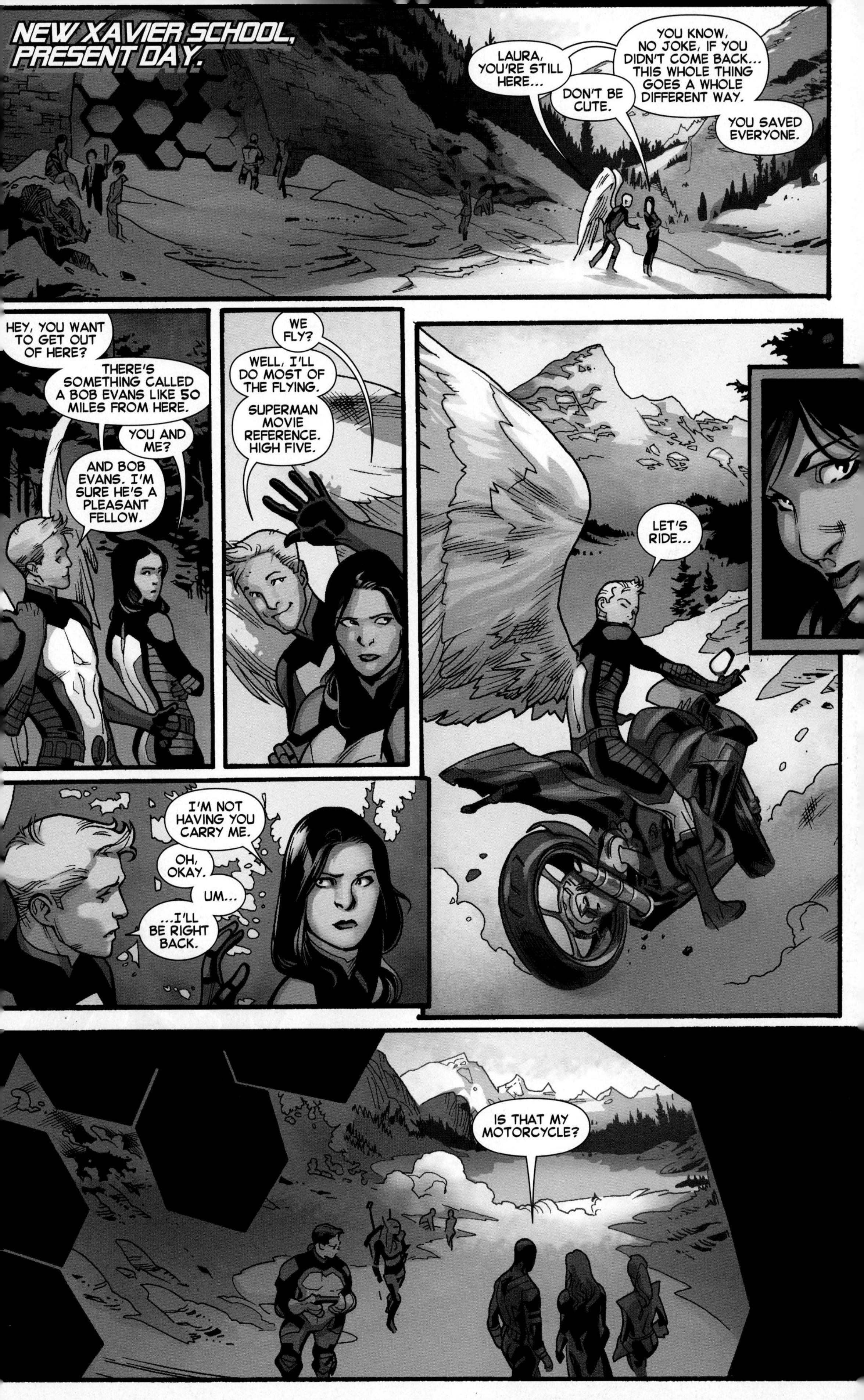
NEW XAVIER SCHOOL, PRESENT DAY.
LAURA, YOU'RE STILL HERE...
DON'T BE CUTE.
YOU KNOW, NO JOKE, IF YOU DIDN'T COME BACK... THIS WHOLE THING GOES A WHOLE DIFFERENT WAY.
YOU SAVED EVERYONE.
HEY, YOU WANT TO GET OUT OF HERE?
THERE'S SOMETHING CALLED A BOB EVANS LIKE 50 MILES FROM HERE.
YOU AND ME?
AND BOB EVANS. I'M SURE HE'S A PLEASANT FELLOW.
WE FLY?
WELL, I'LL DO MOST OF THE FLYING.
SUPERMAN MOVIE REFERENCE. HIGH FIVE.
I'M NOT HAVING YOU CARRY ME.
OH, OKAY.
UM...
...I'LL BE RIGHT BACK.
LET'S RIDE...
IS THAT MY MOTORCYCLE?

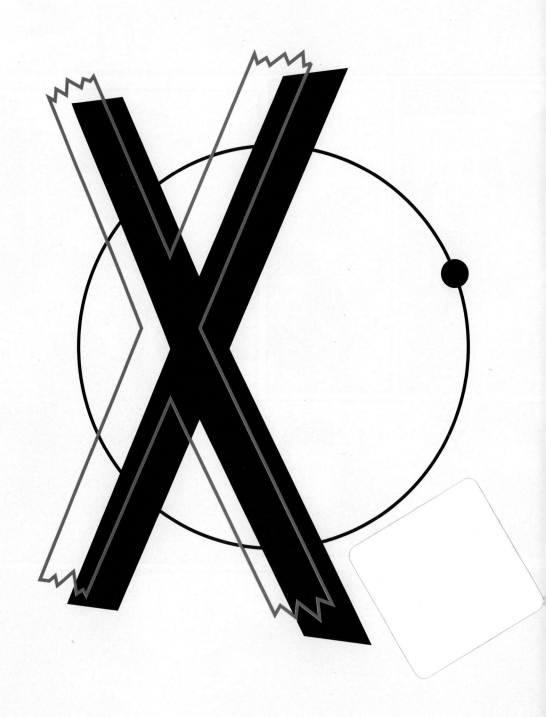

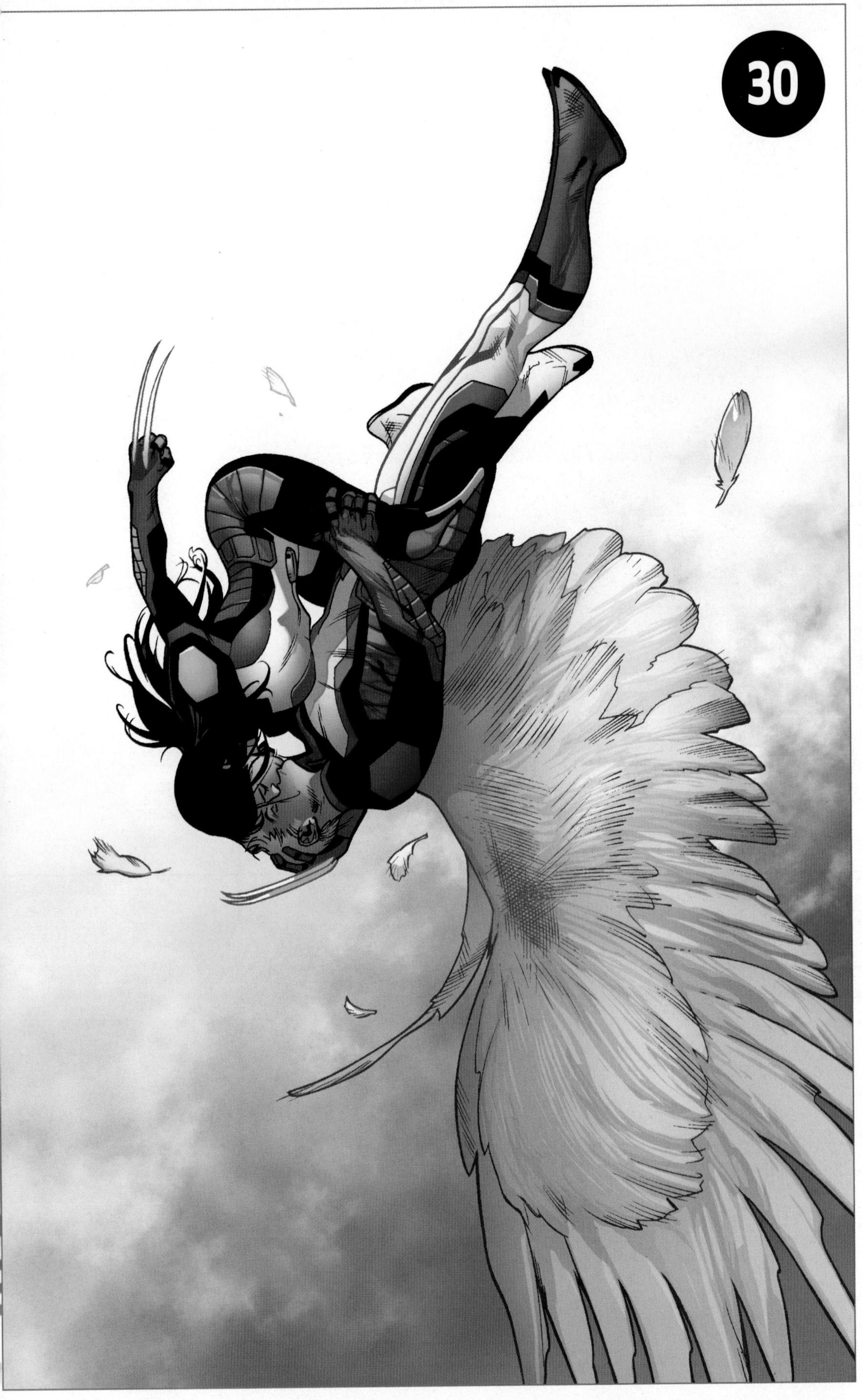
30

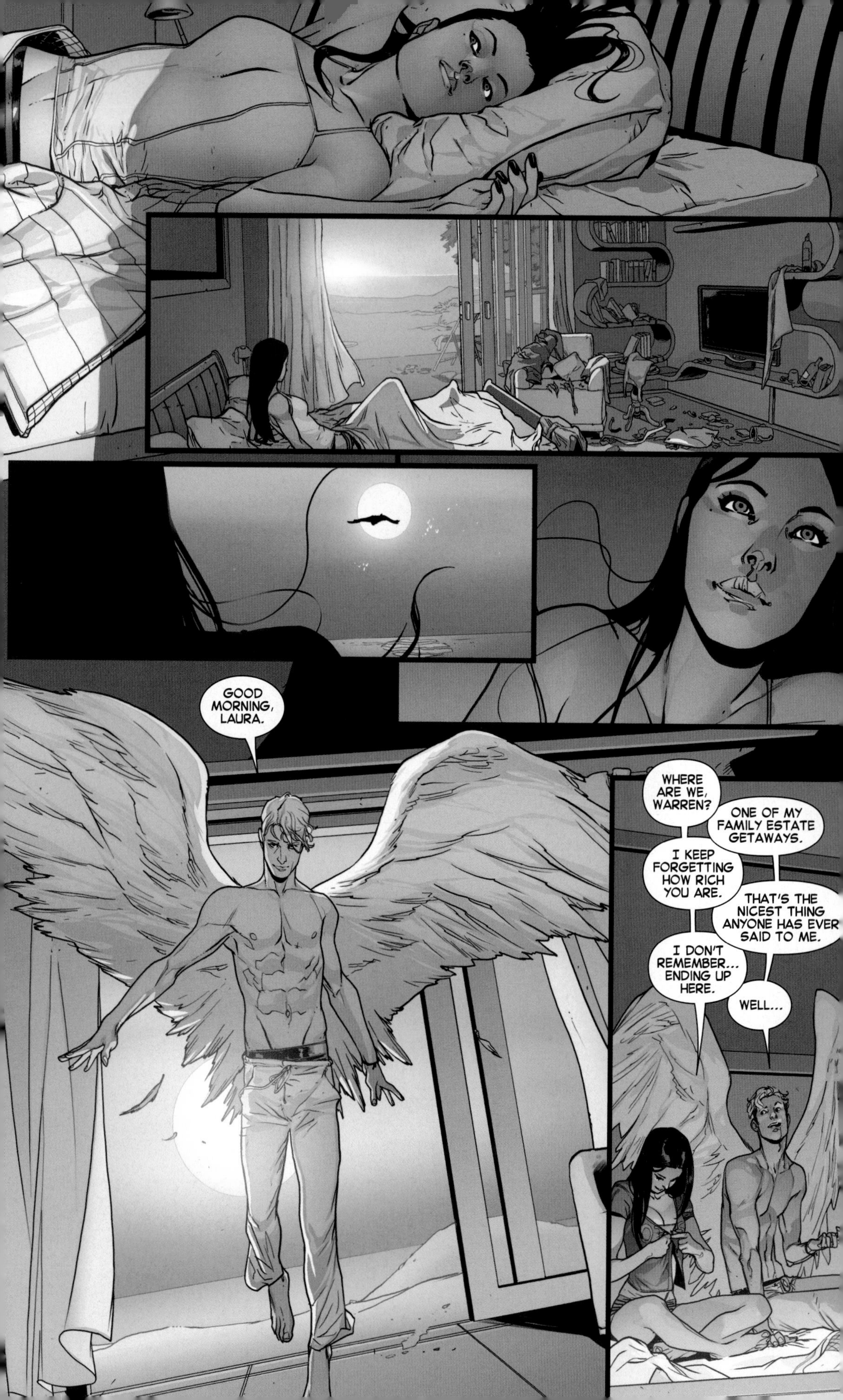

GOOD MORNING, LAURA.
WHERE ARE WE, WARREN?
ONE OF MY FAMILY ESTATE GETAWAYS.
I KEEP FORGETTING HOW RICH YOU ARE.
THAT'S THE NICEST THING ANYONE HAS EVER SAID TO ME.
I DON'T REMEMBER... ENDING UP HERE.
WELL...

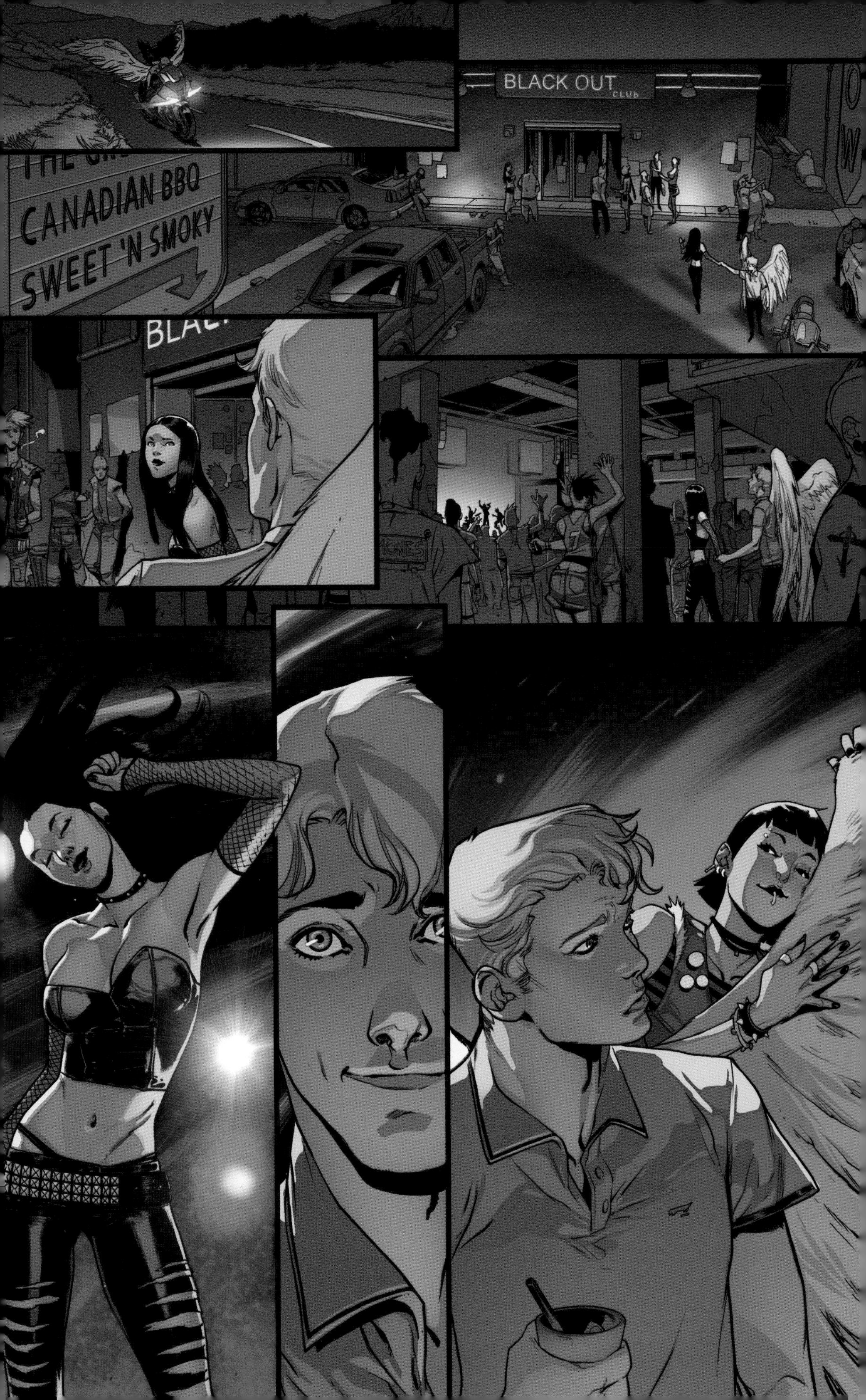
BLACK OUT
CLUB
CANADIAN BBQ
SWEET 'N SMOKY

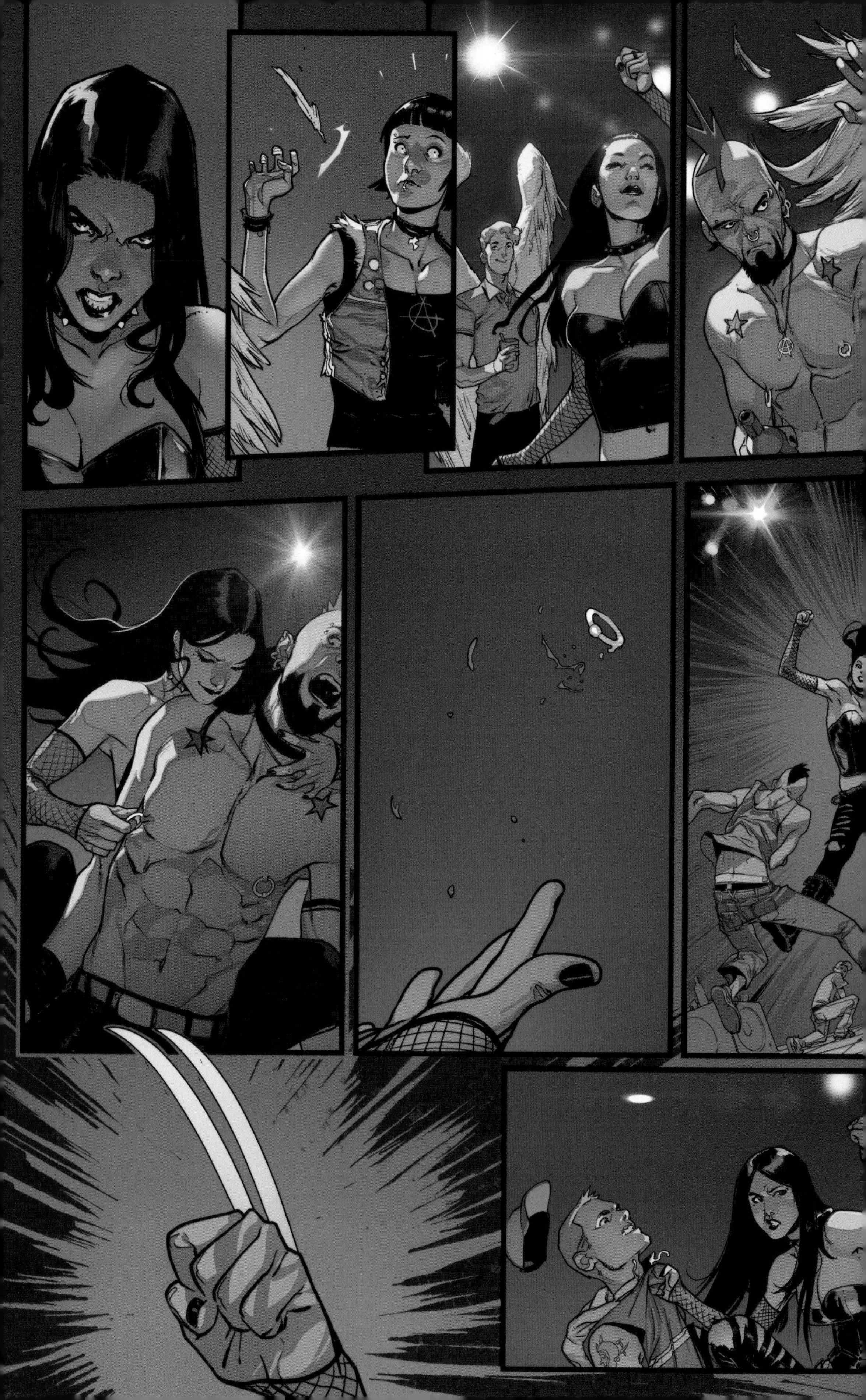

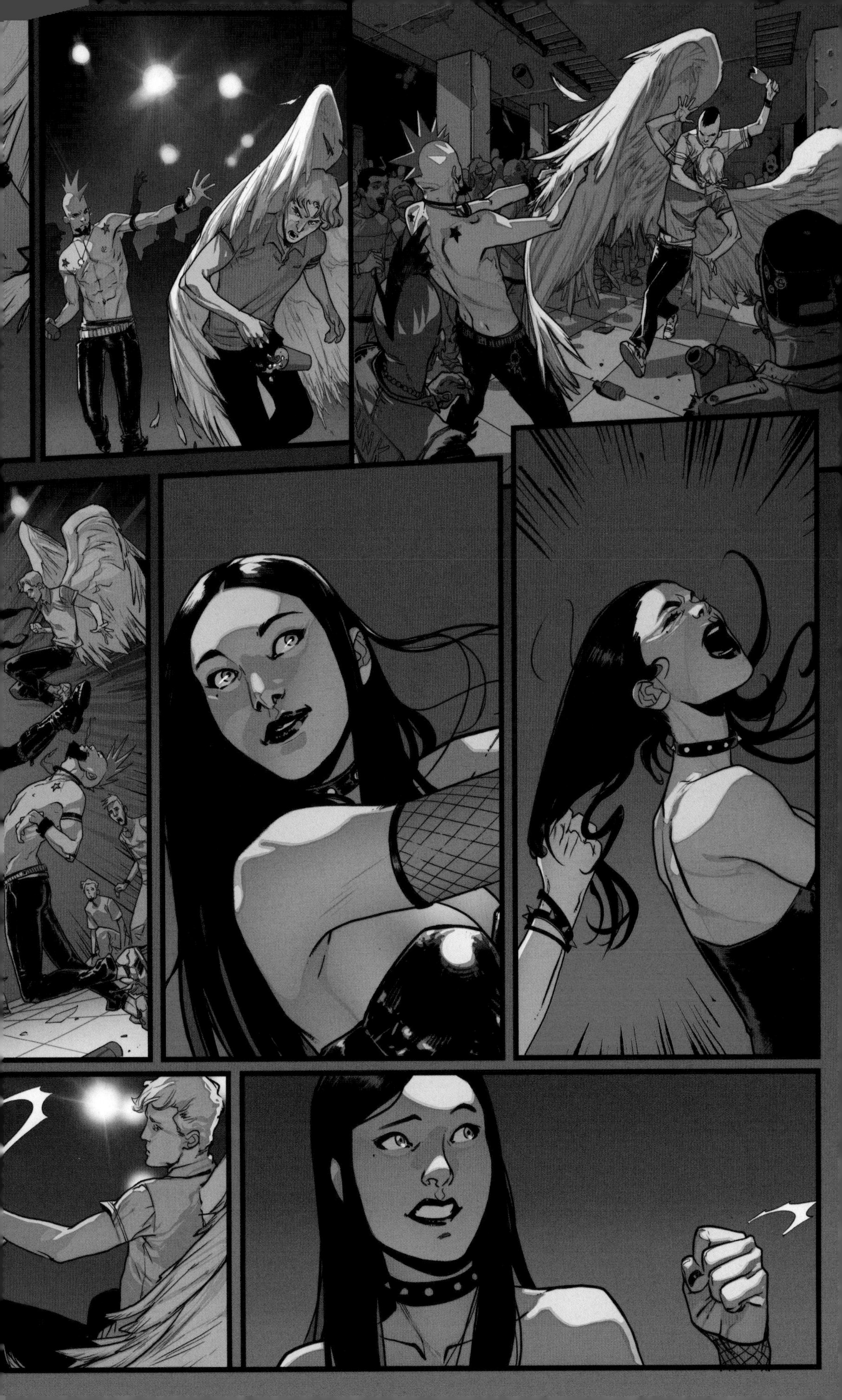

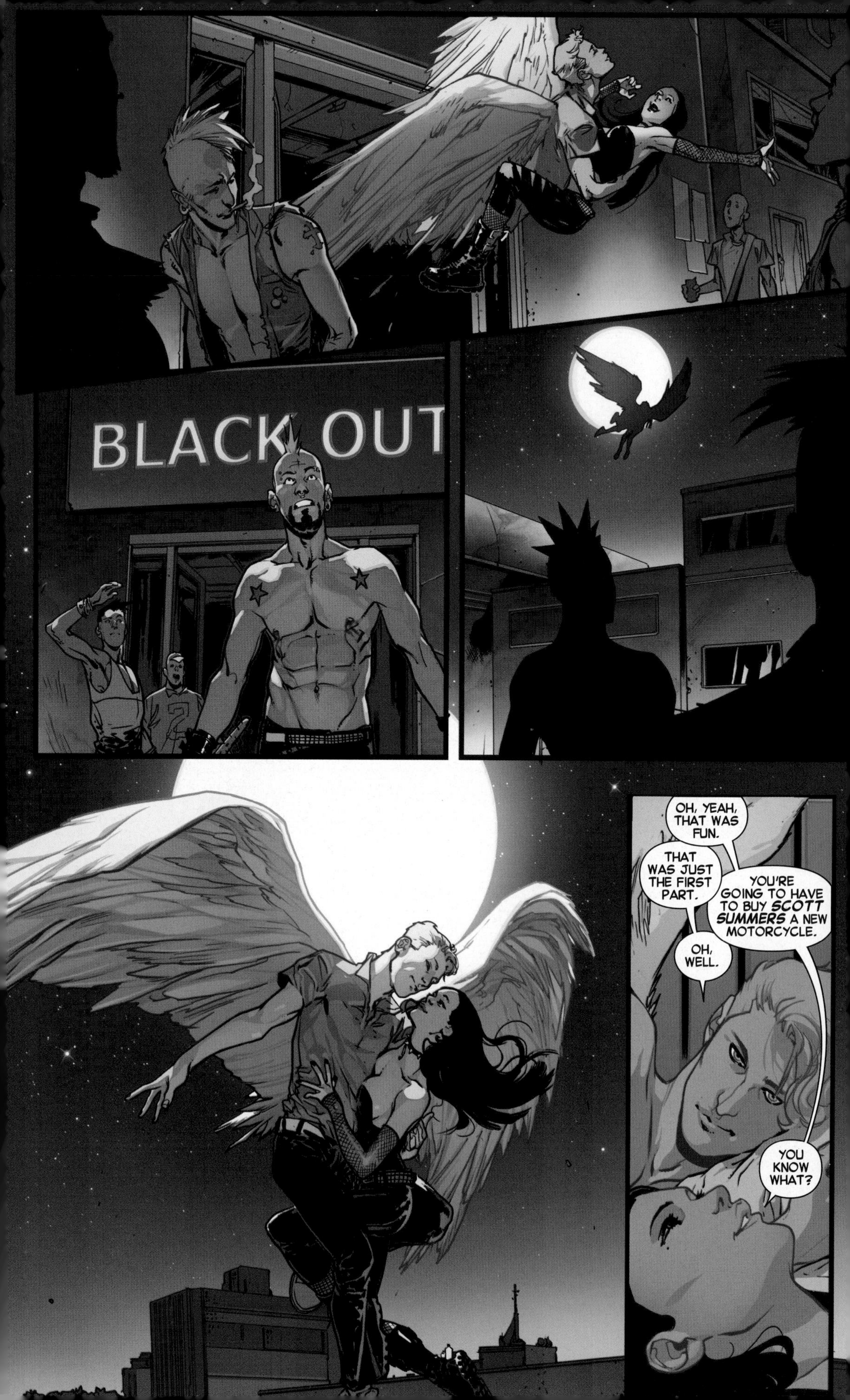
BLACK OUT
OH, YEAH, THAT WAS FUN.
THAT WAS JUST THE FIRST PART.
YOU'RE GOING TO HAVE TO BUY *SCOTT SUMMERS* A NEW MOTORCYCLE.
OH, WELL.
YOU KNOW WHAT?

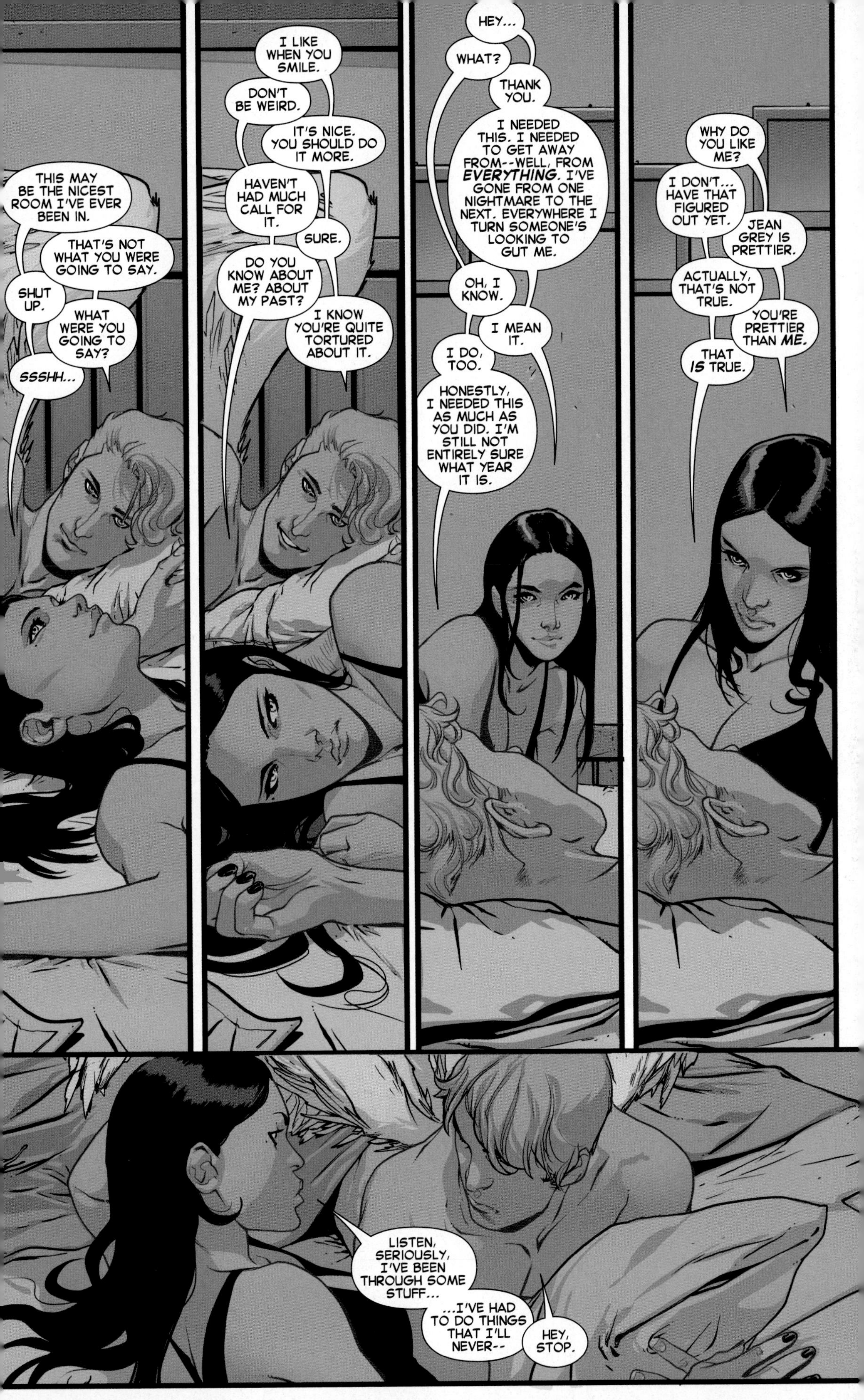
THIS MAY BE THE NICEST ROOM I'VE EVER BEEN IN.
THAT'S NOT WHAT YOU WERE GOING TO SAY.
SHUT UP.
WHAT WERE YOU GOING TO SAY?
SSSHH...
I LIKE WHEN YOU SMILE.
DON'T BE WEIRD.
IT'S NICE. YOU SHOULD DO IT MORE.
HAVEN'T HAD MUCH CALL FOR IT.
SURE.
DO YOU KNOW ABOUT ME? ABOUT MY PAST?
I KNOW YOU'RE QUITE TORTURED ABOUT IT.
HEY...
WHAT?
THANK YOU.
I NEEDED THIS. I NEEDED TO GET AWAY FROM--WELL, FROM *EVERYTHING*. I'VE GONE FROM ONE NIGHTMARE TO THE NEXT. EVERYWHERE I TURN SOMEONE'S LOOKING TO GUT ME.
OH, I KNOW.
I MEAN IT.
I DO, TOO.
HONESTLY, I NEEDED THIS AS MUCH AS YOU DID. I'M STILL NOT ENTIRELY SURE WHAT YEAR IT IS.
WHY DO YOU LIKE ME?
I DON'T... HAVE THAT FIGURED OUT YET.
JEAN GREY IS PRETTIER.
ACTUALLY, THAT'S NOT TRUE.
YOU'RE PRETTIER THAN *ME.*
THAT *IS* TRUE.
LISTEN, SERIOUSLY, I'VE BEEN THROUGH SOME STUFF...
...I'VE HAD TO DO THINGS THAT I'LL NEVER--
HEY, STOP.

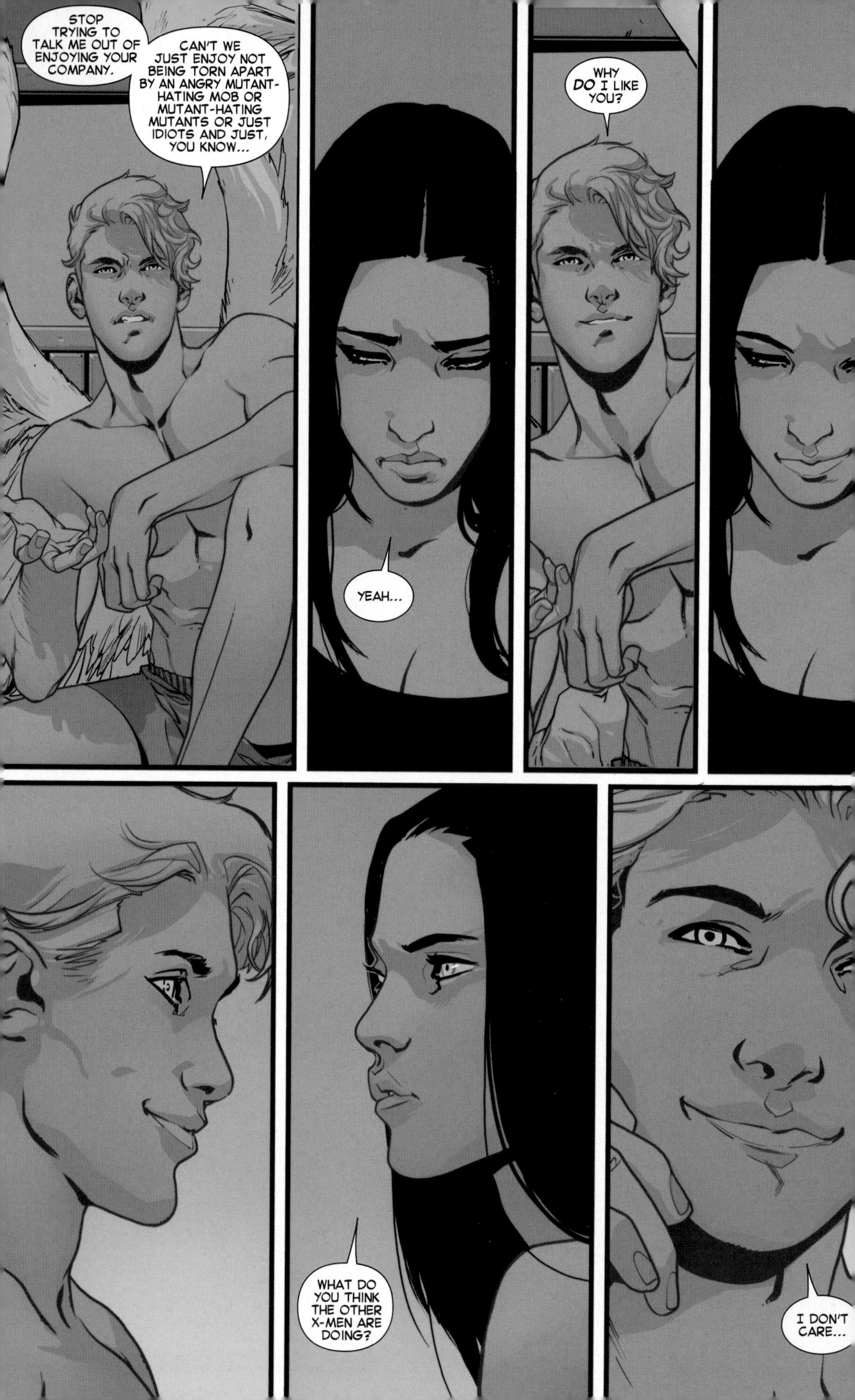
STOP TRYING TO TALK ME OUT OF ENJOYING YOUR COMPANY.
CAN'T WE JUST ENJOY NOT BEING TORN APART BY AN ANGRY MUTANT-HATING MOB OR MUTANT-HATING MUTANTS OR JUST IDIOTS AND JUST, YOU KNOW...
YEAH...
WHY DO I LIKE YOU?
WHAT DO YOU THINK THE OTHER X-MEN ARE DOING?
I DON'T CARE...

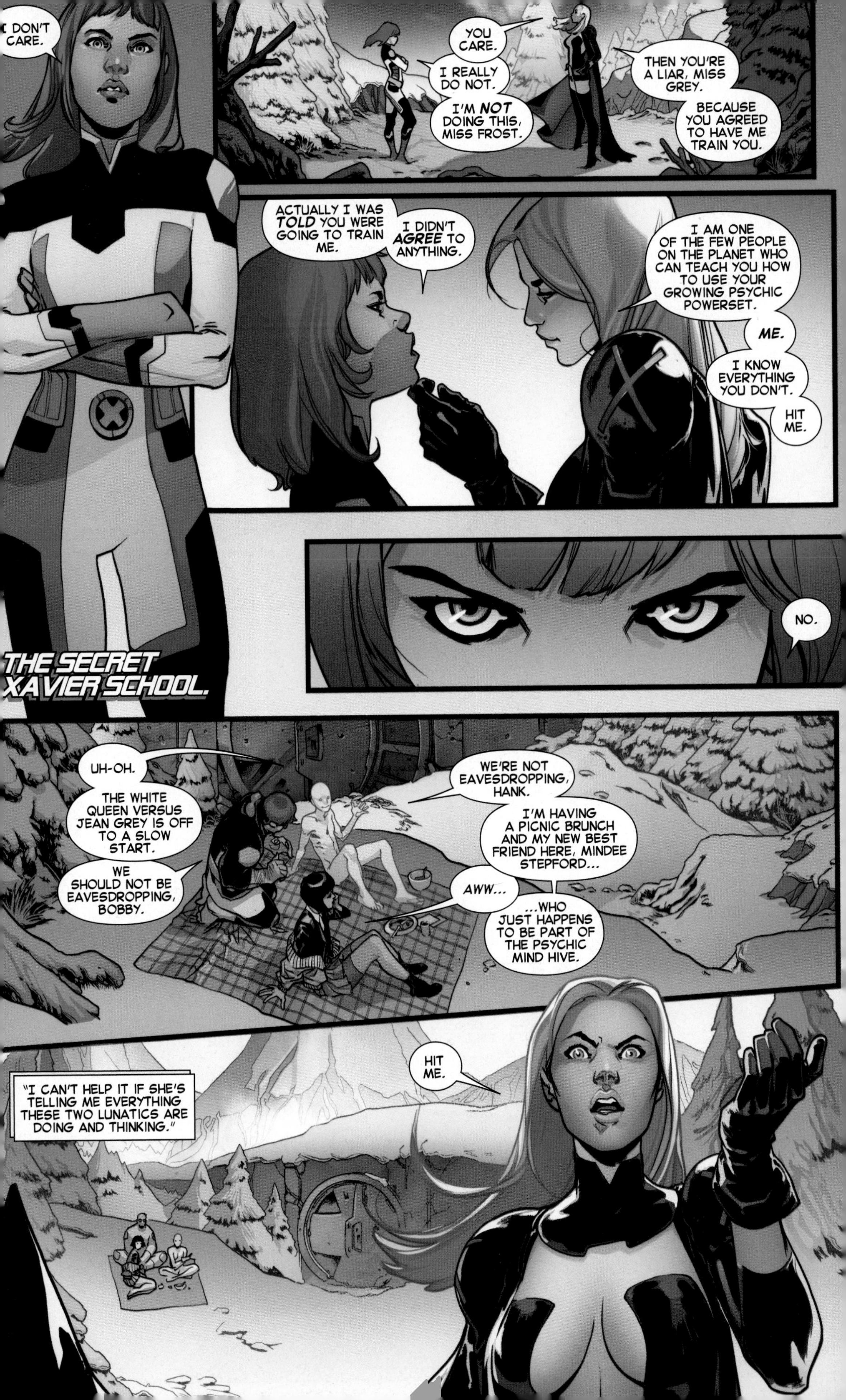
I DON'T CARE.
YOU CARE.
I REALLY DO NOT.
I'M NOT DOING THIS, MISS FROST.
THEN YOU'RE A LIAR, MISS GREY.
BECAUSE YOU AGREED TO HAVE ME TRAIN YOU.
ACTUALLY I WAS TOLD YOU WERE GOING TO TRAIN ME.
I DIDN'T AGREE TO ANYTHING.
I AM ONE OF THE FEW PEOPLE ON THE PLANET WHO CAN TEACH YOU HOW TO USE YOUR GROWING PSYCHIC POWERSET.
ME.
I KNOW EVERYTHING YOU DON'T.
HIT ME.
NO.
THE SECRET XAVIER SCHOOL.
UH-OH.
THE WHITE QUEEN VERSUS JEAN GREY IS OFF TO A SLOW START.
WE SHOULD NOT BE EAVESDROPPING, BOBBY.
WE'RE NOT EAVESDROPPING, HANK.
I'M HAVING A PICNIC BRUNCH AND MY NEW BEST FRIEND HERE, MINDEE STEPFORD...
AWW...
...WHO JUST HAPPENS TO BE PART OF THE PSYCHIC MIND HIVE.
"I CAN'T HELP IT IF SHE'S TELLING ME EVERYTHING THESE TWO LUNATICS ARE DOING AND THINKING."
HIT ME.

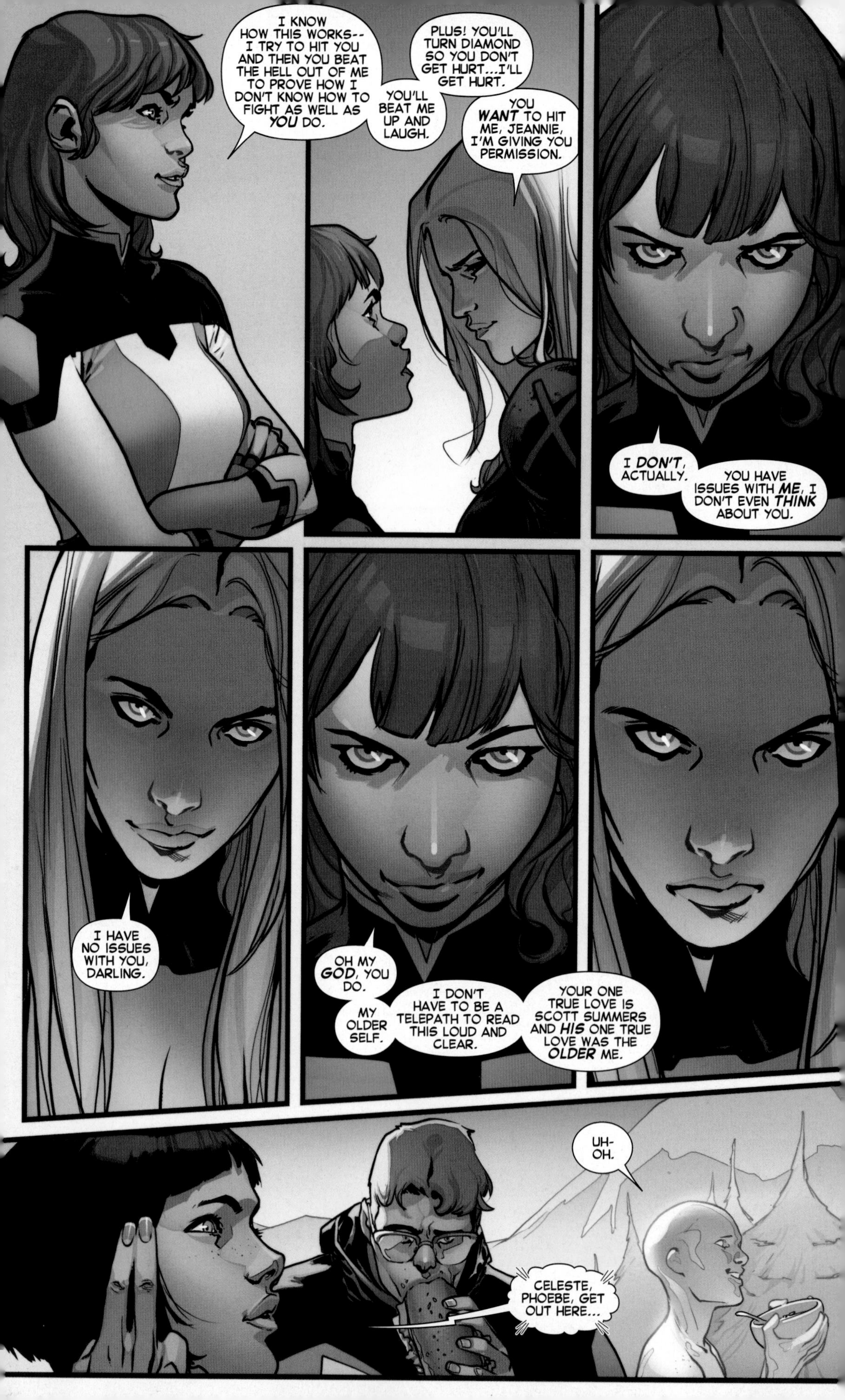
I KNOW HOW THIS WORKS-- I TRY TO HIT YOU AND THEN YOU BEAT THE HELL OUT OF ME TO PROVE HOW I DON'T KNOW HOW TO FIGHT AS WELL AS YOU DO.
YOU'LL BEAT ME UP AND LAUGH.
PLUS! YOU'LL TURN DIAMOND SO YOU DON'T GET HURT...I'LL GET HURT.
YOU WANT TO HIT ME, JEANNIE, I'M GIVING YOU PERMISSION.
I DON'T, ACTUALLY.
YOU HAVE ISSUES WITH ME, I DON'T EVEN THINK ABOUT YOU.
I HAVE NO ISSUES WITH YOU, DARLING.
OH MY GOD, YOU DO.
MY OLDER SELF.
I DON'T HAVE TO BE A TELEPATH TO READ THIS LOUD AND CLEAR.
YOUR ONE TRUE LOVE IS SCOTT SUMMERS AND HIS ONE TRUE LOVE WAS THE OLDER ME.
UH-OH.
CELESTE, PHOEBE, GET OUT HERE...

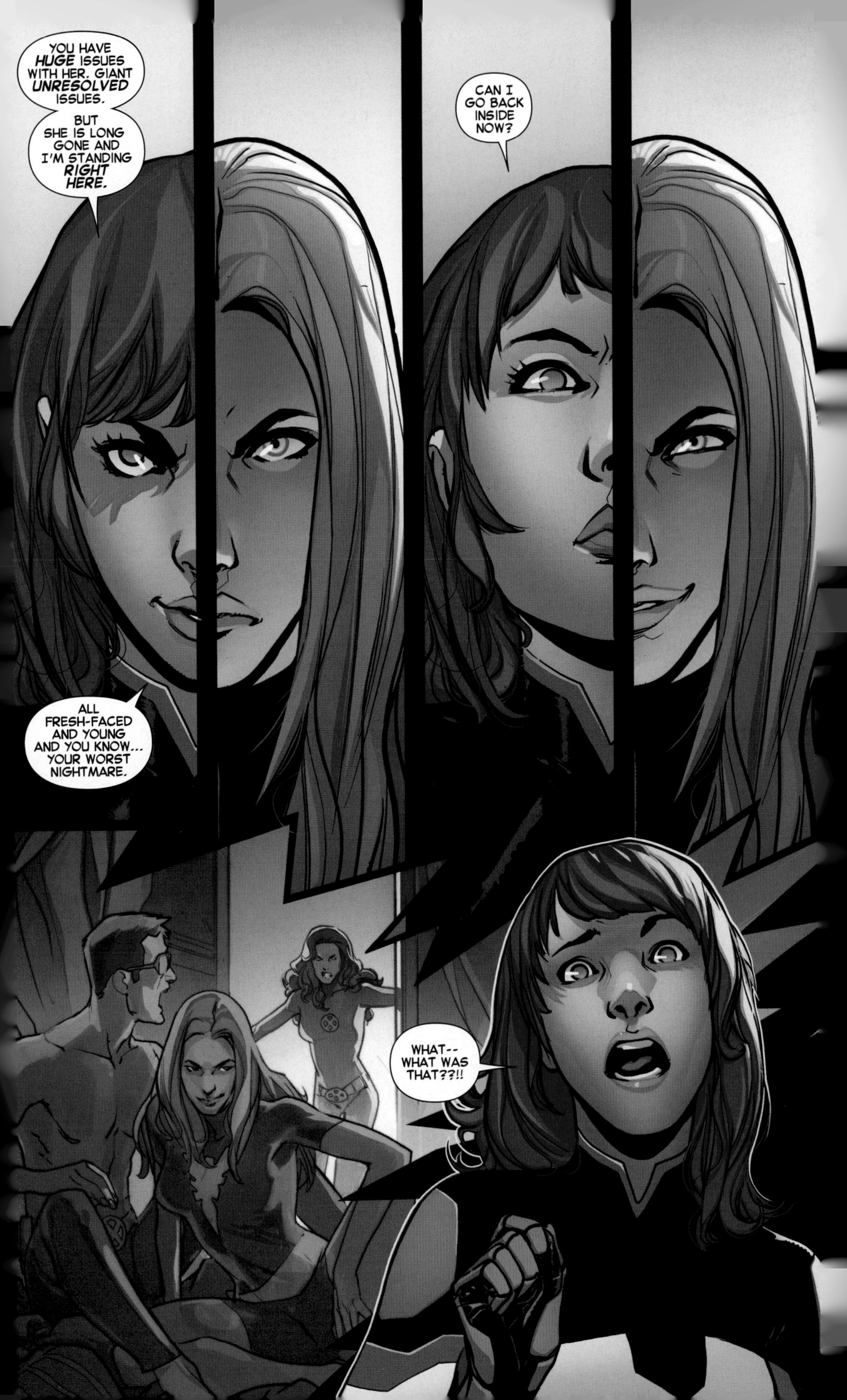

YOU HAVE HUGE ISSUES WITH HER. GIANT UNRESOLVED ISSUES.
BUT SHE IS LONG GONE AND I'M STANDING RIGHT HERE.
ALL FRESH-FACED AND YOUNG AND YOU KNOW... YOUR WORST NIGHTMARE.
CAN I GO BACK INSIDE NOW?
WHAT-- WHAT WAS THAT??!!

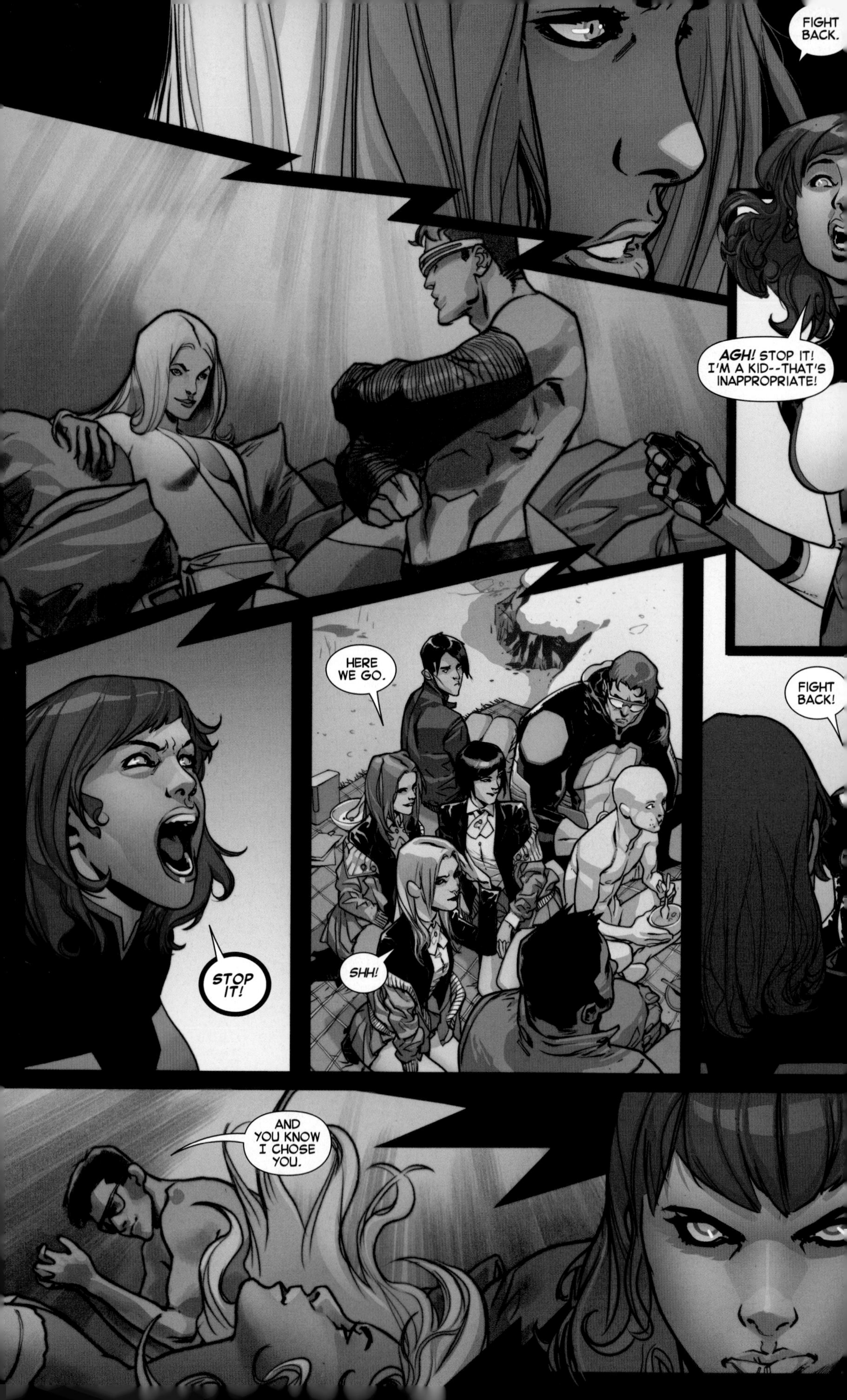
FIGHT BACK.
AGH! STOP IT! I'M A KID--THAT'S INAPPROPRIATE!
STOP IT!
HERE WE GO.
SHH!
FIGHT BACK!
AND YOU KNOW I CHOSE YOU.

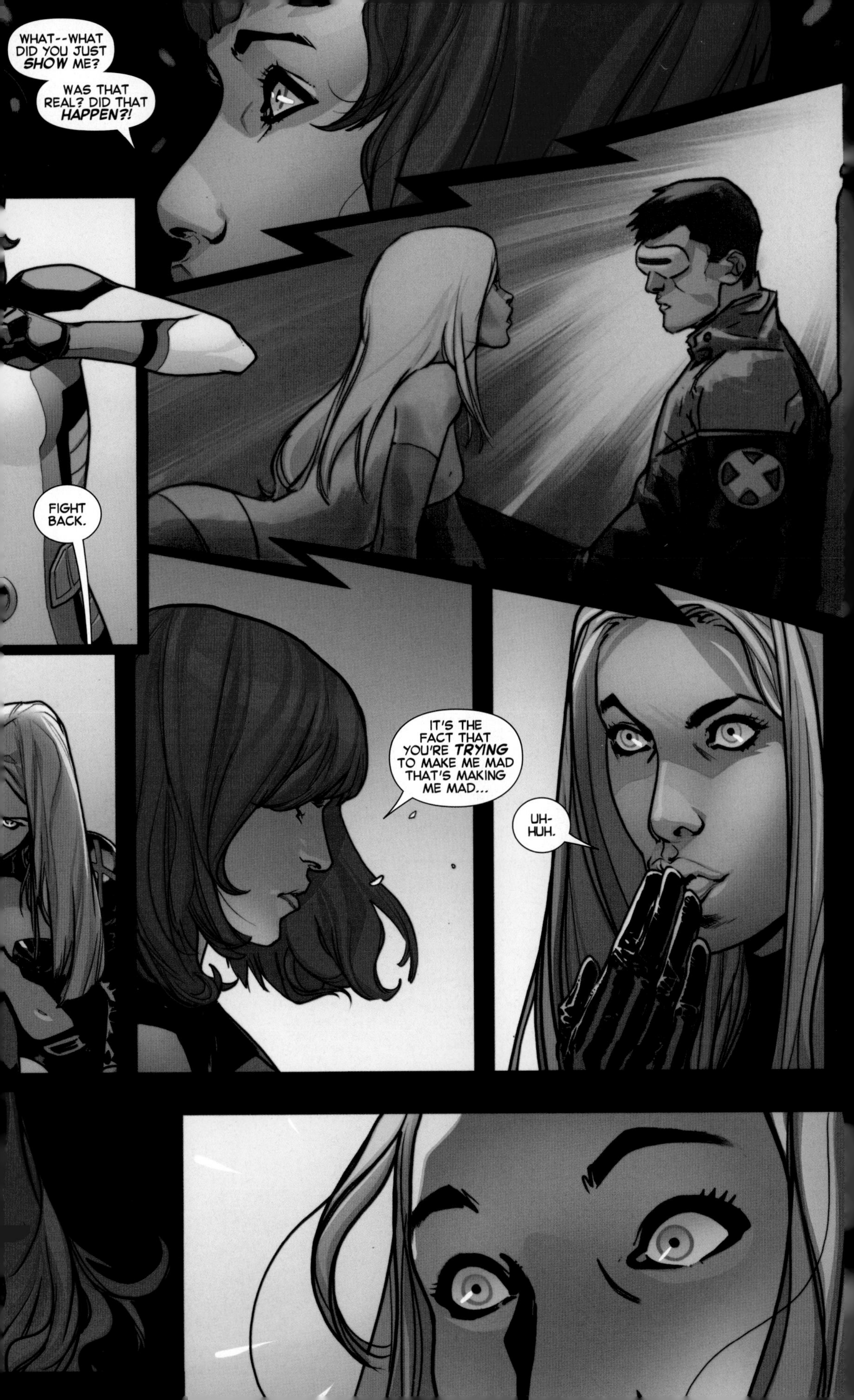
WHAT--WHAT DID YOU JUST SHOW ME?
WAS THAT REAL? DID THAT HAPPEN?!
FIGHT BACK.
IT'S THE FACT THAT YOU'RE TRYING TO MAKE ME MAD THAT'S MAKING ME MAD...
UH-HUH.

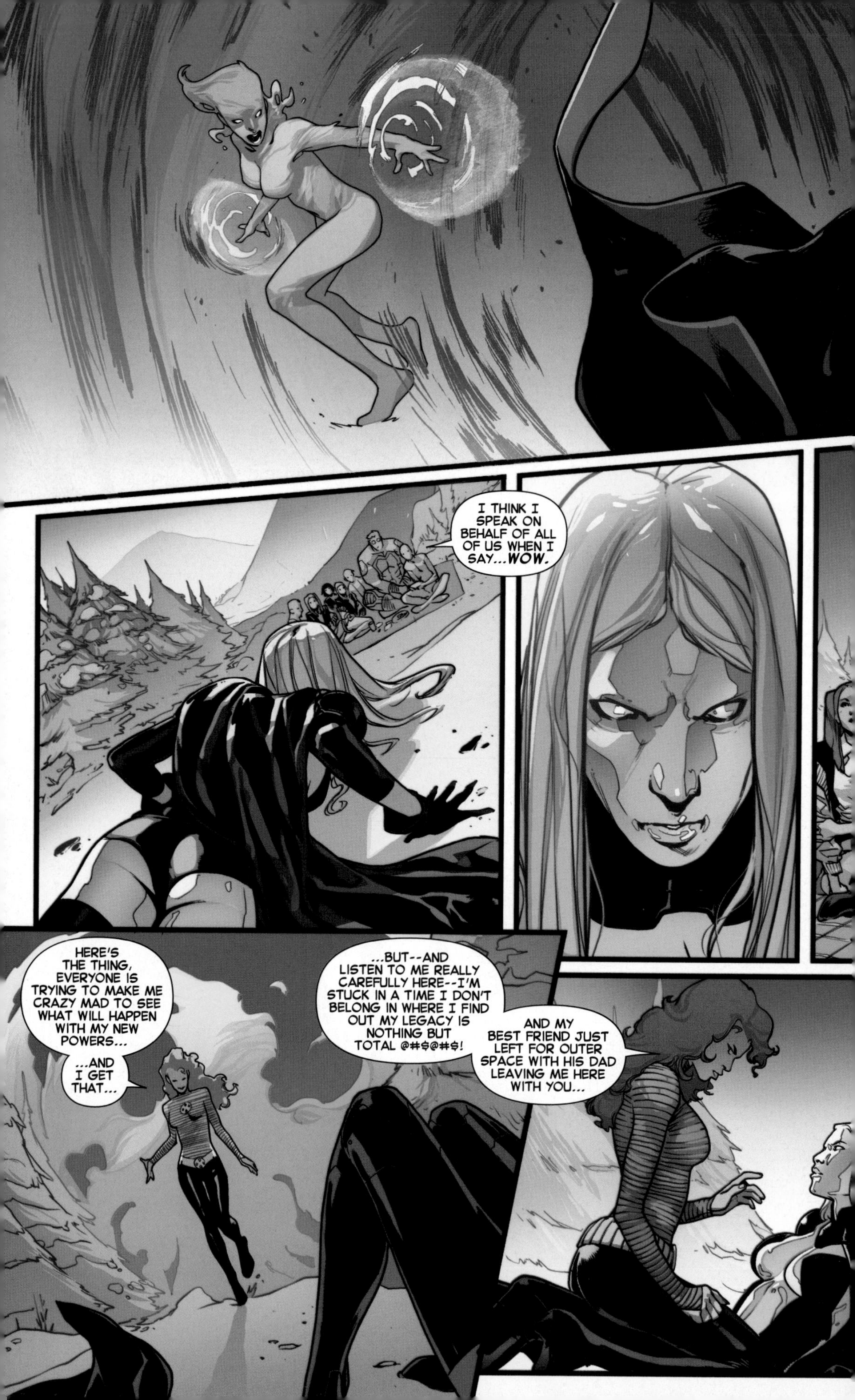
I THINK I SPEAK ON BEHALF OF ALL OF US WHEN I SAY...WOW.
HERE'S THE THING, EVERYONE IS TRYING TO MAKE ME CRAZY MAD TO SEE WHAT WILL HAPPEN WITH MY NEW POWERS...
...AND I GET THAT...
...BUT--AND LISTEN TO ME REALLY CAREFULLY HERE--I'M STUCK IN A TIME I DON'T BELONG IN WHERE I FIND OUT MY LEGACY IS NOTHING BUT TOTAL @#$@#$!
AND MY BEST FRIEND JUST LEFT FOR OUTER SPACE WITH HIS DAD LEAVING ME HERE WITH YOU...

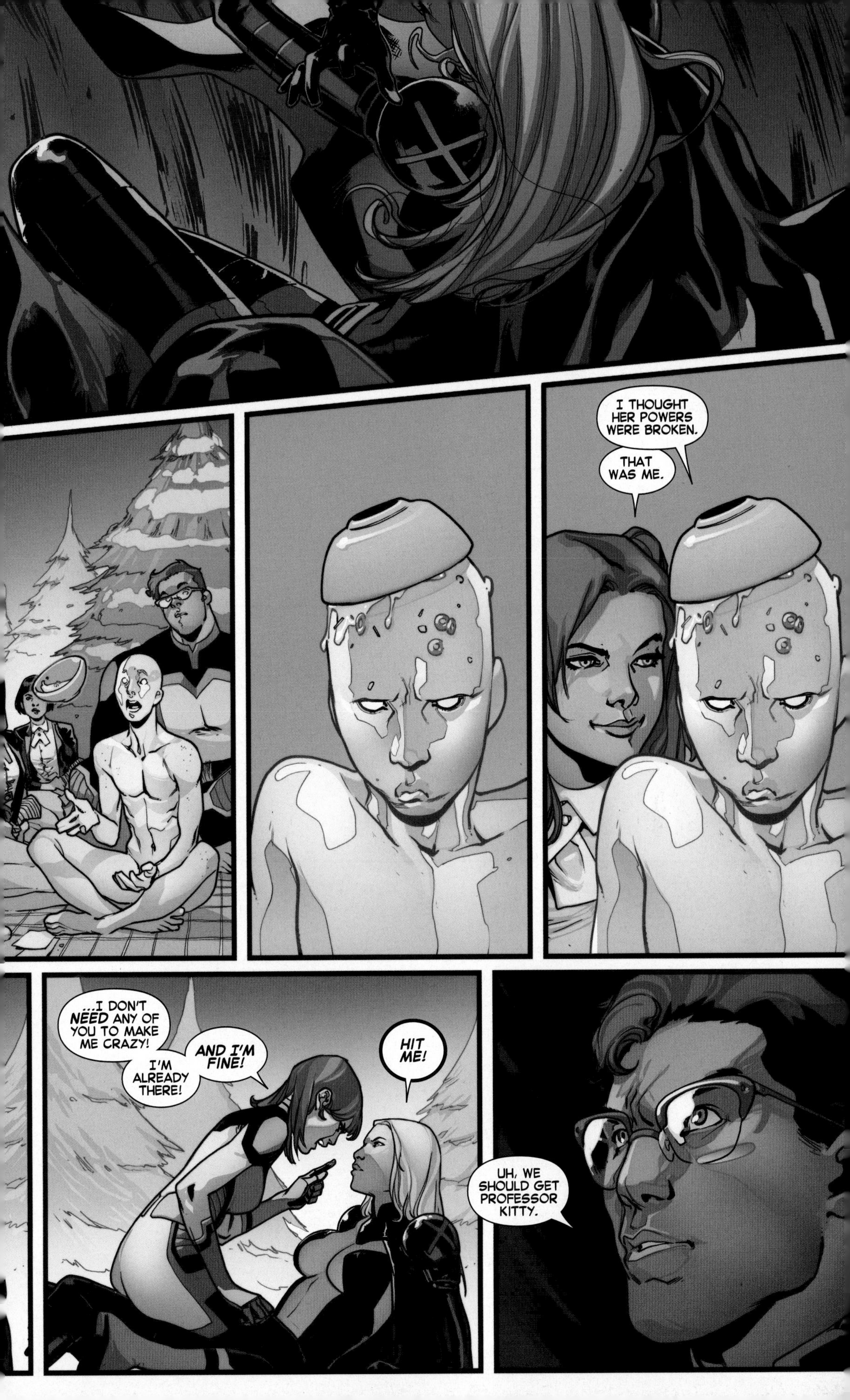
I THOUGHT HER POWERS WERE BROKEN.
THAT WAS ME.
...I DON'T NEED ANY OF YOU TO MAKE ME CRAZY!
I'M ALREADY THERE!
AND I'M FINE!
HIT ME!
UH, WE SHOULD GET PROFESSOR KITTY.

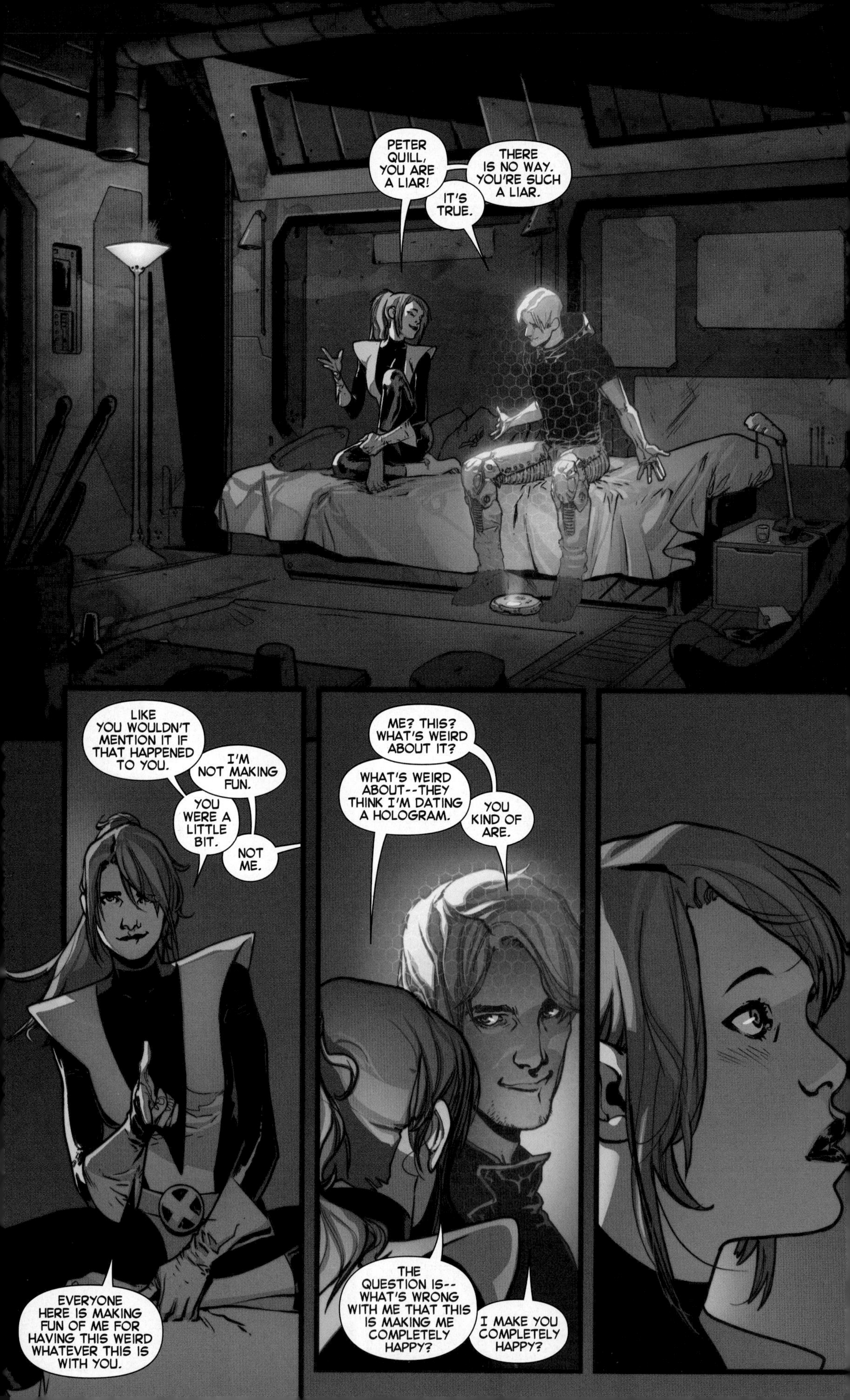
PETER QUILL, YOU ARE A LIAR!
IT'S TRUE.
THERE IS NO WAY. YOU'RE SUCH A LIAR.
LIKE YOU WOULDN'T MENTION IT IF THAT HAPPENED TO YOU.
I'M NOT MAKING FUN.
YOU WERE A LITTLE BIT.
NOT ME.
EVERYONE HERE IS MAKING FUN OF ME FOR HAVING THIS WEIRD WHATEVER THIS IS WITH YOU.
ME? THIS? WHAT'S WEIRD ABOUT IT?
WHAT'S WEIRD ABOUT--THEY THINK I'M DATING A HOLOGRAM.
YOU KIND OF ARE.
THE QUESTION IS--WHAT'S WRONG WITH ME THAT THIS IS MAKING ME COMPLETELY HAPPY?
I MAKE YOU COMPLETELY HAPPY?

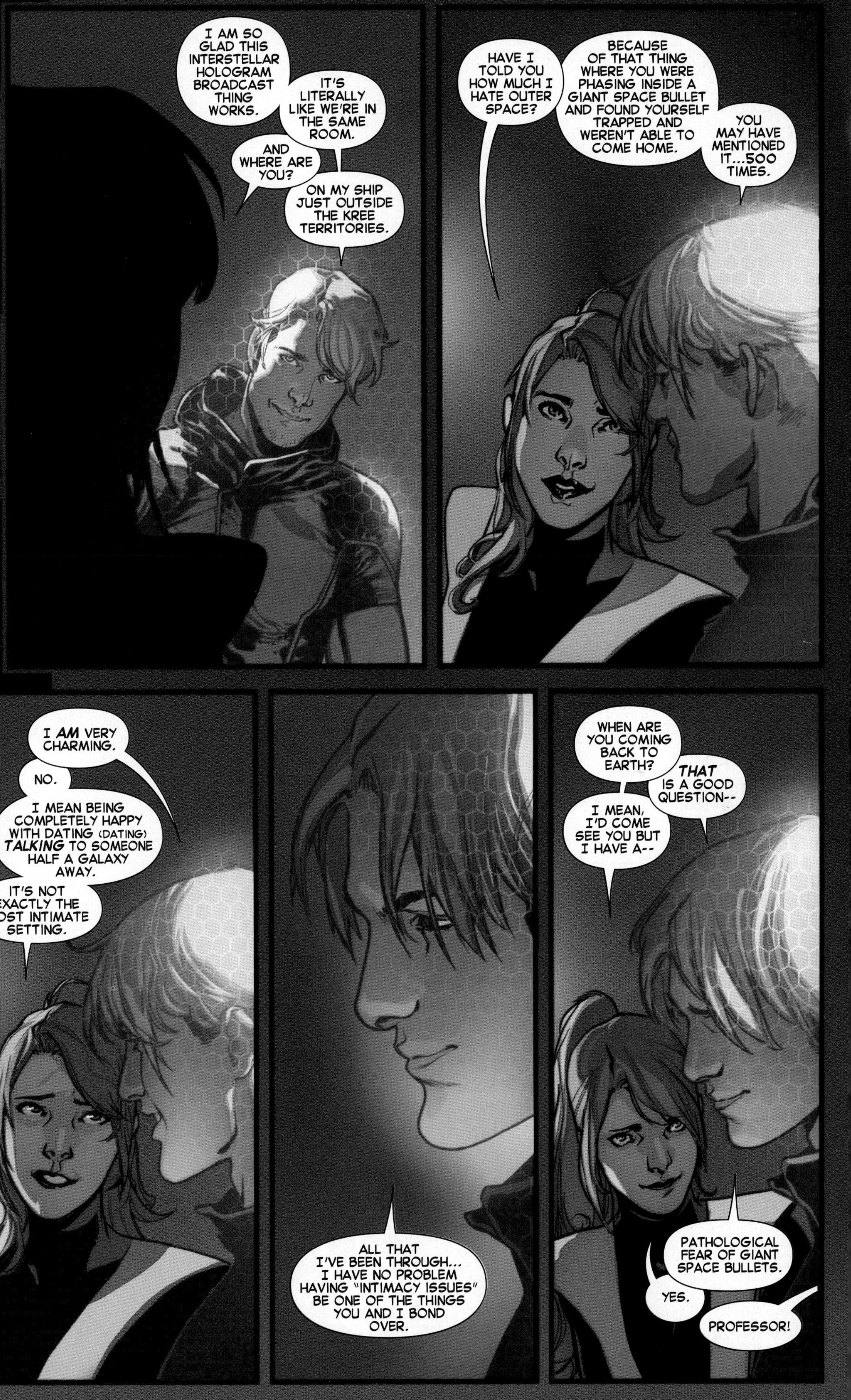
I AM SO GLAD THIS INTERSTELLAR HOLOGRAM BROADCAST THING WORKS.
IT'S LITERALLY LIKE WE'RE IN THE SAME ROOM.
AND WHERE ARE YOU?
ON MY SHIP JUST OUTSIDE THE KREE TERRITORIES.
HAVE I TOLD YOU HOW MUCH I HATE OUTER SPACE?
BECAUSE OF THAT THING WHERE YOU WERE PHASING INSIDE A GIANT SPACE BULLET AND FOUND YOURSELF TRAPPED AND WEREN'T ABLE TO COME HOME.
YOU MAY HAVE MENTIONED IT...500 TIMES.
I *AM* VERY CHARMING.
NO.
I MEAN BEING COMPLETELY HAPPY WITH DATING (DATING) *TALKING* TO SOMEONE HALF A GALAXY AWAY.
IT'S NOT EXACTLY THE MOST INTIMATE SETTING.
ALL THAT I'VE BEEN THROUGH... I HAVE NO PROBLEM HAVING "INTIMACY ISSUES" BE ONE OF THE THINGS YOU AND I BOND OVER.
WHEN ARE YOU COMING BACK TO EARTH?
THAT IS A GOOD QUESTION--
I MEAN, I'D COME SEE YOU BUT I HAVE A--
PATHOLOGICAL FEAR OF GIANT SPACE BULLETS.
YES.
PROFESSOR!

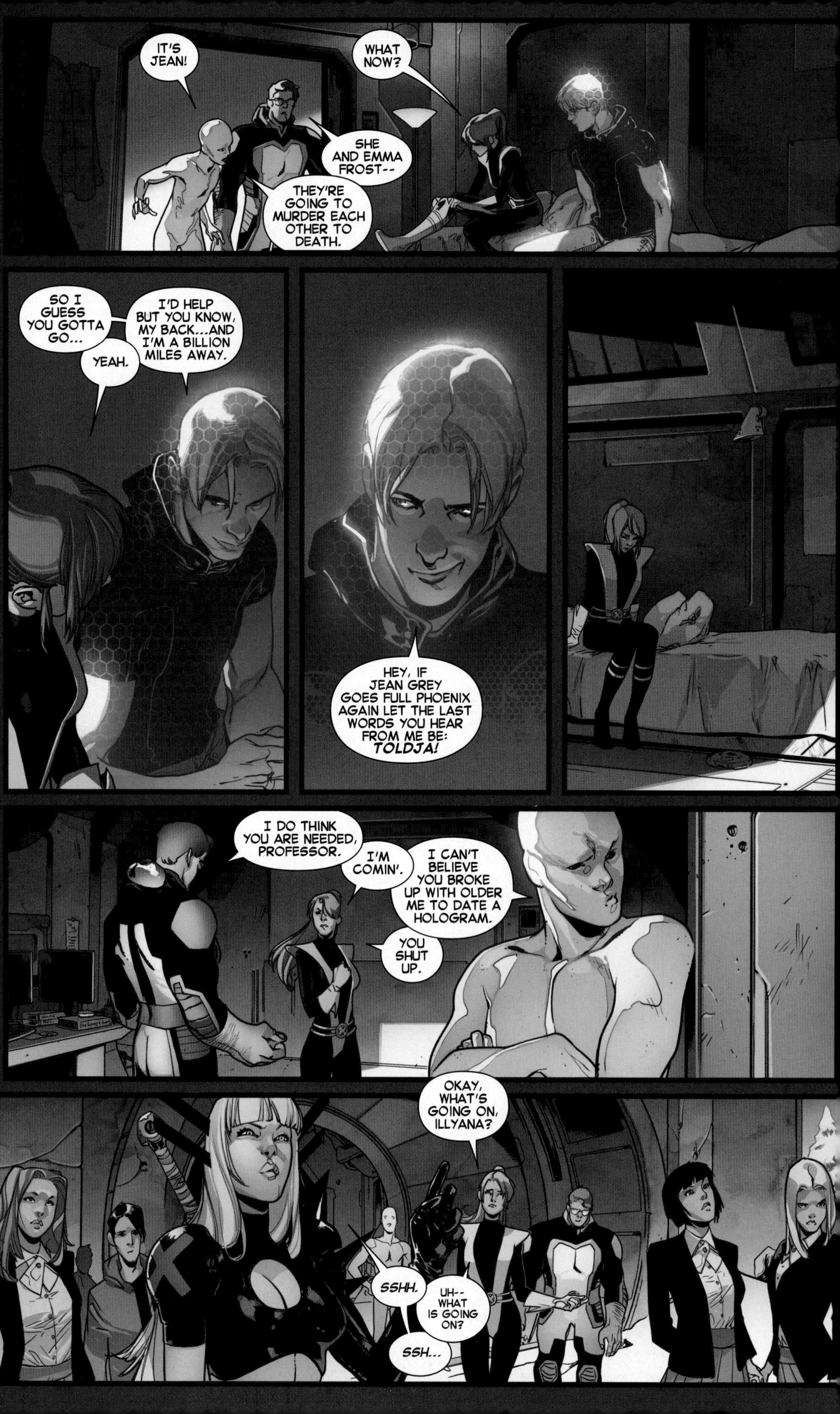
IT'S JEAN!
WHAT NOW?
SHE AND EMMA FROST--
THEY'RE GOING TO MURDER EACH OTHER TO DEATH.
SO I GUESS YOU GOTTA GO...
I'D HELP BUT YOU KNOW, MY BACK...AND I'M A BILLION MILES AWAY.
YEAH.
HEY, IF JEAN GREY GOES FULL PHOENIX AGAIN LET THE LAST WORDS YOU HEAR FROM ME BE: *TOLDJA!*
I DO THINK YOU ARE NEEDED, PROFESSOR.
I'M COMIN'.
I CAN'T BELIEVE YOU BROKE UP WITH OLDER ME TO DATE A HOLOGRAM.
YOU SHUT UP.
OKAY, WHAT'S GOING ON, ILLYANA?
SSHH.
UH-- WHAT IS GOING ON?
SSH...

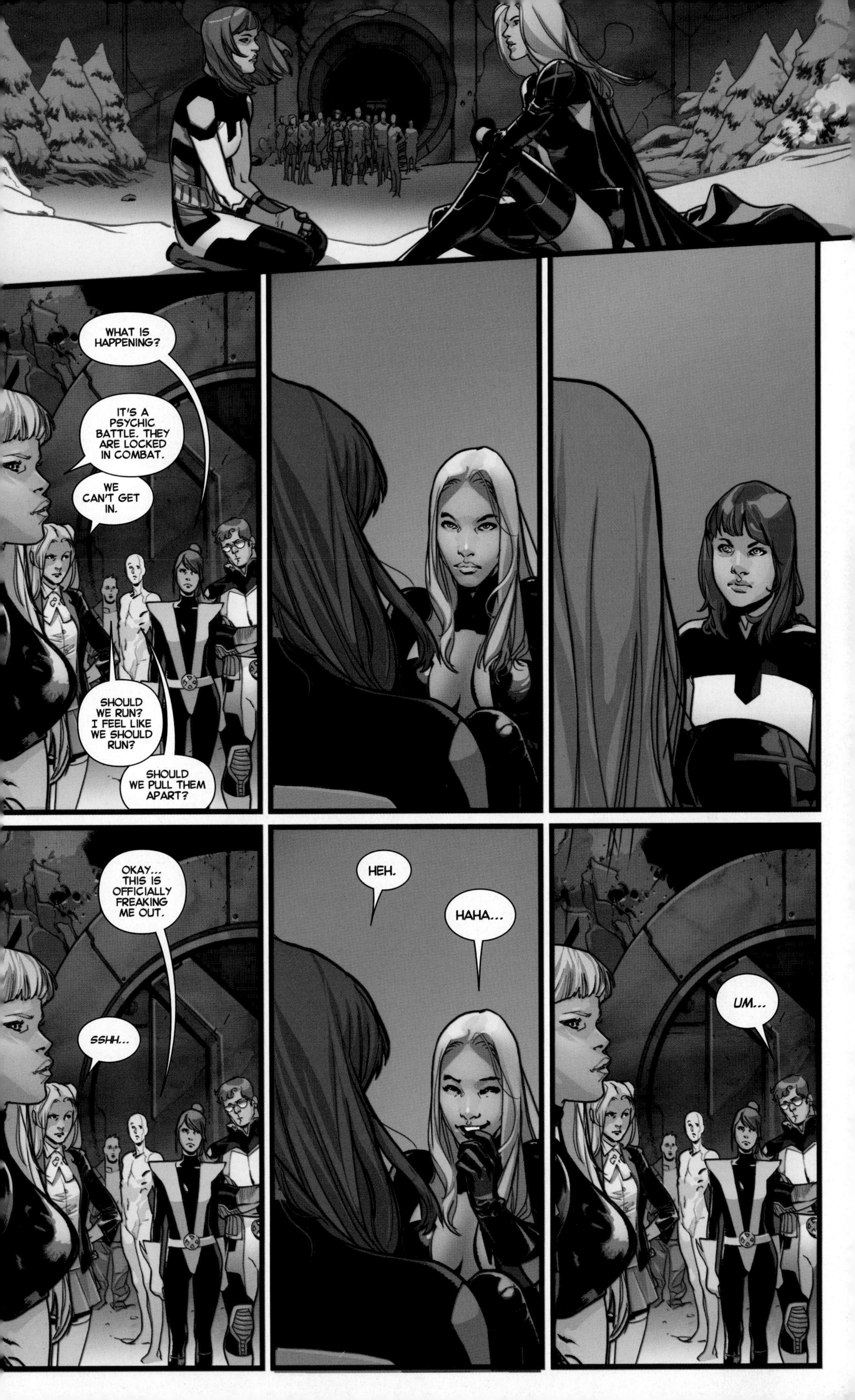
WHAT IS HAPPENING?
IT'S A PSYCHIC BATTLE. THEY ARE LOCKED IN COMBAT.
WE CAN'T GET IN.
SHOULD WE RUN? I FEEL LIKE WE SHOULD RUN?
SHOULD WE PULL THEM APART?
OKAY... THIS IS OFFICIALLY FREAKING ME OUT.
SSHH...
HEH.
HAHA...
UM...

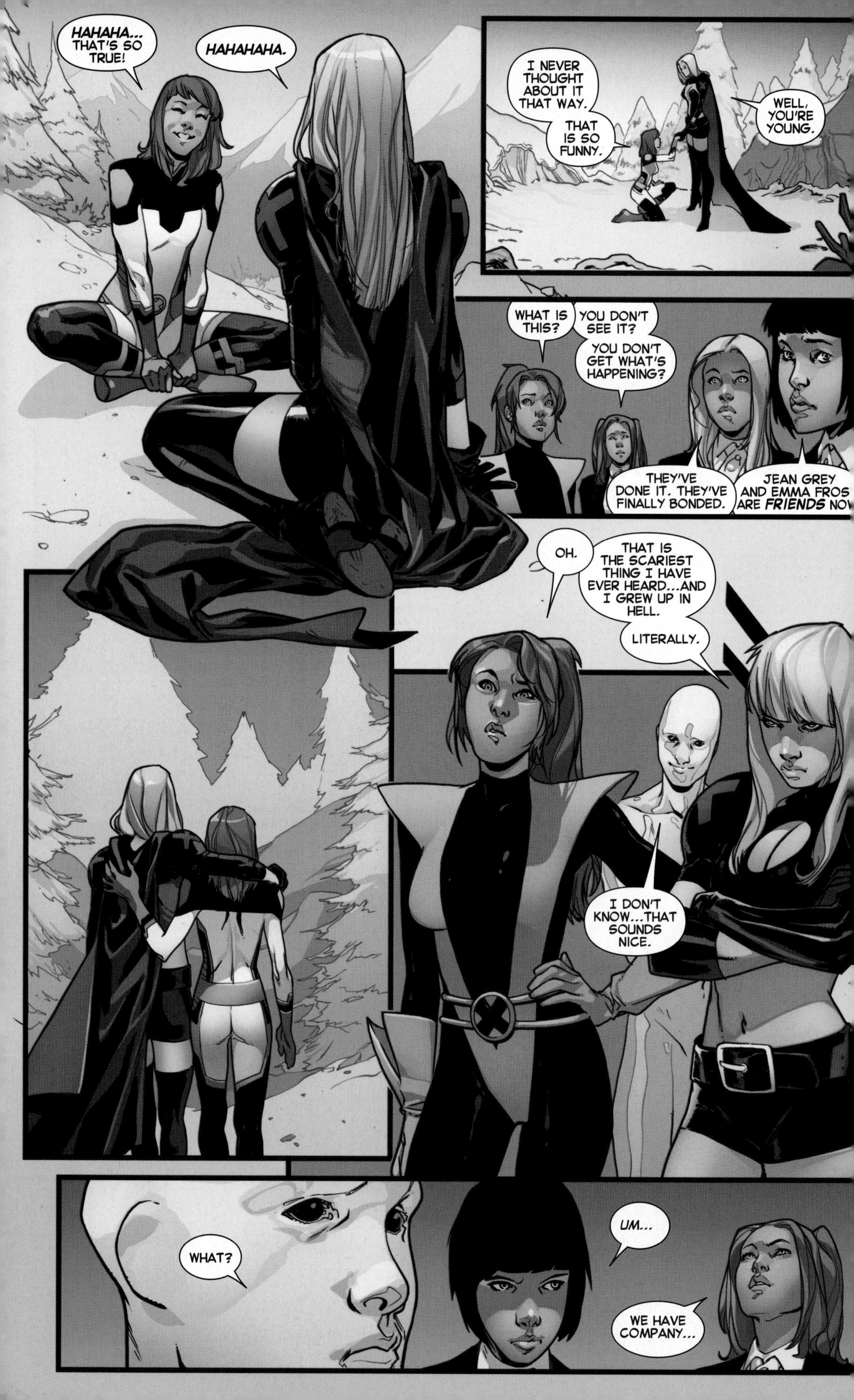
HAHAHA... THAT'S SO TRUE!
HAHAHAHA.
I NEVER THOUGHT ABOUT IT THAT WAY.
THAT IS SO FUNNY.
WELL, YOU'RE YOUNG.
WHAT IS THIS?
YOU DON'T SEE IT?
YOU DON'T GET WHAT'S HAPPENING?
THEY'VE DONE IT. THEY'VE FINALLY BONDED.
JEAN GREY AND EMMA FROS ARE FRIENDS NOW
OH.
THAT IS THE SCARIEST THING I HAVE EVER HEARD...AND I GREW UP IN HELL.
LITERALLY.
I DON'T KNOW...THAT SOUNDS NICE.
WHAT?
UM...
WE HAVE COMPANY...

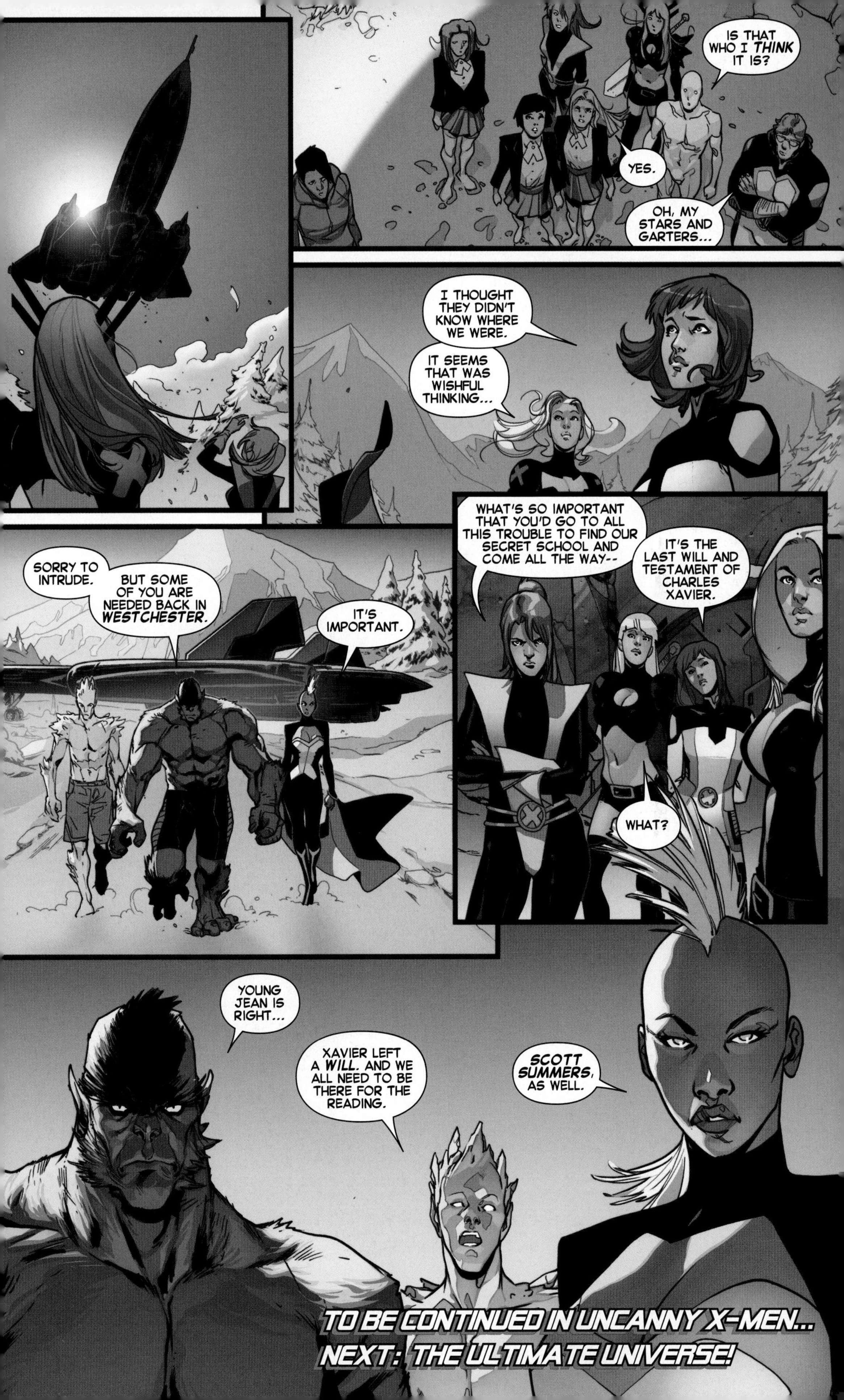
IS THAT WHO I *THINK* IT IS?
YES.
OH, MY STARS AND GARTERS...
I THOUGHT THEY DIDN'T KNOW WHERE WE WERE.
IT SEEMS THAT WAS WISHFUL THINKING...
SORRY TO INTRUDE.
BUT SOME OF YOU ARE NEEDED BACK IN *WESTCHESTER*.
IT'S IMPORTANT.
WHAT'S SO IMPORTANT THAT YOU'D GO TO ALL THIS TROUBLE TO FIND OUR SECRET SCHOOL AND COME ALL THE WAY--
IT'S THE LAST WILL AND TESTAMENT OF CHARLES XAVIER.
WHAT?
YOUNG JEAN IS RIGHT...
XAVIER LEFT A *WILL*. AND WE ALL NEED TO BE THERE FOR THE READING.
SCOTT SUMMERS, AS WELL.
TO BE CONTINUED IN UNCANNY X-MEN...
NEXT: THE ULTIMATE UNIVERSE!

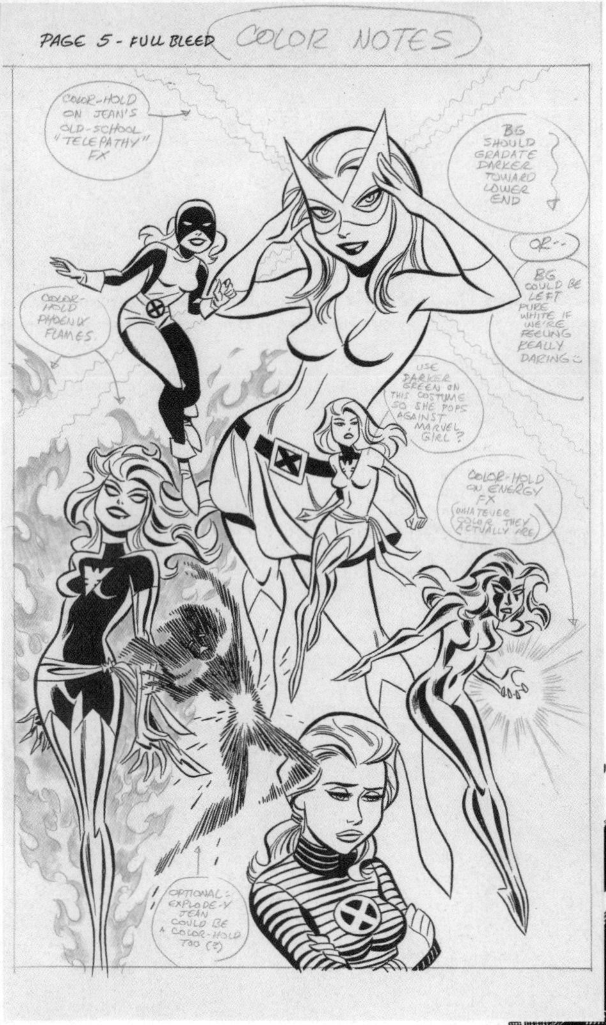
PAGE 5 - FULL BLEED
COLOR NOTES
COLOR-HOLD ON JEAN'S OLD-SCHOOL "TELEPATHY" FX
BG SHOULD GRADATE DARKER TOWARD LOWER END
OR--
BG COULD BE LEFT PURE WHITE IF WE'RE FEELING REALLY DARING :-)
COLOR-HOLD PHOENIX FLAMES
USE DARKER GREEN ON THIS COSTUME SO SHE POPS AGAINST MARVEL GIRL?
COLOR-HOLD ON ENERGY FX (WHATEVER COLOR THEY ACTUALLY ARE)
OPTIONAL: EXPLODE-Y JEAN COULD BE A COLOR-HOLD TOO (?)

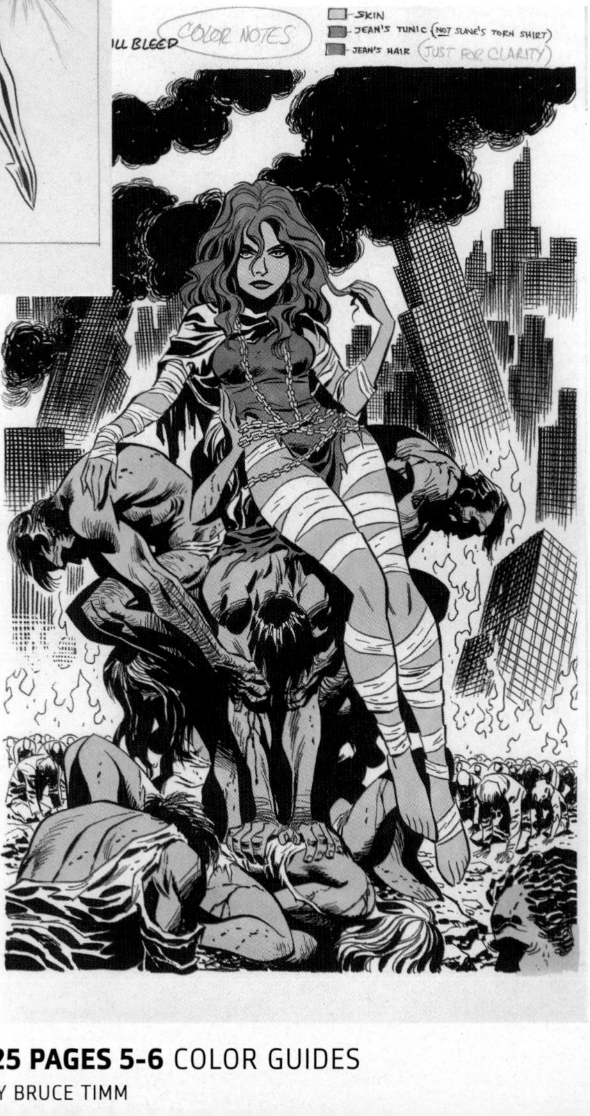
ULL BLEED
COLOR NOTES
SKIN
JEAN'S TUNIC (NOT SLAVE'S TORN SHIRT)
JEAN'S HAIR (JUST FOR CLARITY)

ALL-NEW X-MEN #25 PAGES 5-6 COLOR GUIDES

BY BRUCE TIMM